Understandin
Visual Basic 3
for Windows

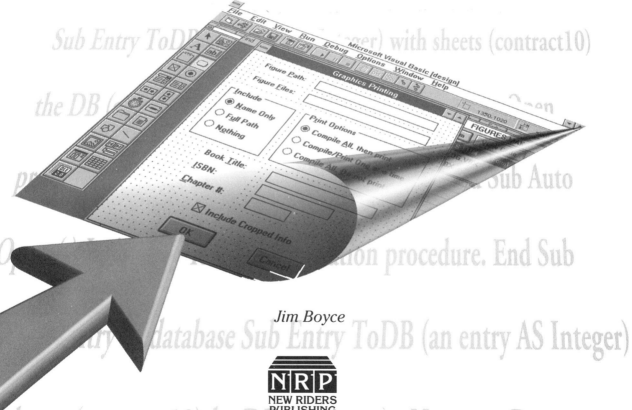

Jim Boyce

NRP
NEW RIDERS
PUBLISHING

New Riders Publishing, Indianapolis, Indiana

Understanding Visual Basic 3 for Windows

By Jim Boyce

Published by:
New Riders Publishing
201 West 103rd Street
Indianapolis, IN 46290 USA

Copyright © 1994 by New Riders Publishing

Printed in the United States of America   2 3 4 5 6 7 8 9 0

Library of Congress Cataloging-in-Publication Data:

```
Boyce, Jim, 1958-
Understanding Visual Basic 3 for Windows / Jim Boyce.
    p.   cm
Includes index.
ISBN 1-56205-310-8 : $24.99
1. Microcomputers—Programming
2. Microcomputers—Visual Basic.  I. Title
QA76.73.B3B69  1994                        94-10169
005.265—dc20                               CIP
```

Publisher	LLOYD J. SHORT
Associate Publisher	TIM HUDDLESTON
Manager of Product Development	ROB TIDROW
Director of Special Projects	CHERI ROBINSON
Managing Editor	MATTHEW MORRILL
Marketing Manager	RAY ROBINSON
Product Director	FORREST HOULETTE
Acquisitions Editor	CHERI ROBINSON
Senior Editor	TAD RINGO
Production Editor	STEVE WEISS
Editor	SARAH KEARNS
Technical Editor	WILLIAM BEEM
Acquisitions Coordinator	STACEY BEHELER
Editorial Assistant	KAREN OPAL
Publishing Assistant	MELISSA LYNCH
Production Imprint Manager	JULI COOK
Production Imprint Team Leader	KATY BODENMILLER
Book Design	ROGER MORGAN

Production Team

NICK ANDERSON	JAMIE MILAZZO
CAROL BOWERS	CHAD POORE
DAN CAPARO	RYAN RADER
STEVE CARLIN	BETH RAGO
JENNIFER EBERHARDT	KIM SCOTT
RICH EVERS	SUSAN SHEPARD
KIMBERLY K. HANNEL	TONYA R. SIMPSON
GREG KEMP	SCOTT TULLIS
DEBBIE KINCAID	ELAINE WEBB

Indexed by	REBECCA MAYFIELD
Production Analysts	DENNIS CLAY HAGER
	MARY BETH WAKEFIELD
Cover Designer	JAY CORPUS

About the Author

Jim Boyce is a contributing editor of *WINDOWS Magazine*, a columnist for *CADENCE Magazine*, and a regular contributor to other computer publications. He has been involved with computers since the late seventies, and has used computers in one way or another as a structural designer, production planner, systems manager, programmer, and college instructor. He has a wide range of experience in the DOS, Windows, and UNIX environments. Jim is the author of the best-selling books *Maximizing Windows 3.1*, *Windows for Non-Nerds*, and *Keeping Your PC Alive,* from New Riders Publishing. Jim has authored and coauthored a number of other books, including the following titles:

- *Hands On AutoCAD*
- *Ultimate Windows 3.1*
- *Inside Windows for Workgroups*
- *Inside Windows 3.1*
- *Windows 3.1 Networking*
- *Maximizing Windows 3.0*
- *Maximizing MS-DOS 5*
- *AutoCAD for Beginners*
- *Inside AutoCAD*
- *Inside AutoCAD LT for Windows*
- *Maximizing AutoCAD Volume 1*

Jim is a transplanted Texan living in Minnesota and enjoying everything except the temperature, which is a scale of magnitude lower than what he's used to. You can contact Jim via his CompuServe ID, 76516,3403, or on the Internet at the address 76516.3403@compuserve.com.

Dedication

This book is dedicated with deep affection to Tina Haugse, a very exceptional person and the best mother three precocious little girls could hope for. You're a lucky man, Don (and now Tina won't let you forget it).

Acknowledgments

Many people helped in the creation of this book in one way or another. I offer my wholehearted thanks to:

Tim Huddleston, Cheri Robinson, and Rob Tidrow, for helping develop this project, and for handling the headaches that always go with a new book project.

Forrest Houlette for his advice and guidance in developing *Understanding Visual Basic 3 for Windows*. Scott Flanders and Lloyd Short, for their willingness to venture into some uncharted territory.

Stacey Beheler, for her usual exceptional job of coordinating the project.

Steve Weiss, for the exceptional and timely job of turning the book into a polished and readable work. Thanks also to Sarah Kearns for her editing contributions.

Bill Beem, for the outstanding job of technical editing. The book is much better because of his thoroughness and testing.

The Production department of Macmillan Computer Publishing, for turning text and illustrations into a real book.

John Schmitt, for advice on stalls, minimum controllable airspeed, crosswind landings, and other fun stuff that has absolutely nothing to do with this book.

Snerdly T. Whipplefoot, who in our last thrilling episode saved the universe from destruction. Snerdly is recovering from his heroics by taking a vacation in Jamaica, where he is trying to learn to tap his feet to reggae. We can be sure that Snerdly will never sport dreadlocks.

Trademark Acknowledgments

New Riders Publishing has made every attempt to supply trademark information about company names, products, and services mentioned in this book. Trademarks indicated were derived from various sources. New Riders Publishing cannot attest to the accuracy of this information.

Microsoft and MS-DOS are registered trademarks, and Windows is a trademark, of Microsoft Corporation.

Trademarks of other products mentioned in this book are held by the companies producing them.

Warning and Disclaimer

This book is designed to provide information about programming using Visual Basic. Every effort has been made to make this book as complete and as accurate as possible, but no warranty or fitness is implied.

The information is provided on an "as is" basis. The author and New Riders Publishing shall have neither liability nor responsibility to any person or entity with respect to any loss or damages arising from the information contained in this book or from the troubleshooting or repair procedures contained in it.

Contents at a Glance

Table of Contents

Part Two: Doing Something Useful   153

New Riders Publishing

The staff of New Riders Publishing is committed to bringing you the very best in computer reference material. Each New Riders book is the result of months of work by authors and staff, who research and refine the information contained within its covers.

As part of this commitment to you, the NRP reader, New Riders invites your input. Please let us know if you enjoy this book, if you have trouble with the information and examples presented, or if you have a suggestion for the next edition.

Please note, however, that the New Riders staff cannot serve as a technical resource for Visual Basic problems or programming techniques. Refer to the documentation that accompanies your Visual Basic package for help with specific problems.

If you have a question or comment about any New Riders book, please contact NRP at the following address.

New Riders Publishing
Macmillan Computer Publishing
Attn: Associate Publisher
201 West 103rd Street
Indianapolis, IN 46290-1097
Fax: (317) 581-4670

New Riders Publishing also maintains a CompuServe forum. We welcome your participation in this forum (**GO NEWRIDERS**). Please feel free to post a public message there if you have a question or comment about this or any other New Riders product. If you prefer, however, you can send a private message directly to this book's product director at 73164,2773.

We will respond to as many readers as we can. Your name, address, or phone number will never become part of a mailing list or be used for any other purpose than to help us continue to bring you the best books possible.

Thank you for selecting *Understanding Visual Basic 3 for Windows*!

VB and the Meaning of Life

Everyone knows that the answer to the question, "What is the Meaning of Life?" is 41. Now that we have that out of the way, let's have a chat about Visual Basic.

I'm going to take a stab in the dark and guess that you're not a programmer, but you would like to learn to write programs with Visual Basic. The second part of my guess is easy, because there are only two reasons why you would buy a book on Visual Basic: you either want to learn to program with VB, or you need a new doorstop. Bricks are cheaper and rocks are free, and both make great doorstops. But, don't let me stop you from buying the book if that's what you really want to use it for... I'm trying to pay off my credit cards. Buy a copy for each door in your house.

I also reason that you're not a programmer because if you were, you would be looking for a Visual Basic book that was about 12 inches thick and full of all sorts of really cool but impossible-to-understand VB stuff. Those types of books are great if you already know about program structure, variables, arrays, controls, events, and all those other computer-geek programming words. If you're not a programmer, or have only worked with BASIC, you'll get just as much enjoyment from a hot coal in your underwear as you will from those types of books, and even less use. So, here's a subtle suggestion:

Understanding Visual Basic Is the Book for You!

Why is this such a great book for you to use to learn Visual Basic? All of the books on Visual Basic that I've seen cover VB functions and statements and show you how to use them in little fragments of program code. That's fine, but most of these books don't do a very good job explaining how a VB program is structured *in general*. Unless you already know what you're doing, it can be next to impossible to teach yourself to program with VB unless you already have a lot of experience with other languages. I've written *Understanding Visual Basic* with that fact in mind.

What's the Approach?

This is the obligatory section that explains what the book is all about and tells you how wonderful it is. *Understanding Visual Basic* takes the approach that you don't know much, if anything, about programming. If you do know something about programming, or you already have some experience with BASIC or some other language, that's great—you're already a few steps ahead. This book is still a great starting point for you to learn Visual Basic, even if you do have that experience.

I'm going to avoid lots of technical jargon and long sections of program code and instead focus on basic concepts. I'll explain the parts of a VB program in general, non-geekazoid terms. When I introduce a new concept like *variables*, for example, I'll explain what they are and why you need them in your program. I won't just tell you what to do; I'll also tell you *why* you're doing it.

In addition to focusing on basic concepts, *Understanding Visual Basic* also uses a task-oriented approach. Maybe you know *what* you want to do, but not what the technical term for it is. Instead of focusing on statements and functions for file manipulation, for example, I'll approach the topic as if you had asked me, "Gee, how do I write a simple program that displays a directory listing and lets me view the files on different disks?"

What's in Here?

Understanding Visual Basic won't teach you everything you probably want to know about Visual Basic (especially at this price...). But that's not the book's goal, anyway. This book will help you get your feet wet and learn basic VB concepts. You'll learn how to write some nifty little programs and become comfortable using VB. You'll learn that with VB, just a few hundred lines of program code can make a really impressive and useful program with which you can impress your friends and influence your enemies. When you've finished the book, you'll be able to read some of those 12-inch-thick VB books without becoming comatose or drooling uncontrollably (at least not more than usual).

Part One, In Which You Learn To Program

Part One, "Simple Ideas and Tasks," is your guided tour around Visual Basic. Chapter 0 (yes, Chapter *0*), "Getting Your Feet Wet," dumps you right in the water without a life jacket and you start creating a program. The water is only six inches deep (that's 15.24 cm for you metric types who aren't stuck with a measurement system that's based on the length of some dead guy's arm or something), so don't worry—you'll have a working program by the end of the first chapter. The other chapters in Part One, "Forms, Controls, and Other Voodoo," "Making Cool Stuff Happen," "Where Does That Code Go?," "Fiddling with Text and Numbers," and "Making Decisions," explain some of the basic parts of a VB program in more detail and teach you how to start writing program code. You also learn about using data like numbers and text strings.

Part Two, Where You Learn To Do Something Useful

In Part Two, "Doing Something Useful," you start writing VB programs for specific tasks. In Chapter 6, "Doing Simple File Stuff," for example, you learn how to create a program that works like a simple File Manager. You learn to work with disks, directory lists, and file lists. The other chapters in Part Two, "Duck with Plum Sauce (Menus)," "Dialog Boxes!," "Even More Dialog Boxes!," "Working with Pictures," and "Printing Stuff," teach you how to include menus, pictures, and dialog boxes in your programs. Part Two also teaches you how to send stuff from your program to your printer. You also learn how easy it is to add menus to your programs.

Part Three, Where You Start Getting Serious and Maybe Need a Pocket Protector

Part Three, "Getting Serious," covers some of the more sophisticated programming tasks and topics. You learn about handling errors and working with large amounts of data in arrays and special data structures. You also learn how to read and write files, which makes it possible for your program to store its data in files. Part Three finishes with a look at some of the debugging tools that Visual Basic gives you to track down those nasty bugs in your program and squash them like... well, bugs.

Getting Help

As you are working through the book, help is never more than a keystroke away. Visual Basic includes an extremely useful Help system that not only explains how to use Visual Basic, but also includes explanations of VB statements and functions and even includes code examples.

To get general Help, choose Contents from Visual Basic's Help menu. This opens the main VB Help file and displays its contents page. If you want to search for help on a specific topic, choose the Search for Help On item from the Help menu. If you want help on a specific function, statement, or keyword, highlight the keyword and press F1. Visual Basic will open the Help file and display a topic page that covers the function you've highlighted. You can browse the topic or display a code example to help you understand how the function or statement works. You can also copy all or part of the code example to the Clipboard so you can paste it into your own program, saving you the time that would otherwise be required to type the code yourself.

Getting Ready...

There isn't a lot you have to do to jump right into *Understanding Visual Basic*. If you don't have Visual Basic, go out and buy it. You can't write VB programs without it. Before you grab your car keys or the phone, though, decide if you want to buy or upgrade to the Professional Edition. The Professional Edition includes a lot of additional gizmos and gadgets that let you add things like 3D controls and animated buttons. It also contains controls for adding mail capability, communications functions, and other sophisticated features to your programs. Here's a list of the extra nifty gadgets included with the Professional Edition:

- **Animated Button.** This control lets you display a series of bit maps to create animated buttons, multi-state buttons, and check boxes.

- **Communications.** This control provides complete serial communication capabilities for your program, including file transfer and other data communication features.

☐ **Gauge.** This control lets you create linear and needle-style gauge indicators to display the progress of tasks in your program.

☐ **Graph.** This control lets you create and display graphs using a wide variety of styles.

☐ **Key Status.** This control displays and modifies the state of the CAPS LOCK, NUM LOCK, INS, and SCROLL LOCK keys.

☐ **MAPI Controls.** These controls let you add Mail capabilities to your program. You can write your own Mail system or add the ability to send and receive mail messages from your programs.

☐ **Masked Edit.** This control is similar to a standard text box, but it provides features that make it easy for you to control and restrict the format of the data entered in the box.

☐ **Multimedia MCI.** This control enables your program to control multimedia devices such as CD drives and others that support the MCI interface.

☐ **Outline.** This control lets you create hierarchical list boxes whose branches can be expanded and collapsed just like the directory lists in File Manager.

☐ **Pen Controls.** These controls enable you to develop programs for the Windows for Pen Computing environment (the version of Windows for pen-controlled devices).

☐ **Picture Clip.** This control displays a portion of a bit map in a picture box or on a form. You can use this control to crop bit map images in your program.

☐ **Spin Button.** This control increments or decrements numbers displayed in a text box, label, or other control.

☐ **3D Controls.** These controls replace standard two-dimensional controls and include three-dimensional check boxes, command buttons, frames and option buttons.

☐ **Data Access.** The Professional Edition includes features that enable you to create and access database files in a wide variety of formats and by various methods.

☐ **Crystal Reports.** This add-on enables you to easily design and integrate reports in your program, and is great for developing database query applications.

Although *Understanding Visual Basic* doesn't cover the Professional Edition, this book is a good starting point to help you learn about the concepts and programming techniques that will enable you to write programs with these extra controls in the future. Many of these extra controls in the Professional Edition are very similar to controls in the Standard Edition, and when you are familiar with the Standard Edition, you should have no trouble picking up the other controls on your own.

Installing the Sample Programs

Understanding Visual Basic uses real programming examples to teach you about VB. The book includes a disk containing sample programs and program code. You'll need these sample programs to work through the examples in the chapters, so you need to install the files on your hard disk. Here's how to do that:

1. Start Windows, and insert the *Understanding Visual Basic Disk* into the system's floppy drive.

2. In Program Manager, choose File, Run.

3. In the Run dialog box, type A:SETUP in the Command Line edit box (use B:SETUP if you inserted the disk in drive B), and choose OK.

4. Follow the instructions in the Setup window to install the files in the directory of your choice.

You really don't need more detailed instructions than that, do you? After all, if you want to be a programmer, you have to learn to think on your feet (although since you'll be sitting down, I suppose you'll have to learn to think on your butt). I promise the instructions in the rest of the book *will* be much more detailed.

Using This Book

You can sit in your favorite comfy chair and read *Understanding Visual Basic*, but you really should sit in front of your computer instead. That way you'll be able to work through the examples as you go along, and the radiation from the monitor will give you a nice "programmer's tan."

Conventions and Strange Typefaces

You ought to know that a couple of different kinds of print are used in this book, and for good reason:

☐ Print that looks like this is program code. Wait—get back here! There's not that much, but where we do have to use it, there's no mistake in finding it.

☐ Print that uses *italics* in programming code (within the text) merely indicates that the italicized word is a variable—the actual word will vary according to the situation. Full code examples in the exercises use italics to indicate comments that explain the code.

☐ Italics are also used to point out *new words* and *terminology that's about to be defined.*

☐ <u>H</u>otkeys (or shortcut keys) have their letters bolded and under-lined.

☐ Text that you type (input) **is shown in bold**.

Should Learning VB be Planned or Random?

You probably should work through the book sequentially, at least through Part One. In Part Two you can jump around and work through the chapters that apply to your programming task at hand. If you don't want to learn about menus right away, for example, you can skip Chapter 7 for now.

The same goes for Part Three; once you've gotten the basics down, you can pretty much skate around and learn about any subject at hand as you feel so inclined. By then you'll be one of the VB initiates.

Of course, that doesn't mean working through this book cover-to-cover is so bad, either. The front-to-back approach will give you a supremely logical, practically thorough, hopefully kinda-fun introduction to Visual Basic. That's what you paid for, right?

And whatever you do, don't panic! Anyone can write Visual Basic programs. It's working out quadratic equations in your head that really turns your eyebrows red hot.

A Tour of the Exercises

This section lists all of the exercises in the book, organized by chapter, and provides a brief description of what each exercise covers. This will help you locate specific topics you'd like to cover right away.

Chapter 0

Drawing the Useless Interface: Create the interface (window) for a simple program by drawing controls on a form.

Setting Design-Time Properties: Set properties of controls and forms as you are designing the program interface to control the appearance and function of controls.

Writing Some Program Code: Add a few simple Visual Basic statements to a small program.

Compiling the Useless Program: Compile a Visual Basic project into a Windows executable (EXE) file.

Testing Useless: Take your first sample program for a test drive.

Chapter 1

Setting a Form's Border Style: Set the border style of a window, controlling the appearance of the window and the user's ability to resize it when the program runs.

Enabling/Disabling a Form: Enable and disable a form at design time to make the form visible but unavailable to the user.

Assigning an Icon to a Form: Assign an icon to a form at design time. This icon represents the program when it is running as a minimized program on the desktop, and represents the program in a program group.

Changing the Pointer: Change the type of mouse pointer used when the pointer is over a specific control or form.

Fooling with Text Box Properties: Create a simple password entry box using a text box and the PasswordChar of a text box.

Playing with Option Buttons: Experiment with option buttons to see how they work together.

Using a Scroll Bar Control: Add a scroll bar control to a program to enable the user to increment and decrement a value.

Chapter 2

Specifying the Startup Form: Specify which form or procedure automatically executes when your program starts. This defines the "entry point" for your program.

Fooling with the Load Event: Use the Load event procedure of a form to define actions that must be executed when a form is loaded into memory.

Unloading a Form: Use the Unload event procedure of a form to execute statements and perform tasks when a program is closed or a form is unloaded from memory.

Click!: Add code to the Click event procedure of a button. When the user clicks the button, the code in the Click event procedure executes.

DblClick!: Add code to the DblClick event procedure of a list box to select an item from the list when the user double-clicks on the list.

Going Through the Change: No, this isn't about growing hair on your palms. Use the Change event of a text box to execute a procedure each time the text in the text box changes.

Making the View Button Work: Add code to a button to make the program display a picture in a picture box control.

Making the Close Button Work: Add code to a button that ends the program when the user clicks on the button.

Making Double-Click Work: Add some code to a file list box that enables the user to double-click on a file and display it in a picture box.

Making the EXE File: Compile a program that displays bit map images in a picture box.

Chapter 3

General Procedures and Yak Juice: Examine a program that uses a general procedure to calculate the cost of yak milk. General procedures simplify a program by letting you write a single procedure that can be used by any other procedure.

Creating a Function Procedure: Examine a program that uses a general function to calculate the cost of yak milk and returns the calculated value to the calling procedure.

Chapter 4

Playing with Data Types: Examine different types of data that you can use in a program, including strings, integers, dates, and more!

Working with Variant Data Types: Use variant data types when the type of data stored in a variable can change type, such as changing from an integer to a real number.

Declaring a Variable Explicitly with Dim: Declare variables explicitly as integers, strings, and other data types using the Dim statement.

Understanding Scope: Work with a program that will help you understand *variable scope*, which illustrates how the way a variable is created defines how it can be used throughout the program.

Fiddling with Text: Experiment with a program that manipulates text strings, teaching you how to do things like split a string into its constituent words.

Chapter 5

Working with If...Then: Check out a program that explains the use of the If...Then structure to execute statements only if a condition is true.

Using If...Then...Else: Add some code to an If...Then structure to make it execute a secondary set of instructions if a condition does not prove to be true.

Exiting a Sub Procedure: Use the Exit Sub statement to exit a procedure without completing it.

Using Select Case: Examine a program that uses the Select Case structure to test a condition for multiple possible values, then executes a set of statements depending on the conditional expression.

Using a For...Next Structure: Experiment with a program that uses a For...Next structure to execute a set of statements a specific number of times (loop through the statements).

Using a Do...Loop Structure: Examine a program that uses a Do...Loop structure to loop through a set of statements until a condition proves True (or False).

Fixing Your Do...Loop: Fix a Do...Loop structure so it terminates properly.

Chapter 6

Drawing File Controls: Draw a directory list box, drive list box, and file list box on a form to create a simple file-browsing utility.

Synchronizing the File Controls: Add code to drive, directory, and file list boxes to make them work together. Selecting a directory in the directory list, for example, changes the file list to display the files in the selected directory.

Handling "Device Not Available" Errors: Add some error-checking code to a procedure to overcome the problem of a disk not being available when the user tries to select it.

Adding an Erase Feature: Use the Kill statement in a simple file utility to erase a file.

Copying and Moving Files: Use the FileCopy and Kill statements to add the ability to copy and move files in a simple file utility.

Renaming a File: Use the Name statement in a simple file utility to rename files.

Modifying FileMan to Start Programs: Add the ability to a file utility to launch programs.

Adding Double-Click to the File List: Give the user the ability to double-click on a program file name in a file list box to launch the program.

Chapter 7

Creating a Menu: Use the Menu Design Window to add a standard pull-down menu to a program.

Adding More Menu Items: Add program menus and menu items to a program's window.

Coding the Delete Menu Item: Add some code to a menu item that enables a user to delete a file. This example issues a Click event for a button when the user selects a menu item.

Assigning Shortcut Keys: Assign shortcut keys to menu items in your menu, such as adding Ctrl+C to a Copy menu item or Ctrl+V to a Paste menu item.

Adding Separators to the File Menu: Modify a menu to include separators. Separators are horizontal lines that separate different sections of a menu.

Completing the FileMan Menu: Add a selection of menu items to complete the menu of a file utility program.

Adding Checks to a Menu: Add some code to a menu Click event procedure to add or remove a check mark from the menu item when the user clicks on the menu item.

Changing the Doc/Text Files Item: Add some statements to a file utility program to provide a selection of predefined file types from which the user can choose to display a list of files.

Completing the Changes: Add some finishing touches to a menu to enable the user to select the file display pattern of a file box by selecting various menu items.

Adding Cascading Menu Items: Create a cascading menu.

Completing FileMan!: Add a few finishing touches to the FileMan program, a file utility program for erasing, copying, moving, and executing files.

Chapter 8

Showing the Settings Dialog Box: Use the Show and Hide methods to make a form appear and disappear like magic.

Stuffing the Dialog Box: Initialize the controls in a dialog box (set the values' controls) before the dialog box is displayed.

Modifying Settings Based on the Dialog Box: Create a procedure that reads the status of dialog box controls after the user has made changes in the dialog box. The dialog box settings are then used to change other program settings and variables.

Setting Up the Control Array: Begin creating a selection of option buttons that function as a *control array*. A control array enables you to create many controls that all share the same event procedures.

Completing the Control Array: Complete a control array consisting of option buttons.

Adding a Procedure for the Control Array: Create a procedure associated with a control array. The procedure performs tasks based on which control in the array generated the event.

Chapter 9

Adding Items to a List: Examine a program that uses the AddItem method to add items to a list box. The items are added when the form containing the list box is loaded.

Taking COMBO.MAK for a Spin: Experiment with a program that adds items to a list box when the program starts.

Initializing the Combo Boxes: Add some statements to a procedure that initializes a dialog box before it is displayed.

Adding Items to List1: Add code to a procedure that places the contents of a text box in a list box when the user clicks a button.

Removing Items from List1: Create a procedure that uses the RemoveItem method to remove items from a list box when the user selects the item and clicks a button.

Adding a Common Dialog Control: Draw a common dialog control on a form. A common dialog control enables your program to use standard dialog boxes for file access, printing, font selection, and color selection.

Adding Open Dialog to COMMDLG.MAK: Create a procedure that displays a common file Open dialog box and reads the status of the dialog box's values, including the Read Only check box, file name, and so on.

Adding a Print Setup Feature: Create a procedure that enables your program to display the Print Setup dialog box and specify the default printer settings.

Enabling the Print Command: Create a procedure that displays the Print dialog box and determines the user's selections in the dialog box.

Using the Font Dialog Box: Create a procedure that enables the user to select a font, font size, and other font characteristics using the common Font dialog box.

Using the Color Dialog: Create a procedure that enables the user to select a color using the common Color dialog box.

Chapter 10

Assigning an Image to a Form: Create a procedure that places a bit map, metafile, or icon image on a form's background.

Assigning an Image at Design Time: Assign an image to a form or other control when you are designing the program.

Adding a Picture Control: Draw a picture control on a form and add code to the program to make the picture control display a picture when the form is loaded.

Sizing a Picture Box to a Form: Create a procedure that automatically resizes a picture box to fit a form whenever the user resizes the form.

Removing a Picture at Run Time: Use LoadPicture to remove an image from a picture box control while the program is running.

Using the Stretch Property: Set the Stretch property of an image control to make the image inside the control stretch to fill the image control.

Saving an Image to a File: Display a Save As dialog box and the SavePicture statement to enable the user to save a bit map, metafile, or icon to a file.

Drawing the Toolbar: Begin creating a toolbar for a program by drawing a picture box to contain the toolbar buttons.

Drawing the Buttons: Draw image controls inside a picture box to use as buttons on a program's toolbar.

Assigning Images to the Buttons: Place images on image controls that are used as buttons in a toolbar.

Making the Toolbar Buttons Work: Add some code to the Click event procedure of image controls to make them function like toolbar buttons.

Repositioning the Image1 Control: Tweak the program a little to make an image control always appear right below a toolbar. This technique is great for placing a control at the bottom edge of a toolbar.

Making the Buttons Look "Pushed": Do some simple graphics switching to make a toolbar button look like it is being depressed when the user clicks on it.

Chapter 11

Setting Top and Left Margins: Use the ScaleLeft and ScaleTop properties of the Printer object to set the top and left margins for printing.

Chapter 12

Adding Error Handling to FileMan: Create a simple error-handling routine that displays an error message when a drive or directory is not available.

Writing the Final Error Handler: Create a more complex and intelligent error handler that tests for specific types of errors and bases its actions on the type of error that occurred.

Creating the DiskErrorHandler Procedure: Create a common error-handling procedure that can be used by any other procedure in the program.

Causing Your Own Errors: Use the Error statement to create errors and test your program and your error handlers.

Chapter 13

Declaring an Array: Use the Dim statement to create a data array. You can use data arrays to store large lists of data.

Using a Variable for the Index: Use a variable to work with a specific item in an array.

Redimensioning an Array: Redimension an array to hold more items. When an array is full, use the Redim statement to make it bigger so you can add more items to the array.

Fixing the Scroll Bar: Tweak a procedure so the Max property of a scroll bar control always matches the number of items in the array. This is a good technique to synchronize an array and a scroll bar.

Adding Delete Capability: Create a simple procedure that enables the user to delete an item from an array. The array contains a list of people's names.

Adding a Select All Feature: Modify a simple text editor to add the ability to select all of the text in a document.

Enabling the Copy and Paste Items: Create procedures that enable the user to copy text to the Clipboard and paste text from the Clipboard.

Programming the Cut Function: Create a procedure that enables the user to cut a selection of text from a text box and place it on the Clipboard.

Chapter 14

Opening an Existing File for Sequential Access: Create a simple procedure that opens a text file for sequential access.

Reading a Text File Into a Text Box: Create a simple procedure that copies the contents of a text file into a text box. This is the first step in creating a text editor.

Saving a Sequential File: Write a procedure that copies the contents of a multi-line text box into a file using sequential access. This enables your simple text editor to save changes to a file or create new text files.

Defining the Data Type and Array: Create a data type that will be used to hold data records for an address book program.

Creating the FileOpen Procedure: Write a procedure that opens a file using random access.

Testing the FileOpen Procedure: Test a FileOpen procedure that opens a file for random access.

Creating the SaveFile Procedure: Write a procedure that stores fixed-length records in a file using random access.

Viewing the OpenFile Procedure: Examine a procedure that opens a file for binary access and copies data from the file into a data structure.

Chapter 15

Fixing a Run-Time Error: Learn how to modify code if a run-time error occurs when you are testing a program.

Resuming Execution with a Different Statement: Control the statement that will execute next after an error has triggered break mode.

Using Single Step: Learn to make a program step through statements one at a time to test and debug the program.

Using Procedure Step: Step through a program one step at a time, except when making calls to other procedures or functions. Procedure step executes called procedures and functions in normal run mode.

Using the Immediate Pane in the Debug Window: Use the immediate pane to modify variables and perform other debugging tasks.

PART

Simple Ideas and Tasks

This first part of the book introduces you to Visual Basic, starting with some very basic (no pun intended) concepts and working toward more complex topics. Here's a list of the chapters in Part I with a quick explanation of what the chapters cover:

0: Getting Your Feet Wet. This chapter doesn't throw lots of deep concepts at you. Instead, it provides some "poke-these-buttons" exercises to help you become familiar with Visual Basic.

1: Forms, Controls, and Other Voodoo. Chapter 1 changes tone a bit and begins concentrating a little more on concepts. You learn about forms and controls and how these objects are important in a Visual Basic program. You also learn about *properties*.

2: Making Cool Stuff Happen. This chapter explains events and event-driven programming. It teaches you to make things happen in your program by creating *event procedures* that are associated with various types of events, such as clicking a mouse button.

3: Where Does That Code Go? Chapter 3 starts getting a little more technical (but not too much). The chapter explains things like where event procedures go, where common functions and procedures are placed, and how a Visual Basic program is generally structured.

4: Fiddling with Text and Numbers. This chapter introduces *variables,* the different types of data you can work with, and techniques you can use to manipulate text and numbers.

5: Making Decisions. Visual Basic provides a number of different structures you can use to control the way a program functions. This chapter will make you an expert on just about all of them.

Getting Your Feet Wet

Are you ready to start programming? Well, give it a shot anyway. This chapter will give you a hand-held tour of Visual Basic. By the end of the chapter, you'll have a working VB program that is absolutely useless and doesn't even look really cool. If you want to create useful, jazzy programs, you'll have to at least read Chapter 1, "Forms, Controls, and Other Voodoo." Here's what we're shooting for in this chapter:

- [ ] Learn to start Visual Basic
- [ ] Recognize what all the gadgets in the Visual Basic interface are for
- [ ] Create a window for a small program
- [ ] Add a few command buttons and a text box to the program window
- [ ] Write a few lines of simple program code
- [ ] Create an executable (EXE) file of the program and test it
- [ ] Become wealthy beyond your wildest dreams

As you read through the chapter, you might run across a few terms that aren't explained in a lot of detail, like *debugging*, which has nothing at all to do with pest control. This is just a "test the waters" chapter, and you'll learn more about these terms in later chapters. For now, just be happy and follow blindly along.

A Tour Around Visual Basic

Starting Visual Basic is a no-brainer for a Windows expert like yourself. Just double-click on the Visual Basic icon in the Visual Basic group (in Program Manager). When Visual Basic starts, it automatically begins a new *project*, which is a collection of working files you use to eventually build a program. VB assumes that you want to create a window for your program, so it displays a *form* for the new project. Forms become the windows and dialog boxes in your program. Figure 0.1 shows a new, blank form named Form1.

 **NOTE**   Your display might look slightly different from figure 0.1. For example, your display might also show the Properties dialog box. Be happy.

Figure 0.1
A new, blank form
and the Toolbox.

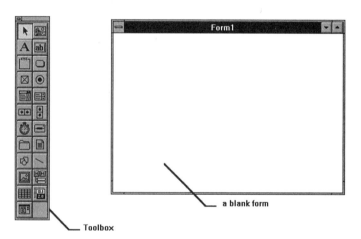

Toolbox

a blank form

Your program might use just a single form, or it might use lots of forms. Each form has a unique name. By default, VB gives your forms really unique and interesting names like Form1, Form2, Form3... you get the idea. You can keep these form names or rename the form to whatever you want. You should rename your forms as soon as you create them, because it will help you keep track of your forms and controls as you write the program's code. Preface form names with the characters *frm*, and follow this with a descriptive name. Here are some examples: *frmMain*, *frmEditor*, and *frmAboutBox*. You'll read more about naming conventions in later chapters.

The Toolbox

In addition to Form1, you also should see the Toolbox (see fig. 0.1) when Visual Basic starts. The Toolbox contains all of the *controls*—such as command buttons, check boxes, list boxes, and so on—that you can add to a form. Controls are in many ways the most important thing in a Visual Basic program. All of the components of your program's interface, such as text boxes, menus, command buttons, scroll bars, and other graphical items, are controls. A large part of writing a Visual Basic program involves writing procedures that execute when the user performs an action on a control, such as clicking a button. The number of tools you see in the Toolbox depends on whether you are using the Professional or Standard Edition of Visual Basic. In the Professional Edition, you'll see a lot of additional control tools. You'll find a list and explanation of the tools in the Toolbox in Chapter 1.

Like forms, controls have names. VB is just as inventive with control names as it is with form names. The first Textbox control you create is called Text1, the second is Text2, etc. Command buttons are Command1, Command2, Command3, and so on. You can keep these names or create your own names for controls. As with forms, you should rename controls to make their names as descriptive as possible to help you identify controls when you are writing the program's code. An OK button, for example, could be named cmdOK. A Cancel button could be named cmdCancel. The **O**pen menu item in the **F**ile menu could be named mnuFileOpen. Using these names will help you know instantly what a control is for when you read a reference to it in your program's code.

The Project Window

The Project window (see fig. 0.2) gives you a list of all of the files that are part of your current project. You can use the Project window to switch between forms (if your project includes more than one form) and to select other files (explained shortly) when you want to remove the files from the project. You also can use the Project window to view a form or view its *code* (program code is the collection of statements you write that form the functioning part of your program). To view a particular form, select it in the Project window, then choose the View Form button. If you want to look at its code, choose the View Code button. Your project might also include *module* files that contain nothing but code (these files have a file extension of BAS). These types of files also show up in the Project window.

NOTE

Time for a note! Each project has a name. When you save a project, Visual Basic creates a text file with a MAK file extension. This text file contains a list of all of the forms and other files that belong in the project, and also lists other information about the project. Visual Basic creates a special MAK file called AUTOLOAD.MAK. It's located in your Visual Basic directory. AUTOLOAD.MAK defines which files are automatically added to a new project each time you start one. If VBX files (custom controls) appear in your project each time you start one, it's because the VBX is listed in AUTOLOAD.MAK. You can edit AUTOLOAD.MAK, adding or deleting references to VBX files, to control whether or not these files are added to each new project that you start.

Figure 0.2

The Project window displays a list of the files in the current project.

The Properties Window

Forms and controls have *properties* associated with them. For example, the title in a form's title bar is its Caption property. The name that appears on a command button is its Caption property. A form's MinButton property determines whether it has a minimize button in the upper right corner of the form. Its ControlBox property determines whether it has a control menu in the upper left corner of the form. You'll learn more about properties in Chapter 1.

The Properties window (see fig. 0.3) displays the properties for the currently selected control or form. To set a property while you're writing the program (called "setting the property at design time"), you just click on the property in the Properties window and change it as needed by typing the new property in the Settings combo box (see fig. 0.3) or by selecting the property from the list provided in the Settings combo box. With settings that have predefined possible values (such as True or False), you can double-click on a property in the Properties window to cycle its value through all of its possible values.

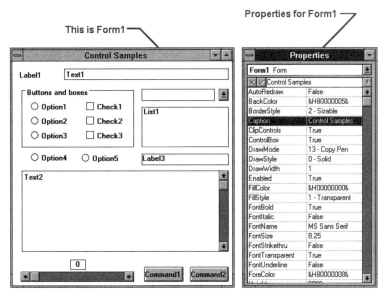

This is Form1 ⌐

Properties for Form1 ⌐

Figure 0.3
The Properties window shows the selected control or form's properties.

The Object box lists the name of the active control and its control type (TextBox, CommandButton, etc.). You can select another control by picking it from the Object box list. Use the Settings box portion of the Properties window to choose a property setting or to type a setting. Use the Properties list to select the property you want to change.

The Code Window

Although some programs don't require a lot of code, you can't avoid writing at least a little bit of code for a typical program. You use the Code window to write program code. You can display the Code window by double-clicking on a form or a control on a form. Or, you can choose a form or control, then click on the View Code button in the Project window to display the Code window. Once the Code window is open, you can use it to view, add, or change any code that is associated with the form. To view the code for another form or module, select the form or module in the Project window, then choose the View Code button.

Figure 0.4

Use the Code
window to write
program code.

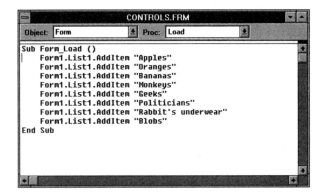

The Menu Design Window

When you want to add or modify a menu on a form, you use the Menu Design
Window (see fig. 0.5) to do so. You can create different menus, add items to
a menu, change the order of items, create cascading items (explained in
Chapter 6, "Doing Simple File Stuff"), and set various properties for the
menu items.

Figure 0.5

The Menu Design
Window.

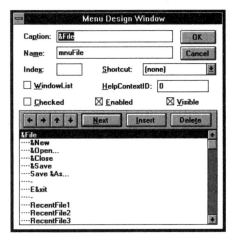

There are other windows that show up from time to time as you work on a
project. You'll read about them in later chapters. Now that you have a little
bit of knowledge under your belt, you're ready to become a Visual Basic
programmer!

Writing Your First Program

Please, try to contain your excitement. You're about to create a completely useless program in Visual Basic. It only has a couple of lines of program code, two command buttons, and a text box. What does this wonderful program do? It displays a message in the text box when you click on one of the buttons, and clears the message when you click on the other button. Pretty cool? No, but it will take you through the motions of creating a program, and you'll see just how easy it is to create a working program with Visual Basic. For want of a better name, we'll name this program Useless.

The general process you use to create a program with Visual Basic is pretty simple. Here are the steps you will take with most programs:

Define your problem. No, you don't need to spend any time on a psychiatrist's couch for this one. You just need to decide what it is you want your program to do and how you want it to look. This is the conceptual part of programming that really taxes your gray matter.

Draw the interface. This means that you create the window(s) and dialog boxes for the program (all of which are forms). Then add controls, such as buttons, text boxes, and check boxes, to the forms.

Set design-time properties. After you have drawn the interface for your program, you need to set properties of most of the controls. For example, you probably need to set the window title or set the names that will appear on command buttons.

Write some program code. You can't get away from it—you'll have to actually write some program code. With simple programs, this means writing small bits of code for different *events* that can occur for the controls and forms in your program. When you click on a button, you generate a Click event for the button. You need to write some code to tell the program what to do when the user clicks that button. In more complex programs, you often have to write lots of other code, also. You'll learn more about code in Chapter 3, "Where Does That Code Go?"

Events are a big part of every Visual Basic program, and a large percentage of writing a program involves writing procedures that execute when events occur. What's an event? If you click a button, a Click event

continues

occurs for that button. If you change the text in a text box, a Change event occurs for that text box. If you select an option button, a Change event occurs for that option button. These are just a few examples of the wide range of events that can happen in a program. You'll learn more about events in later chapters.

Test the program. As you work on the program, you can test it right in Visual Basic without having to create the EXE file (a step called *compiling the program*). If there are any errors in your program, Visual Basic will generate an error message that will help you figure out what's wrong.

Compile the program. When you are ready to turn your program into a working EXE file, you have to compile it. This is an easy one; all you have to do is pick the Ma**k**e EXE File command in Visual Basic's **F**ile menu, specify a few options, then let Visual Basic take over.

Those six steps might take you a few minutes, or they might take you months, depending on the complexity of your program. I don't want to scare you away just yet, so your first Useless program will only take you a few minutes to create. It's important to understand, however, that Visual Basic offers one of the fastest methods for writing many types of Windows programs.

Drawing the Interface

The interface for Useless consists of a single form that contains two command buttons and a text box. Figure 0.6 shows the finished Useless program in action.

Figure 0.6

The Useless
program window.

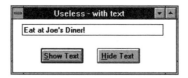

To add a control to a form, just click on the appropriate tool in the Toolbox. To draw a command button, for example, click on the command button tool in the Toolbox (it's the one with the picture of a command button on it).

Then, move the cursor onto the form, click and hold the main mouse button (by default, the left button), then drag the mouse. As you drag the mouse, Visual Basic draws a rectangle on the form. The rectangle shows you the outline of the control you are drawing. When you're happy with the size of the control, release the mouse button and Visual Basic adds the control to the form.

Some controls have a fixed size. A common dialog control, for example, is always the same size because the user doesn't interact with it directly. Many other controls, however, can be drawn at any size. You can make the frame as large as necessary to contain a selection of other controls, for example.

If you need to resize the control, click on it to make it active. Then, place the cursor at the edge of the control. The cursor should change to an up/down, left/right, or diagonal arrow, depending on where you place the cursor. Drag the edge of the control to resize it. To move a control, click on the control and drag it to its new location.

If you're confused about which control is which in the Toolbox, look at the back cover of your *Programmer's Guide* that came with Visual Basic. The illustration on the back cover labels all of the control tools in the Toolbox.

Ready? Start by drawing the interface.

Drawing the Useless Interface

1. Start Visual Basic.

2. In the Toolbox, click on the Textbox tool. Click and drag on the form to place the Text1 control on the form (see fig. 0.6).

3. Click on the Command button tool. Click and drag on the form to place the Command1 button.

continues

4. Click on the Command button tool again. Click and drag on the form to place the Command2 button.

5. Resize and reposition the form and its controls to something roughly resembling figure 0.6.

6. From Visual Basic's menu choose **F**ile, Sa**v**e Project to save the project.

TIP Unless you write some code to specify otherwise, a form pops up on the display at the same location where it was on the screen when you created it. When you're finished with a form, position it on the display where you want it to appear when you run the program.

Now that your program window is finished, you need to set some design-time properties.

Setting a Few Properties

Properties can be set at design time (when you design the program) or at run time (when the program is executed). You set properties at design-time to "predefine" them so they are set correctly when the program starts. For example, you need to set the title of your program window so that it displays something other than Form1 when the program starts. To do that, set the Caption property of the form using the Properties window. You'll learn how to set the Caption property in the next exercise.

You also can set properties at run time. Let's say you write a simple text editor using Visual Basic. When you open a file, you want the title bar to change to display the name of the program as well as the name of the document that's open. To do that, you also set the Caption property of the form, but you have to do it with a line of program code.

In your Useless program, you're going to set properties both at design time and at run time. You'll set the Caption property of Form1 to "Useless." This will cause the title Useless to appear in the program's title bar when it starts. Set the Caption property of Command1 to read "**S**how Text" and the Caption property of Command2 to read "**H**ide Text." Next, set the Text property of the Text1 control to be null (contain nothing). All of these properties are set at design time.

You'll also change a few properties at run-time. When the user clicks the
<u>S</u>how Text button, Useless will display the text "Eat at Joe's Diner!" in the
Text1 textbox. When the user clicks the <u>H</u>ide Text button, the text will
disappear from Text1. You'll accomplish this amazing feat of programming
wizardry by setting the Text property of the Text1 control.

Setting Design-Time Properties

1. Click anywhere on Form1 (but not on one of the controls) to make the
    form active.

2. If the Properties window isn't showing, choose <u>W</u>indow from the Visual
    Basic menu, then Pr<u>o</u>perties to display the Properties window. If you like
    shortcuts, just press F4 instead.

3. In the Properties window, scroll through the list of properties until you
    find the Caption property. Double-click on Caption in the Properties list or
    double-click in the Settings box to highlight the existing caption (Form1).

4. Type **Useless**, and notice that the title in the title bar changes.

5. From the Object box drop-down list, choose Command1.

6. Double-click on the Caption property in the Properties list, and type
    &Show Text. The & causes the letter that follows it to become an under-
    lined hotkey.

7. From the Object box drop-down list, choose Command2.

8. Double-click on the Caption property in the Properties list, and type
    &Hide Text.

9. From the Object box drop-down list, choose Text1.

10. In the Properties list, locate and double-click on the Text property, and
    press the Del key. This clears the text box so it will be blank when the
    program first starts.

11. Resize the buttons if the text doesn't fit on them.

12. Choose <u>F</u>ile, Sa<u>v</u>e Project to save the project.

Figure 0.7 shows the Caption property set for Command2 in the Properties
window.

Figure 0.7

The Caption property set for Command2 in the Properties window.

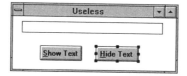

As you are working on a project, you should save it often. This makes it possible for you to take a break from the project and come back to it later, and also helps avoid the possibility that you could lose a lot of work if your PC suddenly goes belly-up because Ben, your pet rat, chewed through the power cord (and ended up with a new hairdo in the process).

Next, write some program code that will execute when the buttons are pushed.

Writing Some Program Code

You're about to write an *event-driven program*. This means that when certain events occur, certain other things happen. This doesn't mean that when a full moon occurs you'll grow hair on your palms. It just means that when specific things happen to the controls in the form, specific pieces of code will be executed. When the user clicks the **S**how Text button (Command1), for example, a Click event occurs for Command1. You're going to write a couple of lines of code that will be associated with this Click event. You'll do the same thing for the **H**ide Text button (Command2).

The easiest way to add code for a control is to double-click on the control. This opens the Code window and creates a new, blank *subroutine* for the default event for the selected control. A subroutine (also generally called a *Sub*) is a set of program statements that Visual Basic recognizes by name. The sub that executes when the user clicks a button that you have named cmdOK is called cmdOK_Click, for example.

Here's an important point, so stamp it on your forehead or your hairy palm: There are a lot of different potential events for a single control. A CommandButton, for example, has eleven different possible events. The default event is Click, because that's generally what you do with buttons. But there are ten other events that can happen to a button, all of which will remain nameless for now to keep your confusion to a minimum.

Now, let's do some *real* programming.

Writing Some Program Code

1. Double-click on the **S**how Text button (Command1) to display the Code window. Notice that the procedure listed in the Proc list box is Click, and that the name of the Sub is *Command1_Click*.

2. Make the code look like the following. Make sure you get all of the quotation marks and periods in the right places:

```
Sub Command1_Click ()
      Text1.Text = "Eat at Joe's Diner!"
      Caption = "Useless - with text"
End Sub
```

3. From the Object drop-down list in the Code window, choose Command2 to display a new Sub for the Command2 control.

4. Make the code for Command2_Click look like the following:

```
Sub Command1_Click ()
      Text1.Text = ""
      Caption = "Useless - no text"
End Sub
```

That's it! Your Useless program is finished. All you have to do now is compile it. But first, let's take a quick look at that code you just wrote. We'll analyze it line-by-line.

```
Text1.Text = "Eat at Joe's Diner!"
```

The Form1.Text1.Text part of the line identifies the Text property of the Text1 control on Form1. All this line does is set Text1 to read "Eat at Joe's Diner!". You're just stuffing some text into the text box. VB takes care of making it show up in the text box when the Command1 button is clicked.

```
Form1.Caption = "Useless - with text"
```

Come on... you can figure this one out. You're setting the caption (the title in the title bar) of Form1 to read "Useless - with text." As with the text box, VB takes care of putting the text in the title bar when the Command1 button is clicked.

```
Text1.Text = ""
```

Here you're fiddling with the Text1 control again. Setting it to "" makes it null, or blank. This clears the text from the text box when Command2 is clicked.

```
Form1.Caption = "Useless - no text"
```

This line sets the caption of the form again, just like the similar line in the Command1_Click Sub.

NOTE In this example, you didn't have to specify the form name in addition to a control name when you set a property. You only have to specify Text1.Text to set a property of this control—you don't have to specify the form name. When you begin working with more than one form in later chapters, you'll learn how to reference controls on different forms in your program. In case you're curious, however, you specify a control on a specific form by prefacing the control name with the form name and an exclamation mark. To reference the Text property of a control on Form2 called Text4, for example, you would use the control reference Form2!Text4.Text.

Do you feel like a real programmer and master or mistress of all you survey? Well, get a grip and get a life. You still need to compile the program, and that's going to be *really* tough to do.

Compiling Your Useless Program

When you compile a program, you take all of the individual files in the project, like the forms, BAS code files, and any other special files, and wad them up into an EXE file. I don't pretend to really understand how it works. After all, who cares? Visual Basic does it for you anyway. Just understand that the EXE file is the executable program file that can stand on its own without Visual Basic. You can install the EXE file as a program item in Windows if you want, or send a copy to a friend or enemy.

But here's where I should bring up one important point: The EXE file can't stand *completely* on its own. It needs a DLL (Dynamic Link Library) in order to run. A DLL is a file that contains various functions that a program can call to perform certain tasks. The DLL required by Visual Basic programs is included with Visual Basic, and with version 3.0 the file is called VBRUN300.DLL. Earlier versions of Visual Basic have similar DLLs with slightly different names (only the number is different). When you run your VB program, Windows must be able to find this DLL. The VBRUN???.DLL files are readily available from information services like CompuServe, America OnLine, etc. If you upload your programs to these services, you don't need to include the DLL.

Now that you've stored that knowledge-nugget away, you're ready to compile your Useless program.

Compiling the Useless Program

1. In Visual Basic's menu, choose **F**ile, Ma**k**e EXE File. This displays the Make EXE File dialog box (see fig. 0.8).

2. In the File **N**ame edit box, type **USELESS** as the name. This is the name of the EXE file VB will create for your program.

3. If you want to put your program file in a different location, select the drive and directory using the Dri**v**es and **D**irectories controls.

continues

4. In the Application **T**itle edit box, type **Useless**. This is the name that will show up in the Task Manager for your program when it is running.

5. Choose OK.

Figure 0.8

The Make EXE File dialog box.

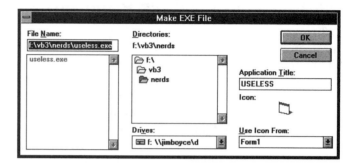

But wait a minute! You say you want to change the icon for the program? Well, too bad—you have to change the Icon property of the form. Visual Basic includes a whole bucket full of icons. If you want to change the icon, select Form1, and open up the Properties window. Double-click on the Icon property and choose an icon from the ICONS directories. Then, recompile the program. The icon you have specified will be used to represent the program when the program is minimized on the desktop, and also will be used to represent the program when it is added to a program group in Program Manager.

TIP If your program uses more than one form, you can assign a different icon to each one. In the Make EXE File dialog box, you can select which of the assigned icons is to be used for the program by choosing a form from the **U**se Icon From drop-down list.

During the compile process, Visual Basic checks your program. If it finds any errors, it displays an error message for you and shows you where the problem is located. You'll have to fix the problem and recompile the program. You'll learn more about fixing problems and killing bugs in Chapter 15, "Da Bugs!" This program is really simple, so you shouldn't have any errors in it. If VB spits out an error message when you compile your Useless program, check your program code and make sure it matches *exactly* the code in the exercises.

Testing Useless

Although you can test your program right in Visual Basic without first compiling it, we skipped that step because Useless is such a simple program. To test it now, run the program file USELESS.EXE that Visual Basic created in the last exercise. You might as well add it as a program item to one of your Program Manager groups.

Testing Useless

1. In Program Manager, select and open the group window where you want Useless to be installed.

2. Choose **F**ile, **N**ew, and in the New Program Object dialog box, choose the Program **I**tem radio button. Choose OK.

3. In the Program Item Properties dialog box, use the **B**rowse button to locate and select the file USELESS.EXE.

4. In the **D**escription edit box, type **Useless**.

5. Choose OK to create the new program item.

6. Double-click on the Useless icon to start the program.

7. When the Useless program window appears, click on the **S**how Text button. The text "Eat at Joe's Diner!" should appear in the text box and the title bar should change to read "Useless - with text".

8. Click on the **H**ide Text button. The text should disappear from the text box and the title bar should change to read "Useless - no text".

If the program didn't work, go back through the exercises and figure out what you did wrong.

TIP A form is almost a stand-alone Windows program in its own right. Visual Basic takes care of making the form behave like a Windows program. If you set the MinButton and MaxButton properties to True, for example, your form will have Minimize and Maximize buttons. You don't have to write any code to make the Minimize or Maximize buttons work. Visual Basic and Windows take care of that for you.

Getting Help

Visual Basic has a wonderful Help system. Whenever you need help on a topic, or you can't remember the exact syntax or purpose of a function, statement, or keyword, you can use the Help system to jog your memory or teach you about the topic. For example, assume you're in the middle of writing a statement that uses the MsgBox function to display a message box, and you can't remember the syntax of the MsgBox function. No problem! Just highlight the text *MsgBox* in the statement, and press the F1 key. Visual Basic automatically displays a Help topic page for the function (see fig. 0.9).

Figure 0.9

The Help topic page for the MsgBox function.

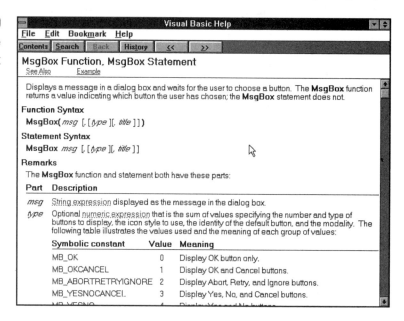

The Visual Basic Help system also is great when you can't remember which properties, methods, or events apply to a specific type of control. Just choose the **S**earch button when the Help window is open and search using the name of the control. The Help topic page for the control will provide a pop-up window that lists all of the properties of the control (see fig. 0.10). You can click on a property in this list to view a topic page that explains the purpose and function of the selected property.

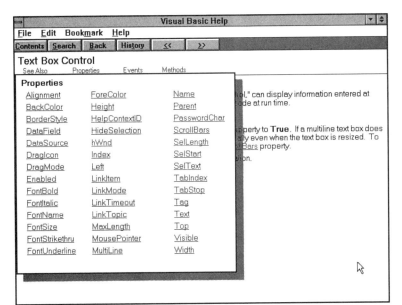

Figure 0.10

The topic page for a control provides a list of its properties.

Many topic pages in the Visual Basic Help file also have code examples. You can copy parts of these code examples into your program to save the time that you would otherwise spend writing the code yourself. In addition, Visual Basic includes many sample projects. You can use portions of the sample projects in your own programs to save time. The sample programs have lots of comments, which make them ideal for helping you to learn how they work.

Forms, Controls, and Other Voodoo

Chapter 0 gave you the nickel tour around Visual Basic. Now it's time to get serious. Sit up straight! Turn off that loud music! Wipe that silly, drooling grin from your face! Ah, that's better.

As if you couldn't figure it out from the chapter title, this chapter explains forms, controls, and other Visual Basic voodoo like properties. It will help you understand what all these things are and what purpose they serve in your programs. Here's a hit list for this chapter:

- ☐ Understand what forms are and how they work
- ☐ See examples of the standard VB controls you can add to a form
- ☐ Understand what properties are and what purpose they serve
- ☐ Learn to solve complex quadratic equations written in red crayon on a hairy cabdriver's back

If you don't get the quadratic equation bit, it's okay. That's kind of a Grasshopper-Zen sort of thing, anyway. You have to be able to hear one hand clapping before you really catch on to quadratic equations written in *any* color crayon. But by then, you don't care....

There is a little bit of code in this chapter, but I've tried to keep it to a bare minimum. Don't worry if you can't figure out how the code works or where it should go in your program. We'll cover that in the next couple of chapters.

Tell Me About Forms, Controls, and Properties

I'm glad you asked. Forms and controls are types of *objects* in Visual Basic. A command button is an object, a text box is an object, and so on. Objects are just items that Visual Basic recognizes as unique entities. Let's start with an important object for almost any program—forms.

Forms

Forms are the program windows and dialog boxes that make up your program. You can have multiple forms in a single program. That makes sense, doesn't it? After all, your program might need a bunch of different dialog boxes in addition to its main program window. Each dialog box or window is a form of its own. When you start a new project, VB creates a new, blank form called Form1. You can create as many other forms as you need. Figure 1.1 shows a small form that can be shown with many others on-screen at once.

Figure 1.1
A small form.

Each form has to have a unique name so it doesn't suffer from an identity crisis. By default, the forms are named Form1, Form2, Form3, and so on, *ad nauseum.* You can keep these names or you can change them. Changing the names can make it a lot easier to write the program. Here's why: A big part of writing a program involves setting and changing properties for controls at run time (changing the contents of a text box, for example). If you have 15 forms in your program, it's a lot easier to specify a control on the FileOpen form than it is to remember that the FileOpen form is Form12. By naming your forms according to their function, you'll be able to keep track of all of those forms much more easily.

How do you set a form's name? That's easy. Just set the form's Name property. Select the form, then scroll through the Properties window until you find the Name property. Double-click on the Name property to highlight the current name in the Settings box and type the new name. Here are some rules for naming objects such as forms:

- ☐ Object names must begin with a letter.
- ☐ Object names can contain only letters, numbers, and the underscore (_) character. You can't use spaces or punctuation marks in an object name.
- ☐ Object names are limited to a maximum of 40 characters, so you can't name an object using the lyrics to Eric Clapton's "Layla." Sorry.

You might want to name your objects using a prefix to identify what type of object it is. You might use the prefix *frm* for a form, for example. So, your FileOpen form might be frmFileOpen. When you're trying to decipher some code you wrote three months (or even days) ago and you see a reference to the object frmFileOpen, you'll know immediately that the object is a form. The Visual Basic *Programmer's Guide* that comes with Visual Basic includes a list of suggested object prefixes. Check it out and use the suggested prefixes religiously. Being consistent will help you keep track of form and control names as you are writing a program.

Controls

Controls are all of the gadgets and doodads that you add to your program's forms to enable the user to perform tasks with the program. Command buttons, check boxes, list boxes, and text boxes are examples of controls. Have a look at figure 1.2—it shows the tools in the Toolbox for the Standard Edition of Visual Basic.

Figure 1.2
Tools in the
Toolbox.

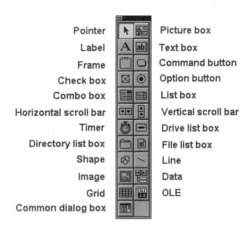

Pointer			Picture box
Label			Text box
Frame			Command button
Check box			Option button
Combo box			List box
Horizontal scroll bar			Vertical scroll bar
Timer			Drive list box
Directory list box			File list box
Shape			Line
Image			Data
Grid			OLE
Common dialog box			

 Pointer. This isn't a control. Use this when you need to select, move, or resize a form or control.

 Picture box. This control displays a bitmap, icon, or Windows metafile. Use it when you want to stick one of these three types of graphics on a form. You also can use it to display text on a form, or use it as a container for other controls (such as a toolbar that contains buttons).

 Label. This control displays text that the user can't change. You can change the text in the label at either design time or at run time. Use this to *label* stuff on the form. Duh.

 Text box. Use this control to display text on the form or to enable the user to input or edit some text. A text box can be single-line or multi-line. If it's multi-line, it can contain more than one line of text. Otherwise, it's limited to a single line of text.

 Frame. This isn't much of a control. It's just a box you can draw around a *group* of controls. You should use one of these when you want to group together a bunch of option buttons that offer choices about a related feature or function in your program, for example (see *option button*).

 Command button. These are those ubiquitous buttons such as OK, Cancel, Help, Push Me, etc. You can add any capability you want to a command button simply by writing a procedure for it. The procedure for a button might execute a single statement, or it might execute many statements, depending on the requirements of the program.

☐ **Check box.** This is a True/False or Yes/No option box. Use it for turning options on and off in your program. Any number of check boxes can be checked (turned on) at one time.

☐ **Option button.** These are also called *radio buttons*. Use a group of them to enable the user to choose from a selection of options. In a group of radio buttons, only one can be selected at one time. When you select one, the rest in the group are deselected (turned off).

☐ **List box.** This control displays a list of items from which the user can select.

☐ **Combo box.** This control combines a text box with a list box. The user can enter text in the text box portion of the combo box, or can select an option from the drop-down list part of the combo box.

☐ **Horizontal scroll bar** and **Vertical scroll bar.** These are also called *slider* controls because you can slide the scroll bar to select a setting. They enable the user to select from a range of predefined values. They're not the same as the scroll bars you see at the bottom and right side of a window. You might use one of these for a volume control, for example.

☐ **Timer.** This control enables you to execute events at specific times. Think of it as an alarm clock control.

☐ **Drive list box.** This control enables the user to select a disk.

☐ **Directory list box.** This control enables the user to select directories and paths.

☐ **File list box.** This control enables the user to select from a list of files.

☐ **Shape.** This control adds a circle, square, rectangle, or ellipse to a form.

☐ **Line.** This control adds a line to a form.

☐ **Image.** This control displays a bitmap, icon, or Windows metafile. It's similar to a Picture box control, but has certain limitations. Check Chapter 10, "Working with Pictures," to learn what these limitations are. The advantage of an Image control over a Picture box control is that the Image control requires fewer system resources (primarily less memory). If your program conserves resources, your users will have more memory free to run other programs while they are using yours. It also behaves like a command button, so you can use it instead of a command button when you need a graphical button in your program.

Data. This control enables you to connect to an existing database to display data from the database on your form.

Grid. This control creates a series of rows and columns such as a spreadsheet. You can display text and graphics in the grid's cells. You can add code for the Grid control to enable the user to change the contents of a cell, just as they can with a spreadsheet.

OLE. This control embeds data into your program using OLE (Object Linking and Embedding). Although OLE is beyond the scope of *Understanding Visual Basic*, OLE provides a program with the ability to easily share information dynamically with other programs, and allows the program to create compound documents that are composed of data from more than one program.

Common dialog. This control provides a set of standard dialog boxes for things like opening and saving files, printing, and selecting colors and fonts. Use this control to save time (you won't have to create the dialog boxes) and make your program consistent with other Windows programs.

Next, take a gander at figure 1.3—it shows each of the controls on a form.

Figure 1.3

Common controls on a form.

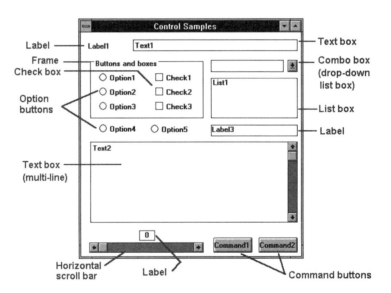

Some controls are always visible on the form, others are always invisible (the user never sees them but you see them at design time), and still others come and go—you can make them appear and disappear as needed.

Controls are a big part of every Visual Basic program. Later in the chapter, you'll read about controls in more detail.

Properties

All objects (forms and controls) in a VB program have *properties*. The text that appears in a text box is its Text property. The font that the text box uses is its FontName property. You can do a lot in a program just by changing control properties. If you want the text to be bold, for example, set the FontBold property to be True. In Chapter 0, you placed text in a text box by changing the text box's Text property. You also changed the title in a title bar by changing the form's Caption property.

The types of properties that an object includes can vary from object to object. A form doesn't include a Text property, for example, because it doesn't contain any text. A text box doesn't have a WindowState property because it's not a window.

You learned in Chapter 0 that you can set an object's properties at design time by using the Properties window (see fig. 1.4). When you select an object and then open the Properties window, all of the properties for the selected object appear in the Properties window and you can change them to your heart's content.

You also can set properties at run time (when the program is running). Setting properties at run time is one of the primary means for making things happen in a program. To set a property at run time, write a line of code that specifies the form name, the control name, the property, and then sets that property to something. Here's an example:

```
Form1!Text2.Text = "Oh, frabjous day!"
```

Form1 specifies the name of the form, Text2 specifies the name of the control, and Text specifies the property for the control. They're hooked together with periods. You're saying, "Go to Form1, select the Text2 control, and set the Text property to...". Then, you're specifying what you want it set to—in this case, it's "Oh, frabjous day!".

Figure 1.4

The Properties window for a TextBox control.

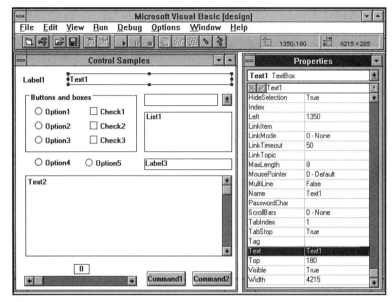

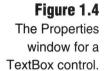
NOTE The Form name is separated from the control name by an exclamation mark. Previous versions of Visual Basic used a period to separate the form name from the control name.

You don't always have to include the form name when you set a control's property. In the previous example, you could have used just Text2.Text instead of Form1!Text2.Text. If you omit the form name, VB assumes that you want to work with the current form. It's a good habit to use the form name anyway to make sure you're dealing with the correct control.

TIP Different types of properties have different types of values. Some use text, others use numbers, and others are either True or False.

Setting Properties for a Form

The beauty of programming in the Windows environment is that development tools like Visual Basic take care of creating a lot of your program's interface. You don't have to actually draw a control menu or code for it, for example; you just have to tell VB you want your program to have a control menu. VB does the rest.

A major part of designing your program's interface includes deciding what its form(s) will look like. You don't have to write a lot of code to make your form(s) look like standard windows and dialog boxes. Instead, you control the appearance and behavior of a form by setting any of its 43 properties. For example, if you want a form to be a fixed size (not resizeable), you can set its BorderStyle property to 1 (Fixed Single) or 3 (Fixed Double).

Let's cover some of the properties you're most likely to fiddle with when you're designing your program's forms.

Setting the Border Style

A typical program window is resizeable. This means that when it's displayed in normal window mode, it has a double-line border around it and minimize and maximize buttons in the upper right corner. Figure 1.5 shows a typical, resizeable program window in its normal state.

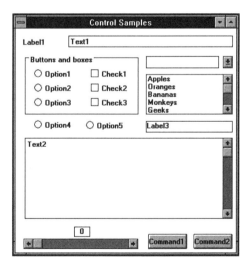

Figure 1.5

A typical, resizeable window.

You also might want your forms to be fixed (not resizeable). There's usually no reason for a user to resize a dialog box, so dialog boxes are often fixed—they don't have any borders, and the user can't grab the border with the pointer to resize them. Figure 1.6 shows a couple of dialog boxes. The one on the left has a single-line fixed border, and the one on the right has a double-line fixed border. Whether you choose to use a single-line fixed border or a double-line fixed border is really a matter of esthetics. Functionally, the two border types are the same.

Figure 1.6

A single-line fixed border and a double-line fixed border.

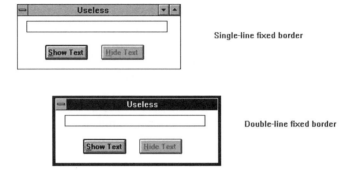

Single-line fixed border

Double-line fixed border

It's easy enough to specify the type of border a form will have; just set the form's BorderStyle property. Try it out in the following exercise.

Setting a Form's Border Style

1. Start Visual Basic, and choose File, Open Project.

2. Locate and select the file NOPANIC.MAK that was provided on the *Understanding Visual Basic Disk.*

3. If you don't see the Controls form on your display, choose CONTROLS.FRM (Form1) in the Project window, and click the View Form window. You should see the form shown in figure 1.7.

4. Select Form1 (Don't Panic!), and open the Properties window to display the form's properties.

5. Locate and select the BorderStyle property, and set it to 1-Fixed Single.

6. Choose Run, Start. The Don't Panic! form should appear on the display with a fixed, single-line border (see fig. 1.8).

7. Choose Run, End.

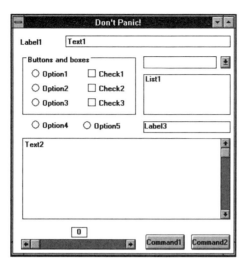

Figure 1.7
The Don't Panic!
form (Form1).

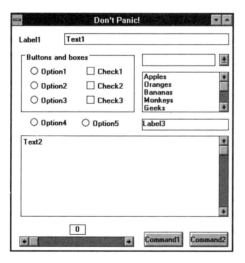

Figure 1.8
The Don't Panic!
form with a single-
line fixed border.

The border of the form doesn't change while you're working on it; it only changes at run time. Do the exercise again on your own, but this time set the BorderStyle property to 3-Fixed Double. Run the program again to see what the Controls form looks like with a Fixed Double border.

This is obvious, but I'll point it out anyway. You just ran a program without compiling it. Visual Basic lets you run a program to test it while you are designing and writing the program. To run a program, choose Run, then Start, or click on the Run button in the toolbar (the one that looks like a right-facing arrowhead). To stop a program and return to the editor again, choose Run, End, or click on the Stop button in the toolbar (the one that has a solid square in the bottom right corner of the button). You'll learn more about this stuff in Chapter 15, which covers testing and debugging.

Enabling and Disabling Forms

Normally when your program is displaying a form, you'll want the form to be *enabled*. When a form is enabled, the user can make it active (set focus to the form), select controls on the form, and so on. Sometimes, though, you'll want a form to be *disabled*. When a form is disabled, the user can't close it, select it, or work with any of the controls on it. Clicking on a disabled form just generates that familiar and obnoxious Windows error beep.

The terms *enabled* and *focus* don't refer to the same thing. If a control is enabled, it is available to the user. If a menu item is enabled, for example, the user can select the menu item. If the menu item is disabled, the menu item appears dimmed and the user can't select it. When a control or form has focus, however, it is the active form or control. In some cases, a control can have the focus even if it is disabled.

Why disable a form? Maybe you want to force the user to do something before the form will go away. Assume that your main form is enabled and the user has been working with it. He then tries to access a feature that you have designed to be password protected. Your program can disable the main form until the user enters a password in another form, or cancels his request for the password-protected feature.

To disable a form, set its Enabled property to either True or False. Try it out in the next exercise.

Enabling/Disabling a Form

1. Open up the NOPANIC.MAK project again if you don't already have it opened.

2. Select the Don't Panic! form (Form1), then open the Properties window and locate the Enabled property.

3. Double-click on the Enabled property to set it to False.

4. Run the program (choose **F**ile, **R**un) and try clicking on the form. You should be rewarded with beeps.

5. Select another window, such as the Project window or Debug window, and try to select the Controls window again. Because the form is disabled, you can't select it.

6. End the program, and set the Enabled property of Form1 back to True.

Let's go back to the password example I mentioned earlier. How do you enable the form when the user enters the correct password? That's easy—just set the Enabled property using a line of code:

```
<if the user enters the right password...>
    Form1.Enabled = True
<end if>
```

Don't worry about the If/End If stuff for now. That's covered in Chapter 11, "Printing Stuff." For now, just understand that you can enable a form at run time just by setting its Enabled property to be True.

Assigning an Icon to a Form

No program is complete without its own custom icons. When you minimize your program window, you probably want to have it represented by an incredible, astonishing, and even better-than-average icon of your own choosing. No problem—just set the form's Icon property. But where do you find the icon?

Visual Basic comes with a truckload of icons for just about every purpose. If you don't like those icons, you can modify them or create your own. But you say you don't have an icon editor? No problem! Visual Basic includes its own icon editor as a sample program. Just hunt in the \VB\SAMPLES\ICONWRKS directory and load the project file ICONWRKS.MAK. Compile the program (choose **F**ile, **M**ake EXE File), and you'll have a nifty icon editor. Figure 1.9 shows IconWorks with an icon opened for editing.

Figure 1.9

IconWorks with an icon opened for editing.

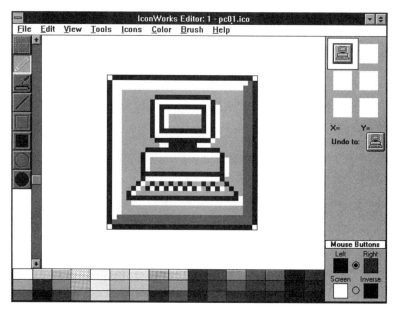

Are you all set to check out some icons? Assign one to Form1 in NOPANIC.MAK.

Assigning an Icon to a Form

1. Open NOPANIC.MAK (yes, again).

2. Click on Form1 to select it, then open the Properties window and locate the Icon property.

3. Double-click on the Icon property in the Properties window to display the Load Icon dialog box (see fig. 1.10).

4. Select the file \VB3\ICONS\MICS\BULLSEYE.ICO, and choose OK (your VB3 directory may be named something else, depending on where you installed Visual Basic).

5. Run the program, and minimize the Don't Panic! window. You should see a bullseye icon at the bottom of the display. Isn't that *special*? End the program when you've seen all you need to see of the bullseye icon.

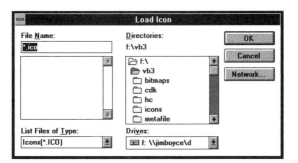

Figure 1.10
The Load Icon
dialog box.

You can assign a different icon to each form in your program, but you probably won't want to assign icons to forms that are used as dialog boxes. Why would a dialog box need an icon? You probably will set its properties so it can't be minimized, anyway. To do that, set the MinButton and MaxButton properties to be False.

When you compile the program, you can specify which icon to use for the program itself: click on the Use Icon From drop-down list and specify which form's icon will be used for the program. This is the icon that will show up in Program Manager for the program.

Changing the Mouse Pointer over a Form

Do you want the pointer to change when the user moves it over one of your program's forms? That's another easy one; just set the MousePointer property for the form. You can set the pointer to one of 13 different pointers. If you set it to 0-Default, the pointer acts like a normal Windows pointer when it's hovering over the form. That means it changes according to the type of control it's sitting on. If it's on a text box, for example, it changes to an I-beam pointer. If it's on a blank area of the form, it's an arrow pointer.

If you set the MousePointer property to one of the other 12 options, the pointer will always look like the assigned pointer when it's hovering over the form—it won't matter what type of control is underneath the pointer.

Changing the Pointer

1. Open NOPANIC.MAK (are you getting bored with this project yet?).

2. Select Form1, then open the Properties window and locate and select the MousePointer property.

3. Click on the Settings box drop-down list and choose 2-Cross (or double-click on the MousePointer property twice to cycle through the choices to 2-Cross).

4. Run the program and move the pointer over the controls on the form. You should see a cross pointer *most* of the time.

5. Move the pointer over the control menu, title bar, and minimize/maximize buttons. The pointer should change to an arrow pointer again.

6. Move the pointer over the Command1 control. It should change to an arrow pointer.

7. End the program (choose **R**un, **E**nd).

The cursor changed to an arrow pointer when you moved it over the control menu, title bar, and minimize/maximize buttons because that's built into the program automatically by Visual Basic. But, why did it change when you moved it over the Command1 button? That's because Command1 also has a MousePointer property, and it's set to 1-Arrow. So, the Command1 button always makes the pointer change to an arrow pointer.

Yes, you can change the MousePointer property of a control at run time (I knew you'd ask). Just set the object's MousePointer property to the integer (whole number) value that corresponds to the pointer you want. Here's a line of code that would set Form1's pointer back to the default when Command2 is clicked:

```
Sub Command2_Click ()
    Form1.MousePointer = 0
End Sub
```

Other Common Form Properties

There are a lot of other form properties that you can set. Some of them are really simple, and don't require much explanation or an exercise. Here's a list of some of these other form properties with suggestions on how to use them:

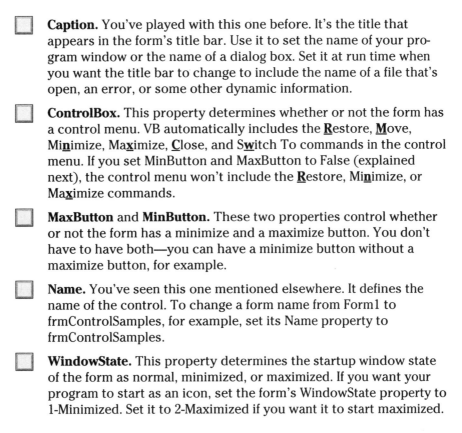

Caption. You've played with this one before. It's the title that appears in the form's title bar. Use it to set the name of your program window or the name of a dialog box. Set it at run time when you want the title bar to change to include the name of a file that's open, an error, or some other dynamic information.

ControlBox. This property determines whether or not the form has a control menu. VB automatically includes the Restore, Move, Minimize, Maximize, Close, and Switch To commands in the control menu. If you set MinButton and MaxButton to False (explained next), the control menu won't include the Restore, Minimize, or Maximize commands.

MaxButton and **MinButton.** These two properties control whether or not the form has a minimize and a maximize button. You don't have to have both—you can have a minimize button without a maximize button, for example.

Name. You've seen this one mentioned elsewhere. It defines the name of the control. To change a form name from Form1 to frmControlSamples, for example, set its Name property to frmControlSamples.

WindowState. This property determines the startup window state of the form as normal, minimized, or maximized. If you want your program to start as an icon, set the form's WindowState property to 1-Minimized. Set it to 2-Maximized if you want it to start maximized.

That's enough about forms to get you started. You'll experiment with some of the other properties in later chapters. Now you need to learn some more about controls.

Using Specific Types of Controls

There are 23 controls in Visual Basic Standard Edition. Some of these 23 controls are explained in other chapters. The drive list box, directory list box, and file list box controls, for example, are explained in Chapter 5, "Making Decisions." This section of the chapter gives you an idea of how some of the most common controls are used and provides some tips on using them in your programs. It doesn't cover all of the properties for all of the controls, because we'd be here all day if it did. Figure 1.11 shows a sample with some controls on it.

Figure 1.11

The Don't Panic!
form with some
controls.

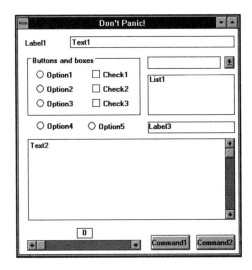

Start Visual Basic and open the file NOPANIC.MAK (yes, again) so you can
check out the properties for its controls.

Labels

Label controls are great any time you need to display some text that the user
can't directly change. Use a label when you want to label something on a
form (duh...) or when you want to display some text that is generated by
your program. There's a label control in NOPANIC.MAK named Label1. Click
on it, and open the Properties window so you can check out the properties
listed in the following list:

AutoSize. If this property is set to False (the default), the size of the
label control won't change if the text changes. If set to True, the size
of the label control *will* change horizontally if the text changes. Set
this property to True if you expect to change the contents of the
Label while the program is running. Remember to make room on the
form for the label to grow.

Borderstyle. If this property is set to 0 (the default), the label won't
have a border around it. If set to 1, the label will have a border
around it and look a lot like a text box.

Font???. There are six different font properties for a label. Use these
properties to control the appearance of the label's text. Check out
the Properties window for a label to find out what these font

properties are. They're self-explanatory by their property names: FontBold, FontItalic, FontSize, FontName, FontStrikethru, and FontUnderline.

☐ **WordWrap.** If this property is set to False (the default), the label won't change size vertically to accommodate lengthy text (but it will change horizontally if AutoSize is set to True). If set to True, the size of the label control will change vertically to accommodate the amount of text in it, but will retain its original horizontal size.

Remember that label controls aren't just for labeling things on a form. Use a label instead of a text box any time you need to display text on a form, but don't want the user to be able to change the text.

Text Boxes

Text boxes are usually used to get some input from the user. It may be the name of a file, a password, or some other text. Text boxes can be either single-line or multi-line. As if you couldn't guess, a single-line text box can contain a single line of text. Multi-line text boxes can contain multiple lines of text. When you need to get a small piece of text from the user, do it with a single-line text box. You might use a multi-line text box if you're creating a simple text editor.

You've already read about some text box properties such as Text (the contents of the text box). Text boxes also share some properties with Labels, such as BorderStyle and all those font properties. There's a text box called Text1 on the Don't Panic! form. Click on it, and check out these additional properties in the Properties window:

☐ **MaxLength.** This property specifies the maximum amount of text (in number of characters) that can be entered in the text box. When the maximum number is reached, the user is rewarded with an obnoxious beep. Use this property to limit input. If you're prompting for an eight-character password, for example, set MaxLength to 8.

☐ **Multiline.** Set this to True if you want the user to be able to enter multiple lines of text in the box. Set it to False (the default) if you want to get just a small piece of text on a single line.

☐ **PasswordChar.** This one is great if you're prompting for a password with a text box. When the user enters text in the text box, the program displays the character specified by this property instead of the actual text. A lot of programmers use an asterisk (*) for this.

ScrollBars. This property is only useful for multi-line text boxes, and it puts scrollbars on the text box according to the value of the property. You can set it to 0-None, 1-Horizontal, 2-Vertical, or 3-Both. Include scrollbars if you are using a multi-line text box and expect the user to enter lots of text.

Let's play with the text boxes in NOPANIC.MAK.

Fooling with Text Box Properties

1. Open the file NOPANIC.MAK, click on the Text1 text box control, and open the Properties window.

2. Locate the PasswordChar property and double-click on it to select it and make the Settings box active.

3. Type * (that's an asterisk) and press Enter. Notice that the caption in Text1 changes from Text1 to *****.

4. Locate and double-click on the MaxLength property and set it to 8.

5. Run the program and type a bunch or characters in the Text1 control. You'll only see asterisks in place of what you type, and you'll get a beep when you try to enter more than eight characters.

6. End the program, and in Form1 (Don't Panic!), select the control Text2.

7. In the Properties window, select the ScrollBars property and set it to 3-Both. You should see a horizontal scroll bar appear on the control.

Here are some world-shattering, terribly important points about text boxes and scroll bars: If you set the MultiLine property of the text box to False, you won't see any scroll bars at all, regardless of the value of the ScrollBars property. If you don't include scroll bars, or include only a vertical scroll bar, text will automatically word-wrap in the text box. If you include a horizontal scroll bar, text won't word-wrap in the text box, but the user will be able to scroll the text box to read long lines of text.

TIP If you're using a multi-line text box for a simple note editor, make it big enough to contain 80 characters and eliminate the horizontal scroll bar. That will force text wrap to be on and still let the user enter plenty of text. Hey, who needs more than an 80-character-wide document in a simple text editor? If you want to wrap your brain around the text editor concept, open and explore the project \VB\SAMPLES\MDI\MDINOTE.MAK that comes with Visual Basic. It's a text editor that enables you to open and edit multiple ASCII documents. You might use it as a starting point to create your own special-purpose text editor.

Command Buttons

Command buttons are everywhere in Windows. You've seen 'em: **O**K, **H**elp, **K**ick Me, **P**ush This Button to Implode Your Head and Learn Why Rabbits Don't Wear Underwear, **C**ancel, and so on. Command buttons will probably be a big part of any program you write. Here are some of the most important properties for Command buttons:

Cancel. Set this property to True if you want the button to be the default Cancel button. If a button is the default Cancel button, pressing the Esc key when the program is running clicks the button, even if it doesn't have focus (isn't the active control). Then, write some code for the button's Click event that does whatever needs to be done when the user cancels the operation.

Caption. This property sets the text that appears on the face of the button. Add an ampersand (&) character in front of any letter you want underlined as a hot key for the button. Using E&xit as the caption, for example, will give you a button with the text E**x**it on it. Pressing Alt+X will choose (click) the E**x**it button.

Default. Set this property to True if you want the button to be "clicked" when the user presses Enter. In many cases, it's a good idea to set the OK button's Default property to True. When the user presses the Enter key, it's the same as clicking the OK button. This isn't true, though, if another command button is highlighted when the user presses Enter. If that's the case, the highlighted button is clicked and not the Default button.

Enabled. Set this property to True if you want the user to be able to click on the button. Set it to False if you want to prevent the user from clicking on the button. When a button is disabled, it still appears on the form, but the text is *dimmed* (it's gray instead of black, for example).

Font???. Yep, these are those font properties again. Change them when you want to change the appearance of the button's caption.

Experiment on your own with the Command1 and Command2 buttons in the NOPANIC.MAK project. For example, set Command1's Default property to True and Command2's Cancel property to True. Then run the program to see how the two buttons behave when you press Enter and Esc. You'll be rewarded with a message box (sorry, no banana-flavored pellets for you in this exercise).

Frames

Frames are boxes that you can use to group other controls together. In fact, a bunch of controls inside a frame is called a *group*. Use a frame to group together options and controls that logically relate to one another. Frames also are important for controlling the way option buttons (radio buttons) work. Option buttons that are inside a frame act with one another—if you select one, all the others are deselected.

All option buttons that are outside of a frame act with all other option buttons that are also outside of any frames. Just think of the form's border as serving like a frame for these buttons, and you'll get the idea. You'll also experiment with the concept shortly. But first, here are a couple of **H**ighly **S**ignificant properties for frames:

Caption. This is the title of the frame. If you're grouping together a bunch of controls that control line spacing, for example, set the Caption property to Line Spacing to let the user know what all those controls are for. You can use an ampersand to add a hot key to the frame's caption. If the user presses the hot key, the first selected control in the group receives focus. If you have a bunch of option buttons in the frame, for example, whichever option button is currently selected (turned on) receives focus (becomes the active control) when the user presses the hot key for the frame.

Enabled. Set this property to False if you don't want the user to be able to access the controls in the group. This is a lot easier than disabling the controls in the group one-by-one.

TIP

Here's a big tip: If you put controls inside a frame, you can move all of the controls at design time just by moving the frame. Idinat *special?* If you need to rearrange some controls on the form, you can drag a frame and all of the controls in it move along with the frame. To include a control inside a frame, however, the frame must be selected when you draw the control. You can't drag a control from another location on the form and into a frame.

To place controls in a frame, you first have to draw the frame. Next, draw the other controls inside the frame. You can't just drag a control into a frame; if you do, there won't be any association between the control and the frame.

Option Buttons

These used to be called *radio buttons*. Options buttons enable a user to select options in a program. Use these whenever you want the user to be able to pick only one choice from a selection of choices. Place option buttons inside a frame to keep them from affecting other option buttons on the form.

Enabled. You can disable individual option buttons by setting the Enabled property to False, but many times it's easier to disable their frame, instead. The exception is if you want to disable one option button without disabling the rest of the option buttons inside the frame.

Value. This property is True if the option button is selected and False if the button is deselected. You can set this property at run time with a line of code to preset the value of an option button before you display the form. If you set an option button's Value property to True, all other option buttons in the group are automatically set to False.

Take a minute to play with the option buttons in NOPANIC.MAK.

Playing with Option Buttons

1. Open NOPANIC.MAK for the umpteenth time if it isn't already open.

2. Run the program and click on Option1, Option2, and Option3. Notice that picking one clears whichever other one is selected.

3. Click on Option4 and notice that it doesn't affect Option1, Option2, or Option3.

4. Click on Option5; there's still no effect on the option buttons that are inside Frame1 (Buttons and boxes).

5.   End the program, and select the Frame1 control.

6.   Open the Properties window and change the Enabled property to False.

7.   Run the program again and try to select any of the controls inside Frame1 (buttons and boxes). You can't select any of the controls because the entire frame is disabled.

Check Boxes

Check boxes are similar to option buttons, but you can have more than one check box checked (turned on). Check boxes are like toggle switches that you can use to turn features on or off. Use a check box any time you want the user to be able to turn an option on or off but don't want the option to be dependent on any other.

Here are some useful properties of check box controls:

Enabled. As with option buttons, disabling a check box prevents the user from being able to change its value. If you want to disable all of the check boxes and other controls in a frame, disable the frame instead; it's easier and quicker.

Value. If this property is set to True, the check box has a check in it. If set to False, the check box is cleared.

List Boxes

Use a list box whenever you want to display a selection of predefined choices in a list. Your list box can be single-column or multi-column. In either case, scroll bars appear on the list whenever there are too many items to display in the box.

An empty list box isn't much use, so you'll have to fill the list box at some point. Right now you don't need to know *where* in your program that code should be located; you'll read about that in Chapter 2, "Making Cool Stuff Happen." For now, just take a look at some code that would fill a list box named List1 on Form1 with some values:

```
Sub Form_Load ()
    Form1!List1.AddItem "Apples"
    Form1!List1.AddItem "Oranges"
    Form1!List1.AddItem "Bananas"
    Form1!List1.AddItem "Monkeys"
```

```
        Form1!List1.AddItem "Geeks"
        Form1!List1.AddItem "Politicians"
        Form1!List1.AddItem "Rabbit's underwear"
        Form1!List1.AddItem "Blobs"
   End Sub
```

It's really simple: just specify the name of the object (in this case, List1) and use the AddItem method to add the item to the list. If you also have to specify the form name because it isn't the active form, include it and separate it from the control name by an exclamation mark. But wait a minute—the items aren't sorted alphabetically. How would you sort them? You just have to set the Sorted property for the list box to be True.

Here are some properties of list boxes you should know:

Columns. This property specifies the number of columns in the list. Figure 1.12 shows a list box with two columns. If the list box isn't wide enough to display all of its columns, VB automatically adds a horizontal scroll bar to the list box.

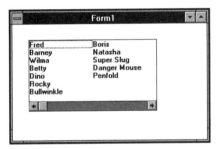

Figure 1.12

A two-column list box.

MultiSelect. This property is really useful. If it's set to True, the user can select multiple items from the list. You'll read more about MultiSelect in Chapters 5 and 10.

Sorted. If this property is set to True, VB automatically sorts the items in the list in alphanumeric order.

Combo Boxes

Combo boxes are a combination of a text box and a drop-down list. There are three different styles of combo boxes (see fig. 1.13). Style 0 is called a *drop-down combo box.* A drop-down combo box looks and works like a drop-down list. The user can click on the down arrow on the control and select an item from the list. The user also can enter some text directly in the text box part of the combo box.

Figure 1.13

Styles of combo boxes.

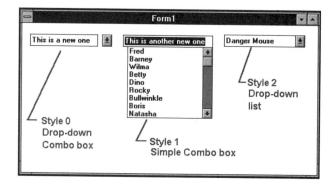

A style 1 combo box is called a *simple combo box.* The list in a simple combo box doesn't drop down; it's always open. The user can select from the list or enter text in the text box portion of the combo box.

A style 2 combo box is called a *drop-down list box.* This type of combo box works just like a style 0 combo box with one exception: the user can't enter text in the text box portion of the control. He can only select an item from the list.

There is a lot you'll need to know about working with the contents of a combo box. Because they're a big part of dialog boxes, combo boxes are covered in Chapters 8 and 9.

Scroll Bars

Scroll bar controls are not the same as scroll bars that appear on list boxes, text boxes, and other controls. Scroll bar controls are *slider controls.* The vent control on your car's air conditioner is a slider control. You slide the control up and down (vertical scroll bar) or left and right (horizontal scroll bar) to change its value.

When should you use a scroll bar control? They're great any time you want to enable the user to graphically choose from a range of values. Maybe you want the user to pick a percentage in your program. Just use a scroll bar control that has a minimum value of 0 and a maximum value of 100.

There's a horizontal scroll bar in the NOPANIC.MAK project. When you slide the control, it changes the value in the Label2 control right above the scroll bar. Check it out.

Using a Scroll Bar Control

1. Open NOPANIC.MAK and run the program.

2. Click on the right scroll arrow of the horizontal scroll bar as many times as you like. The value in the label above the scroll bar should increment by 1 each time you click on the scroll bar.

3. Click on the left arrow of the scroll bar as many times as you like. The value in the label should decrement by 1 each time you click the scroll bar.

4. Click on the right side of the scroll bar, just to the right of its thumbtrack (the thumbtrack is the square gadget that slides along the middle of the scroll bar). The value should increment by 1.

5. End the program.

6. Select the scroll bar control on Form1, and open the Properties window.

7. Change the LargeChange property from 1 to 10.

8. Run the program again and click on the right side of the scroll bar. The value in the label should increment by 10 each time you click on the scroll bar. If you click one of the arrows, the value increments or decrements by 1.

9. End the program.

The way the scroll bar is now set up, clicking on one of its two arrows increments or decrements the value by 1. Clicking on the scroll bar itself increments or decrements the value by 10. You probably already understand what's going on, but read about the following properties to get a good grasp of how the scroll bars work.

☐ **Min.** This property sets the lower limit for the scroll bar value. If your user is picking a number between 1 and 100, for example, set the Min property to 1.

☐ **Max.** This property sets the upper limit for the scroll bar. Using the previous 1 to 100 example, you would set Max to 100.

☐ **SmallChange.** This property sets the amount the value will increment or decrement if the user clicks on one of the scroll bar's arrows.

☐ **LargeChange.** This property sets the amount the value will increment or decrement if the user clicks on the scroll bar itself.

☐ **Value.** Aha! This is where the actual value of the current scroll bar position is kept. There's a line of code in NOPANIC.FRM associated with the Change event for the scroll bar that sets Label2's Caption property equal to the Value property of the scroll bar.

Okay! Have you had enough for now? You don't know everything there is to know about these controls, and you still know nothing at all about some of the other controls. But, at least you have enough knowledge to be dangerous.

2

CHAPTER

Making Cool Stuff Happen

You had a glimpse in Chapter 1 at how easy it is to make things happen in a Visual Basic program. In a lot of cases, all you have to do is set some control or form properties to make the program do somersaults. This chapter won't make you quite ready for any serious programming, but it will give you some background in *events*, *methods*, and *procedures*, all of which are Visual Basic voodoo words. Here's a hit list for this chapter:

- [ ] Understand what events are and why they're a big part of a VB program
- [ ] Learn about specific types of events
- [ ] Understand what a procedure is and where it lives
- [ ] Understand what methods are and how they are different from properties, events, Granny Smith apples, and little red wagons
- [ ] Play around with some events in a VB program
- [ ] Calculate the number of angels that can dance on the head of a pin

You might need a calculator with trigonometric functions for that last one.

This chapter contains small bits of code. Sorry, but I couldn't help it. Don't worry if you have absolutely no clue where the code is supposed to go. "Yea, fear not, for all things shall become clear in Chapter 3."

This Is an Event

Windows is an *event-based environment*, and Visual Basic programs are *event-driven.* "Huh?" you say, as a puzzled look slides onto your face from the deepest recesses of your psyche. It's really a simple idea: The different parts of your program only execute when certain *events* happen. These events include actions like clicking the mouse, moving the cursor onto a form, changing the text in a text box, or selecting an item from a list.

By far the biggest part of writing a Visual Basic program involves writing program code for the multitude of possible events that can occur to your forms and controls when the program is running. There also are other things you have to consider (which are covered in Chapter 3, "Where Does That Code Go?"), but you can do a lot of nifty stuff just by programming for a few events.

The types of events that apply to a particular form or control vary. A form, for example, doesn't have a Change event, because the form doesn't have an overall value that can change. A text box *does* have a Change event, because the user might click inside the text box and change its contents. This chapter doesn't cover all of the possible events, but it does cover the common ones for specific types of objects, starting with forms.

Events That Happen with Forms

There are 23 different events that apply to forms. In simple programs, the most common form events are Load and Unload.

The Load Event

You can't use a form at run time until it's *loaded.* No, that doesn't mean the form tosses down a bottle of good-to-the-last-drop Cuervo Gold. It just means that the form is loaded into memory where it becomes available to your program. Your program code can then start setting values for the controls on the form, such as filling up list boxes.

When is a form loaded? One form, called the *startup form*, loads as soon as your program starts running. Can you define which form is the startup form? Sure you can! Here's how:

Specifying the Startup Form

1. Open the project in Visual Basic and choose **O**ptions, **P**roject. This displays the Project Options dialog box (see fig. 2.1).

2. Click on Start Up Form, and use the Setting drop-down list to choose the form which you want to be the startup form.

3. Choose OK.

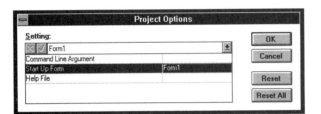

Figure 2.1

The Project Options dialog box.

TIP

If you tried this exercise, you probably noticed that in addition to being able to choose one of the project's forms to be the startup form, you also can choose Sub Main as the startup form. Sub Main isn't a form; it's a section of code that doesn't apply to any particular form. You'll learn more about it in Chapter 3. For now, just understand that *none* of the forms have to load right away or show up on the display if you don't want them to. If you don't specify otherwise, Form1 will be the startup form.

So, what is significant about the Load event? Mainly, it's a good time for the code that sets up the form to be executed. Maybe you want the program to check the disk for a registration file or fill a list box with values when the form is loaded. Attach the necessary program code to the Load event for the form. If you want some code to execute as soon as you start the program, attach that code to the Load event for the startup form.

Check out the code for the Load event in the project EVENTS.MAK.

Fooling with the Load Event

1. Open the project EVENTS.MAK.

2. Display Form1 (open the Project window, choose EVENTS.FRM, and choose the View Form button).

3. In the Project window, choose the View Code button (or double-click on any blank area of Form1).

4. Examine the code for the Load event (see fig. 2.2).

5. Run the program and click on the OK button in the message box that appears on the display.

6. Examine the EVENTS window and notice that the list box is filled in.

7. End the program.

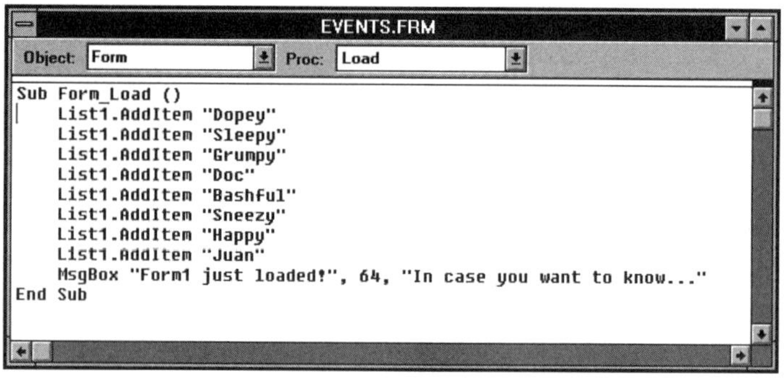

Figure 2.2

The code for the
Load event of Form1.

```
EVENTS.FRM

Object: Form          Proc: Load

Sub Form_Load ()
    List1.AddItem "Dopey"
    List1.AddItem "Sleepy"
    List1.AddItem "Grumpy"
    List1.AddItem "Doc"
    List1.AddItem "Bashful"
    List1.AddItem "Sneezy"
    List1.AddItem "Happy"
    List1.AddItem "Juan"
    MsgBox "Form1 just loaded!", 64, "In case you want to know..."
End Sub
```

When Form1 loads, eight items are added to the list box named List1 with the AddItem method. At this point the MsgBox statement displays a message on the screen. In case you're wondering, the 64 causes the message box to have an information icon and an OK button. You'll read about message boxes in Chapter 8, "Dialog Boxes!"

Now that you know how to make things happen when a Load event occurs, check out the Unload event.

The Unload Event

Forms take up memory. To conserve memory, you can get rid of forms that the program isn't using. To remove a form from memory, you *unload* it. You can unload the form by executing a line of code that generates an Unload event for the form:

If you double-click on a form's control menu when the program is running, an Unload event is generated for the form and the form goes away. That's easy enough, but what if you need to have the program execute some code when a form is unloaded? Maybe you need to close a file that the form had opened, for example. If so, add some code for the form's Unload event:

```
Sub Form1_Unload ()
     'put some code here that closes the file
End Sub
```

Check out a specific example in EVENTS.MAK. The Unload procedure for Form1 includes a line of code that displays a message box when the Unload event occurs.

Unloading a Form

1.   Open EVENTS.MAK if it is not already open.

2.   Open the code window for Form1, click on the Proc drop-down list, and choose the Unload procedure from the list. You should see the code shown in figure 2.3.

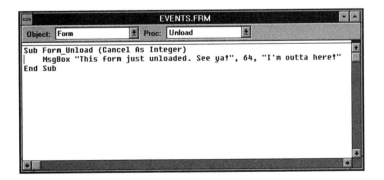

Figure 2.3

The Form1_Unload event procedure for Form1.

When you close the program by double-clicking its control menu, or choose **C**lose from the control menu, an Unload event occurs. When that event occurs, the program displays the "See ya!" message box.

There are lots of other events associated with forms, but Load and Unload are enough for now. Next, read about some of the events that are associated with controls.

Events That Happen with Controls

You're always fiddling with controls in a Windows program: clicking buttons, choosing something from a list box, double-clicking on a file name, clearing a check box, typing text in a textbox, and so on. This means there are a bunch of events that apply to controls.

Click

The Click event happens when you click on an object. When you choose a command button, for example, a Click event is generated for that button. How is the Click event useful? Consider a command button as an example: In a file-browsing program that you might write, you want the Erase button to erase a file whose name appears in a text box. Write some code for the Click event for that button (I'll use some real code this time):

```
Sub btnErase_Click ()
    'Get the name of the file from the contents of a text box
    DeadFile$ = Text1.Text
    'Erase the file
    Kill DeadFile$
End Sub
```

Take a look at a specific example in EVENTS.MAK.

Click!

1. Open EVENTS.MAK and display Form1.

2. Double-click on the **C**lick Me! button to open the Code window for the object. You should see the code shown in figure 2.1.

3. Examine the code for the button's Click event, and run the program.

4. Click on the **C**lick Me! button. You should be rewarded with a message box.

5. End the program.

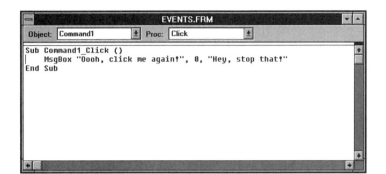

Figure 2.4
The code for Command1_Click ().

When you click on **C**lick Me!, a Click event is generated for the button. When that event occurs, the code in Sub Command1_Click() is executed, displaying a message box.

DblClick

The DblClick event happens when you double-click on an object. Most objects that have a Click event also have a DblClick event, although buttons do not have a DblClick event. A drive list box is a good example of a control that can use a DblClick event. Assume you're working on your file browser program again and you want the user to be able to start a program by double-clicking on the program's file name in a file list box. Write some code for the drive list box's DblClick event:

```
Sub Command1_Click ()
    'Use the Shell statement to execute the file that is selected
    'in the drive list box named drvListBox1
    ReturnCode = Shell(drvListBox1.FileName, 1)
End Sub
```

You'll learn more about file list boxes and using the Shell statement in Chapter 6, "Doing Simple File Stuff." For now, play with the DblClick event in EVENTS.MAK.

DblClick!

1. Open EVENTS.MAK, display Form1, and double-click on List1 (the list box). The code window should appear with the the DblClick procedure shown (see fig. 2.5).

2. Examine the code, and close the code window.

3. Run the program and double-click on any item in the list box. You will be rewarded with a message box.

4. End the program.

Figure 2.5

The code for Sub
List1_DblClick( ).

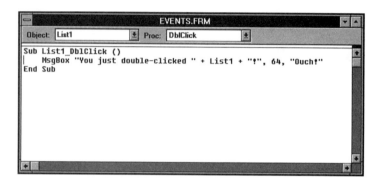

When you double-click on the list box, a DblClick event is generated for the list box. This makes the code in Sub List1_DblClick( ) execute, which displays a message box informing you on which item you double-clicked.

Change

The Change event is useful for responding to changes in a control. In Chapter 6, you'll use the Change event with a directory list box to change the contents of a file list box. For now, see what effect the Change event has on the text box in EVENTS.MAK.

Going Through the Change

1. Open EVENTS.MAK and display Form1.

2. Double-click on Text1 to display the code window with the code for Sub Text_Change( ) (see fig. 2.6).

3. Examine the code, then close the code window and run the program.

4. Highlight the text in Text1 and try to type **This is irritating** in the text box.

5. When you finally give up trying, end the program.

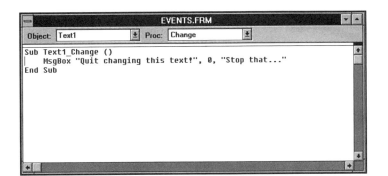

Figure 2.6

The code for Sub Text1_Change( ).

As you can see from the exercise, the Change event is often not very useful for keeping track of changes that the user makes to a text box. This is because a Change event occurs each time a new character is added or removed from the text box. Even so, the Change event is useful if the text in the text box is changed within the program. For example, if your program issues the code Text1.Text = "Hello!", only a single Change event is generated. You'll see examples of this technique in other chapters.

TIP

Okay, the Change event *can* be useful for a text box, even when the user is making the changes. You can use the Change event to monitor and respond to each character the user types.

Other Control Events

There are a lot of other events that are associated with controls, and you will experiment with many of these other events in other chapters. If you want to view the events that apply to a particular type of control, create the type of control you're curious about, then double-click on the control to display a code window. Click on the Proc drop-down list in the Code window and browse through the list until you find something of interest. This list displays all of the events supported by the selected control. Events that are bold in the list have code associated with them. If you want to learn about a specific event, open Visual Basic's Help file and click on Events on the Contents page.

Some Important Things About Events

An important point to understand about a control's events is this: If you don't write some code for a specific event, that event will have no effect on your program. If you forget to write some code for the Click event of a button, for example, the user can click the button all day long and nothing at all will happen. The *event* will still occur, but no code will be executed when it happens. This also means that there are a lot of events you can ignore. You don't have to write any code for the DblClick event for a form, for example, unless you want something to happen when the user double-clicks on the form. If not, you can pretend the DblClick event doesn't exist for the form.

Here's the other big point about events: They don't have to be generated only by the user. You can generate events from within your program. Assume that you have a dialog box in your program that contains a file list box and an OK button. When the user clicks the OK button, the program opens the selected file. You probably want to give the user the shortcut of being able to just double-click on the file in the list to open the file. How do you handle the double-click event? In the code for the file list box's DblClick event, generate your own Click event for the command button. Assume that the name of the OK button is Command1:

```
Sub File1_DblClick()
    Command1_Click
End Sub
```

If the user double-clicks in the file list box, a DblClick event is generated. The program code for the DblClick event then generates a Click event for the button.

This Is a Procedure

Now you know about events and are probably feeling a bit cocky. You probably still haven't calculated how many angels can dance on the head of a pin, but that's okay. That question won't be on the test. But there will be some questions about *procedures*.

In the last section you read that you have to write some program code if you want the program to do something in response to an event. Actually, you have to write an *event procedure* for the event. You may have already figured this out on your own, but an event procedure is a chunk of program code that is associated with a specific event for a control.

Each event procedure that you write has a name. The name consists of the name of the control and the event for which the procedure applies. The name of the procedure for the Click event of a button named Command1, for example, is Command1_Click. Here's an example:

```
Sub Command1_Click()
        '...some code that executes when the Click event occurs
End Sub
```

The word Sub (for SubProcedure) marks the beginning of the procedure, and the words End Sub mark the end of the procedure. There can be any number of program statements between the Sub and End Sub lines. The procedure might consist of just one statement, or there may be hundreds of statements. It all depends on what the procedure must do when the event occurs.

Here are the steps for the best way to start writing an event procedure for an object:

1. Create the form or control.

2. Double-click on the form or control to open a code window for the control.

3. From the Proc drop-down list in the Code window, choose the event for which you want to write a procedure.

4. Visual Basic automatically inserts the appropriate Sub *control_event( )* and End Sub statements—just start adding the necessary program statements between the Sub and End Sub statements.

You'll learn a lot more about procedures and other program code magic in Chapter 3.

This Is a Method

Another Visual Basic voodoo word you need to know is *method*. A method is a predefined action that operates on a specified object. Huh? Okay, it's like this: A method is an action. The program statement `frmGreenFrogs.Show` displays the form named frmGreenFrogs. The statement `frmGreenFrogs.Hide` hides the form (makes it disappear). A method is just a single word that tells the program to do something to an object such as a form or control. There are a lot of methods in Visual Basic.

Some Useful Methods for Forms

There are a handful of methods that you will routinely use with forms. One of these methods—Show—makes a form appear on the display. You would use this method when you want to display a dialog box.

Exposing Your Form

Loading a form doesn't display it—it just sticks it in memory. To show a form on the screen, use the Show method. To simplify things a bit, the Show method also loads a form; you don't have to load a form before you show it. Just use the Show method, and Visual Basic will load it *and* show it:

```
frmGreenFrogs.Show
```

So why would you ever want to use the Load method instead of the Show method? Sometimes you'll want to load a form but keep it hidden. That way you can reference the controls on the form but not show it on the screen. Also, a form shows more quickly if it is already loaded when you use the Show method to show it. By preloading the forms your program will need, your program will appear to function more quickly whenever a form must be displayed.

Here's an example: A user of your program clicks a button named btnFungus. This button displays a dialog box named frmFungusDialog that offers a list of edible fungi. But before you can show the dialog box on the display, you have to fill the list box with the names of your favorite, succulent morsels. Here's an example of how the procedure might be structured (the lines that start with an apostrophe are comments—statements that do not execute):

```
Sub btnFungus_Click()
      'First, load the form
      Load frmFungusDialog
      'Next, add an item to the list box
      frmFungusDialog!List1.AddItem "Shitaki mushroom"
      'Add another item to the list box
      frmFungusDialog!List1.AddItem "Gray stuff growing on a tree"
      'Add yet another item to the list box
      frmFungusDialog!List1.AddItem "Green stuff under a rock"
      '...more statements to fill the list box
      'Now, show the form on the display
      frmFungusDialog.Show
End Sub
```

NOTE In case you haven't guessed, AddItem is a method. The previous example uses the AddItem method to add items to the list box named List1 on the fungus dialog box.

Hiding a Form

Great! Now how do you get rid of a form? If you just want to take it off of the screen (hide it) but leave it loaded in memory so you can still use it, apply the Hide method to it:

```
frmFungusDialog.Hide
```

The form will disappear from the screen but will remain in memory. You can continue to set values of its controls and manipulate the form in other ways, even though it isn't visible.

If you're finished with the form and want to release the memory the form is using, unload the form by applying the Unload

```
Unload frmFungusDialog
```

If you need the form again, you can always reload it with the Load or Show methods.

The Show, Hide, and AddItem methods are just a few of the many methods available in Visual Basic. At this point you should have a good understanding of what a method is. In later chapters, you'll use other types of methods.

A Little Hands-On Stuff

You're probably chomping at the bit to start writing your own Visual Basic program. For some experience in working with events and procedures, take some time to put together a small program that enables you to preview bit map (BMP) files. I've set up the file controls for you, because you won't learn about file controls until Chapter 6. Although you will be working with a picture box control in the program, you won't deal with this type of control in depth until Chapter 10.

The project BMPVIEW.MAK is your starting point for the bit map viewer. BMPVIEW.MAK contains a form with file controls, a couple of buttons, and a picture box. Your job is to write the event procedures that will make the program functional. Here's a list of the things the user of your program will be able to do:

- **Use the drive, directory, and file controls to select a file.** This part of the program is written for you. You'll learn how to set these controls up yourself in Chapter 6.

- **Click on the View button.** The Command1 button will be labeled View. The Command1_Click() procedure will display the selected BMP file in the Picture1 picture box control.

- **Click on the Close button.** The Command2 button will be labeled Close. The Command2_Click() procedure will end the program.

- **Double-click on a file in the file list.** If the user double-clicks on a file in the file list box, the File1_DblClick() procedure will display the selected file in the picture box. This procedure will have the same effect as selecting a file from the list, and choosing the Open button.

Those four actions will make a useful program. All you have to do is write some very simple event procedures. Trust me—10 minutes from now you'll have a working program.

Taking Care of the View Button

Start by writing an event procedure to handle the <u>V</u>iew button.

Making the <u>V</u>iew Button Work

1. Open the project BMPVIEW.MAK and display Form1.

2. Double-click on the <u>V</u>iew button to open the Code window. Visual Basic will automatically begin a new event procedure for the Click event.

3. Add the following code between the Sub and End Sub statements for the event procedure Command1_Click. Make sure you get all of the periods, equals signs, parentheses, and other characters in the right spots:

```
If Right(File1.Path, 1) = "\" Then
Picture1.Picture = LoadPicture(File1.Path & File1.FileName)
Else
Picture1.Picture = LoadPicture(File1.Path & "\" + File1.FileName)
End If
```

Are you wondering what those program statements do? Good! The first line uses the Right function to determine if the rightmost character in the path is a backslash:

```
If Right(File1.Path, 1) = "\" Then
```

Why? If the last character in the path is a backslash, the program doesn't have to add a backslash before combining the file path and file name. Instead, all the program needs to do is *concatenate* the path and file name (like sticking C:\ together with PHOOEY.BMP to get C:\PHOOEY.BMP) and load that file into the picture box:

```
Picture1.Picture = LoadPicture(File1.Path & File1.FileName)
```

Next, you need an Else statement to tell the program that it needs to do something *else* if the If statement evaluates as False (if the last character is *not* a backslash):

```
Else
```

If the last character in the path is something other than a backslash (\), it means the program needs to add a backslash between the file name and path. Therefore, you need to concatenate the path, a backslash, and file name together to derive the full pathname of the file to be displayed. An example would be concatenating "C:\WINDOWS" with "\" and "PHOOEY.BMP" to get the full pathname "C:\WINDOWS\PHOOEY.BMP". You're just gluing together little pieces of text, using that text to load a file into the picture box:

```
Picture1.Picture = LoadPicture(File1.Path & "\" & File1.FileName)
```

That's all for this If condition, so:

```
End If
```

I promise that is the longest procedure you will have to write. The other procedures contain only one statement each.

Taking Care of the Close Button

When the user clicks the <u>C</u>lose button, the program should unload the form and end the program. You only have to add one statement to the Command2_Click procedure.

Making the <u>C</u>lose Button Work

1. With the Code window still open, click on the Object drop-down list and choose Command2. VB will automatically start a new procedure for the Click event of Command2.

2. Add the following statement between the Sub and End Sub statements:

```
End
```

That's all there is to it! When the user clicks the <u>C</u>lose button, the Click event is generated for Command2. The End statement ends the program and destroys the form.

Taking Care of the Double-Click

When you double-click on a file in a file list in nearly any Windows program, the program selects the file and then does something to it. If you double-click on a file in the Open dialog box, for example, the program opens the file. In this program, double-clicking on a file should display the file in the picture box. That's exactly the same as selecting a file with a single-click, and pressing the **V**iew button. You could write that code again, but why duplicate it? When the user double-clicks on a file, just make the program click the **O**pen button for the user.

Making Double-Click Work

1. In the Code window, select File1 from the Object drop-down list.

2. We don't want to write a procedure for the Click event, so select DblClick from the Proc drop-down list. This will start a new procedure named File1_DblClick.

3. Add the following statement between the Sub and End Sub statements of the File1_DblClick procedure:

```
Command1_Click
```

That's all there is to it! The program is finished. All you have to do now is compile it to make an EXE file. I've taken the liberty of assigning an icon to the form.

Compiling the Program

With the program finished, you're ready to create an EXE file and test it.

Making the EXE File

1. Choose **F**ile, and Ma**k**e EXE File.

2. In the Make EXE File dialog box, verify the path and name of your new EXE file in the File **N**ame box.

3. Choose OK.

continues

4. If you receive any error messages, go through the previous exercises again to make sure you haven't written the code incorrectly.

5. After the program compiles successfully, minimize Visual Basic.

6. From Program Manager's <u>F</u>ile menu, choose <u>R</u>un.

7. In the Run dialog box, enter the path and file name of your new EXE file, or use the <u>B</u>rowse button to locate it. Choose OK to run the new program.

8. When your BMP Viewer appears, use the file controls to locate a BMP file (there should be a bunch in your Windows directory). Click on a BMP file with a single-click, and choose <u>V</u>iew. The file should appear in the picture box.

9. Double-click on another BMP file. The file should appear in the picture box.

10. When you're finished looking at all of those nifty BMP files, choose the <u>C</u>lose button.

I'd feel pretty confident if I were you. You just wrote the majority of a program's code all by yourself. And, you now know how easy it is to write a really useful program with just a few lines of program code. You're only in Chapter 2—just imagine the programs you'll be able to write when you're finished with this book!

Okay, I know this is probably eating at you. How did I set up the file list box so it only displays BMP files? Take a look at the Form1_Load procedure. It sets the Pattern property of the file list box to "*.BMP." It's too easy!

3

CHAPTER

Where Does That Code Go?

You now know about forms, controls, events, and methods, all of which are fairly easy to understand. But what about all that program code you're going to have to write? You may be feeling that procedures, functions, and program statements are big speed bumps on the road of Life. There is no doubt about it—they're going to slow you down until you have some experience writing VB programs. Just understanding where all that code is supposed to go can be pretty confusing.

Take heart. In this chapter, All Will Be Revealed! You learn how a VB program is put together and where you have to put different types of program code. This chapter will prepare you for the programming Big Time by answering these questions:

- What types of files make up a VB program?
- How does a VB program run?
- Where should the code go?
- What are code modules and procedures?
- What are the steps for writing a VB program?
- Why do cats make that horrible yowling noise when they're in heat?

Okay, maybe we won't go into that last one. I'm not sure I really wanted to know, anyway. They sound like they're possessed....

Here's How VB Programs Work

To understand how you put together a Visual Basic program, you need to understand how a VB program works. The first topic you should understand is the types of files that make up a VB program.

Forms, Code Modules, and VBX Files

If you paid attention through Chapter 2 and didn't doze off, you should have a fairly solid understanding of forms and events. As you work on a project, its forms are stored in files, one form to a file. The controls that reside on the form also are saved in the form's file. The form's file name can be any valid DOS file name, and the form file has the file extension FRM. The form files that make up a project are listed in the Project window. When you want to work with a particular form, you simply select it in the Project window, then choose either the View Code or View Form button, depending on whether you want to view the form's code or the form itself. In the unlikely event that you have forgotten what the Project window looks like, you can have a look at figure 3.1 to jog your memory.

Figure 3.1

The Project window containing various types of files.

In addition to the form and its controls, the form file contains the Visual Basic statements that make up any procedures and functions you have written for the form's events, including events that apply to the form and those that apply to specific controls on the form. If yours is a simple project, it could only contain a single form, and all of the program code could be contained in the form file. Therefore, the Project window would only show a single file—the form file.

Because they contain code, form files are called *form modules*. In addition to form modules, a program can also contain code modules.

Code Modules, Too

Form files are not the only types of files that can be included in a Visual Basic project. In addition to form modules, your project might also contain *code modules*. A code module is a file with a BAS file extension. The code module contains procedures and functions that are part of your program.

"But wait," you say, wagging your finger at me. "The procedures and functions are already in the form file. Where do these other files, procedures, and functions come from?"

I was hoping you'd ask. The event procedures and functions that you write for a form are sometimes not the only procedures, functions, and other program code that you will need to write for a program. If there are functions that are common to many of your forms, for example, you don't want to duplicate them in each form. Doing so would increase the size of your application and also make it difficult for you to manage the code-writing and debugging process. If you have an error in the same code in four different forms, you'll have to change the code four times.

How do you avoid duplicating the procedure or function in each form that needs it? Just create a *module file* that contains all of the procedures, functions, and other program stuff that needs to be accessible to all of your forms. So, your project might include form files and one or more module files. You'll learn more about modules later in the chapter.

...and VBX Files

In addition to forms and modules, a VB program might include one or more VBX files. A VBX file contains all of the code necessary to make special controls work. If you add a grid, OLE2, or third-party control to your application, your project will include a VBX file for each of those special controls. You can't view the code in a VBX file. In fact, there's nothing you can do with a VBX file. It just appear's in your project if you are using the special control with which the VBX file is associated.

By default, Visual Basic adds the OLE2.VBX, CMDIALOG.VBX, and GRID.VBX files to any new projects you create. If you're using the Professional Edition, Visual Basic adds many more controls and VBX files to each project you create. If your program doesn't use the control associated with a particular VBX file, you can remove that VBX file from your project. If you're not using a grid control, for example, you can remove the file GRID.VBX from your application to make its compiled EXE file smaller.

TIP

To remove a VBX file from a project, open the Project window and select the VBX file to be removed. Choose **F**ile, **R**emove File. Visual Basic will remove the file from your project and will remove the associated control from the Toolbox. If you want to add a new VBX file to your project (or one you have previously removed), just choose **F**ile, A**d**d File. VB will display a dialog box you can use to locate and select the file to be added. The VBX files that are included with Visual Basic will be located either in your \WINDOWS or \WINDOWS\SYSTEM directory.

If you want to prevent VB from automatically loading specific VBX files and controls each time you start a new project, start Notepad and open the file AUTOLOAD.MAK, which is located in the Visual Basic directory. Figure 3.2 shows Notepad with AUTOLOAD.MAK loaded for editing.

Figure 3.2

Notepad with AUTOLOAD.MAK opened for editing.

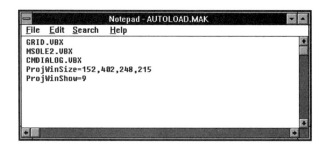

Delete the line(s) in AUTOLOAD.MAK which list the VBX file(s) that you do not want Visual Basic to load each time it starts a new project. Then, resave AUTOLOAD.MAK and restart Visual Basic.

How the Program Runs and Stops

In addition to knowing what goes into a Visual Basic program, you should understand how a VB program works, at least in general terms. First, you need to understand what code is first executed when the program starts. This is the "entry point" or starting point for your program.

The Startup Form

You read about the startup form in Chapter 2. You can assign one of the forms in your program as the startup form. If a form is assigned as the startup form, it is loaded as soon as the program starts. Any code in the Load procedure for the form is executed automatically as soon as the form is loaded.

When should you assign a form as the startup form? If your program uses a main program window and you want that window to display immediately when the program starts, assign it as the startup form. In the Load procedure for the form, add any statments that you want to have executed as soon as the program starts. These statements might set up variables, load other forms, fill in items in list boxes, or perform other startup tasks.

A Main Sub

You also can assign a Sub procedure called Main as the startup form (although it isn't a form at all). Sub Main is a procedure just like any other procedure you create. The only differences are that its name is Main and it's located in a code module—not in a form. If you assign Sub Main as the startup form, no forms will automatically load when the program starts. Instead, the statements in Sub Main will execute.

 You can only have one Sub Main in a program. If your project contains more than one module file, only one of the module files can contain a Sub Main procedure.

What goes into the Main procedure? Include in it any statements that you want to have executed when the program starts. Think of Sub Main as the Load procedure for a program. If you need to set up some variables or perform other actions before any forms are loaded, include the statements in Sub Main to perform those actions, then assign Sub Main as the startup form. If your program uses an INI file to store its settings, for example, you may need to add some code to Sub Main that causes your program to read the INI file to determine how it should run, which form it should open, and so on.

Stopping the Program

At some point, you'll want your program to stop. If the user chooses File, Exit from your program's menu, for example, the program should stop. You can use the End statement to end the program. Here's a sample Sub procedure for a mnuFileExit object. Assume that the name mnuFileExit has been assigned to the menu item Exit in the File menu of your program:

```
Sub mnuFileExit_Click()
    'if the user clicks File, then Exit, end the program
    End
End Sub
```

Another way to end the program is to include the End statement in the main form's Unload procedure. When the form is unloaded, either by your program unloading it through code or by the user closing the window (form), the End statement in the Unload procedure will execute, ending the program.

A Quick Summary...

Here's a quick summary of the things that happen in the life of a VB program:

1. The program starts and automatically loads the startup form, executing the statements in the startup form's Load procedure. Or, the statements in the Sub Main procedure are executed if you have assigned Sub Main as the startup procedure.

2. An event occurs, either because you generate the event as part of the program code or because the user performs some action (like clicking a button) that triggers the event.

3. If you have written a procedure to respond to the event, the code in that procedure executes. If there is no procedure code for the event, the program waits for the next event to occur.

4. When the user is finished with the program, he performs some action—such as choosing Exit from the program's File menu or closing the startup form—to end the program. The End statement, which you have placed in the appropriate place in the program code, then executes and terminates the program.

Simple enough? Good! Now, let's try to decide where all of your program code should go.

Where Should the Code Go?

Part of the process of planning and creating a program includes deciding what procedures and functions are needed and where you should put them. Later in this chapter you can work through a specific example and design a program. For now, read about the types of code you can add to a program and where that code should go. Figure 3.3 gives you a graphical representation of how a program's code can be structured.

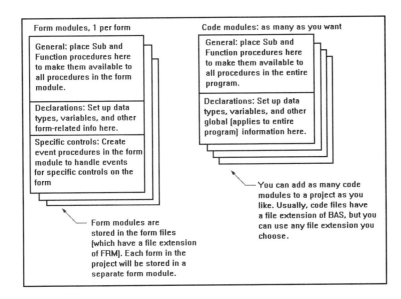

Figure 3.3

Where program code can live in a VB program.

First, you need to understand procedures.

Procedures

By now you probably understand that a *procedure* is a block of Visual Basic statements that are assigned a name like Form1_Load, Command1_Click, txtHairyLizards_Change, FileOpenProc, Main, and so on. Your program can execute the statements in a procedure to perform the various actions that the program is required to do. Procedures belong either in a form module or in a code module. How do you decide where a procedure should go? It depends on which type of procedure it is.

Event Procedures

An event procedure is associated, by name, with a particular control and event. The procedure named txtHairyLizards_Change, for example, is executed only when the text in the text box named txtHairyLizards changes. When that text changes, a Change event is generated, which causes the procedure txtHairyLizards_Change to be executed. Event procedures enable you to *trap* and handle specific events for a control or form. Event procedures only execute when the event with which they are associated occurs, or when you specifically cause the event to occur by executing an appropriate statement in your program.

As an example, here are two instances in which the procedure btnBaldLizards is executed:

1. The user clicks on the button named btnBaldLizards, generating a click event for the button.

2. Your program executes the statement `btnBaldLizards_Click` in another procedure.

Because they are associated with specific events for a form, event procedures should be placed in the form module that contains the control associated with the event.

General Procedures

A *general* procedure is one that isn't associated with a particular event. Instead of being executed when a specific event occurs, a general procedure executes only when your program directs it to execute. Why create general procedures? General procedures are useful when you need to make a procedure available to many other procedures.

Assume that you want to write a procedure that calculates the cost of yak milk based on some obscure formula. Also assume that many of the events in your program will require the program to calculate the cost of yak milk. Perhaps the cost must be calculated when a data file is changed, when a button is clicked, and when some information is printed. You could add the yak milk calculation code to each of the procedures for those three events, but that means you'll be duplicating a lot of code. Instead, create a general procedure named YakJuiceCalc that calculates the cost of yak milk. Then, call this procedure whenever you need to calculate the cost of that yummy yak juice.

To give you some experience with yak juice, your sample files include a project called YAKJUICE.MAK. Open it in the next exercise and check out its general procedures. Figure 3.4 shows Form1 for YAKJUICE.MAK.

Figure 3.4

Form1 for
YAKJUICE.MAK.

General Procedures and Yak Juice

1. Start Visual Basic and open the project YAKJUICE.MAK.

2. In the Project window, choose Form1, and click the View Code button to display the Code window.

3. In the Code window, choose General from the Object drop-down list.

4. From the Proc drop-down list, choose YakJuiceCalc.

5. Examine the code in the YakJuiceCalc procedure to see if you can determine what it does (I'll explain it shortly). Figure 3.5 shows the Code window for YakJuiceCalc.

6. From the Object drop-down list, choose Command1 to display the code for the click event of Command1. Examine the code.

7. From the Object drop-down list, choose Command2 to display the code for the click event of Command2. Examine the code.

8. From the Object drop-down list, choose Command3 to display the code for the click event of Command3. Examine the code.

9. Run the program, then click on Command1, Command2, and Command3 in turn. Notice the resulting value in Text1.

10. End the program.

What's going on in this program? The event procedures for Command1_Click, Command2_Click, and Command3_Click all call the YakJuiceCalc procedure, but each one passes a different number to the procedure. The YakJuiceCalc procedure then multiplies the passed value by .2435 and stores it in a variable. The original calling procedure then displays the results in Text1. By placing YakJuiceCalc in the General procedures section of the form module, all of the event procedures in the form module can use the YakJuiceCalc procedure.

Figure 3.5

The Code window
for YakJuiceCalc.

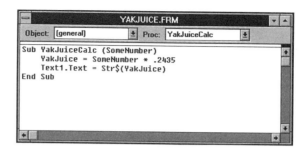

```
—                           YAKJUICE.FRM                    ▼ ▲
Object: [general]          ± Proc: YakJuiceCalc          ±
Sub YakJuiceCalc (SomeNumber)
    YakJuice = SomeNumber * .2435
    Text1.Text = Str$(YakJuice)
End Sub
```

Sub Procedures and Function Procedures

You can create two types of procedures: Sub procedures and Function procedures. Both types of procedures work very much the same way, but there are some differences. Sub procedures do not return a value, but Function procedures do return a value. That difference can be confusing to a non-programmer, so here's a layman's explanation.

A Sub procedure is a self-contained procedure. When a Sub procedure executes, some of its statements may calculate values or perform other tasks. And, the Sub procedure may set the properties of controls or forms being used by the program. But, the Sub procedure does not generate a single value that represents the sum of its efforts. You can't run a Sub procedure and generate a result of, say, 41.

A Function procedure, however, *does* generate a return value. Think of a Function procedure as a magic black box. You pour some information into the box; the box chews on the information for a while and then spits out an answer. That answer is the *return value* of the Function procedure. To sum it up: A procedure calls a Function procedure and passes it some information; the Function procedure runs through its paces, chewing on the information, and returns the value to the procedure that called it.

When is one procedure type required instead of another? If you are writing a procedure that calculates values internally or just sets properties of controls, but doesn't pass a value back to the procedure that called it, you probably should use a Sub procedure. The YakJuiceCalc procedure in the previous exercise was a good example of a Sub function. Although YakJuiceCalc calculated a value, it didn't return it to the procedure that called YakJuiceCalc in the first place. Instead, it used the result of its calculation to change the Text property of a text box.

If you need to write a self-contained procedure that evaluates information that you pass to it and returns a value, create it as a Function procedure. In the next exercise, examine a modified version of the Juicy Yak program. Instead of using a Sub procedure to calculate the cost of yak juice, it uses a Function procedure.

Creating a Function Procedure

1. Open the project YAK2.MAK.

2. Open the Code window, and choose the procedure YakJuiceCalc from the Proc drop-down list.

3. Examine the code for the Function procedure—it calculates a value by multiplying the variables SomeNumber and SomeOtherNumber. Figure 3.6 shows the code for Function YakJuiceCalc.

4. Choose the DisplayAnswer procedure from the Proc drop-down list. This procedure displays the results of YakJuiceCalc in Text1. Figure 3.7 shows the code for the DisplayAnswer Sub procedure.

5. Choose Command1 from the Object drop-down list. The first line of the procedure calls the function YakJuiceCalc using the values 1 and 2, then stores the answer in the variable Answer. The second line passes the variable Answer to the DisplayAnswer Sub procedure to display it.

6. Choose Command2 from the Object drop-down list. This event procedure calls the function YakJuiceCalc using the values 2 and 4 (the result is 8).

7. Choose Command3 from the Object drop-down list. This event procedure calls the function YakJuiceCalc using the values 3 and 5 (the result is 15).

8. Run the program and choose buttons Command1, Command2, and Command3 to display the answers 2, 8, and 15 in the text box.

9. End the program.

What's going on in this program? When you click on Command1, the event procedure Command1_Click is executed. This event procedure calls the Function procedure named YakJuiceCalc, passing it two values—1 and 2. The YakJuiceCalc function multiplies those two numbers and returns the value to the Command1_Click procedure. The Command1_Click event procedure then passes the answer to the Sub procedure named DisplayAnswer, which displays the answer in the text box.

Figure 3.6

The YakJuiceCalc
Function procedure.

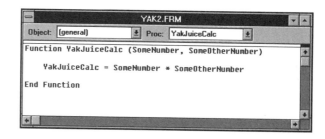

Figure 3.7

The DisplayAnswer
Sub procedure.

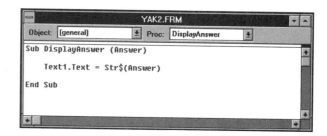

Why use a Sub procedure instead of a Function procedure for
DisplayAnswer? The procedure DisplayAnswer doesn't return a value—it
simply performs an action and terminates. Because it doesn't return a value
to the procedure that called it, DisplayAnswer should be a Sub and not a
Function.

If you're still scratching your head over the code in the previous two exercises, don't worry. You probably are having a hard time understanding the
use of *variables*. Variables are explained in Chapter 4, "Fiddling with Text
and Numbers." Chapter 4 also explains how to pass values between procedures.

Public and Private Procedures

A procedure can be either *public* or *private*. The procedures in a form
module are private to that form; only the procedures within the form module
can call them. Procedures in a code module are public; any procedure in the
program can call them, regardless of the form in which it's contained. When
you want a procedure to be available only to the procedures in a form, place
the procedure in the form module, either as an event procedure or as a
general procedure. If you want a procedure to be available to all procedures
in the program, create it as a general procedure in a code module. Before
you start creating a bunch of procedures, though, think about how you are
going to name them.

Because procedures in a form module are private to their form, they can have the same procedure names as procedures in other forms. Two forms can both have a Form_Load procedure, for example. Public procedures, however, must have unique names. You can't use the same name for two different procedures in a code module (or in more than one code module).

If you want to explicitly make a procedure in a code module private, preface the name of the Sub or Function with the keyword Private:

```
Private Sub YakJuiceCalc ()
    'this is a private Sub procedure
End Sub


Private Function YakJuiceMilk ()
    'this is a private Function procedure
End Sub
```

There isn't any way to make a procedure in a form module public. If you need to call the procedure from another form, move the procedure to a code module.

NOTE A project can contain many code modules. By using multiple code modules, you can add a logical structure to your project while you are working on it. You might put all of the general procedures related to calculation in one code module, for example, and place all of the procedures related to display updating in another code module. When the program is compiled, however, it makes no difference whether your code is contained in a single code module or in many code modules—all of the procedures are combined together in the program as if they came from a single code module.

Declarations

While you were working with the Juicy Yak programs, you may have noticed the word (declarations) in the Proc drop-down list. The declarations section of a module is for declaring constants, types, variables, and DLL procedures. You can't place any executable statements (like Subs or Functions) in the declarations section.

Constants, types, and variables are explained in Chapter 4. For now, just understand that the declarations section is where you declare (define) information that your program will use.

DLL procedures are not covered in *Understanding Visual Basic*, although you should know that you can call functions that are stored in Windows DLL files. Many complex tasks can't be handled directly by Visual Basic, but the Windows API (Application Programming Interface) does provide functions that handle these complex tasks. For example, you can't make a Visual Basic program window float on top of the display when it doesn't have focus, but you can cause it to behave that way by using a call to one of the Windows DLLs. For more information on calling procedures that are stored in DLLs, check out the Visual Basic API Reference item in your Visual Basic program group.

The Mechanics of Writing Code

You've written a little bit of code in previous chapters, but without much explanation of what you were doing. In this section, you learn about some of the mechanics and conventions used in writing Visual Basic program code.

Sprinkle Your Code with Comments

In program code, a *comment* is a small bit of text that explains what the program code is doing. By adding comments to your program, you make it much easier for you or someone else who will be working with your source code (the program code that you write) to follow the logic of the program. If you put a program away for a few weeks, then begin working on it again, having comments in the code will make it much easier to pick up where you left off.

Comments can be on a line of their own, or you can add comments at the end of a statement. To add a comment, precede the comment with an apostrophe ('). Here are some examples of comments in a procedure:

```
Sub KillerRabbits_Attack ()
    'This is a comment on a line by itself.
    'The next line displays a value in a text box
    txt1.Text = "Killer Rabbits"
    txt2.Text = "Attack!" 'This is a comment on the same line
End Sub
```

In the example, the comments are shown in italic. When you add comments to your program, however, the comments will appear in a different color from the program statements. By default, Visual Basic displays comment text in green, but you can specify a different color if green doesn't suit you. To specify a different color for comment text or for other options, choose **O**ptions, **E**nvironment. In the Evironment Options dialog box (see fig. 3.8), click on Comment Text in the list box, and choose a color from the Settings drop-down list. Choose OK to make your changes take effect.

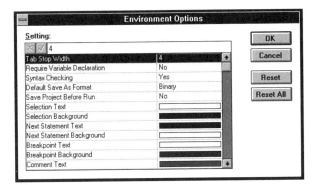

Figure 3.8

The Environment Options dialog box.

Make liberal use of comments in your code. Even if you remember right now what a program statement is for, you probably will forget two months from now when you want to make a change to the program. If you have comments in the code, you won't have to spend a lot of time trying to remember how your program works, what its variables represent, and so on.

Breaking Up Your Code

No, you don't have to attend the Standup School of One-Liners for this one. This section explains how your program statements are structured within the procedure.

Normally, your program statements will be added to a procedure one line at a time, with each statement on its own line:

```
Text1.Text = "This is one statement."
Text2.Text = "This is another statement."
Form1.Show
Form2.Hide
```

You also can combine multiple statements on one line by placing a colon (:) between the statements:

```
Form1.Show : Form2.Hide : Text3.Text = "Victim of killer rabbits"
```

It's usually a good idea to put your program statements on their own lines to visually set them apart from one another. This will make it easier for you to follow the logic of your program. There really is no reason to place multiple statements on one line.

Organizing Your Code with Tabs

It's a good idea to use tabs to organize your program's code and to help you visualize the logical flow of the program. Tabs are particularly useful in helping you understand the flow of a *decision structure* or *loop structure*. You'll read more about these types of control structures in Chapter 5, "Making Decisions." For now, here is an example of some code that uses tabs to show the organization of the control structure:

```
Sub NestedControls ()

Text1.Text = "Oh, frabjous day!"
If slimeyGreenFrogs = 1 Then
    For x = 1 to 1000
        Text2.Text = "Counting frogs..." + Str$(x)
    Next x
End If
Text1.Text = "Thank you for letting me count your frogs."

End Sub
```

Pressing the Tab key shifts the statement over to the fifth character in the line. It does not insert a tab character; instead, Visual Basic inserts spaces in the line. Using the Tab key to structure the appearance of your code makes it much easier to read at a glance the flow of the program's logic. You also may want to add a blank line at the beginning and end of a Sub or Function procedure as shown in the previous example to make it easy for you to determine where the procedure begins and ends.

CHAPTER

Fiddling with Text and Numbers

Probably the most common task that any program performs is manipulating text and numbers in some way. When you place some text in a text box, you're working with text. When you click on a scrollbar (increment its value), you're working with numbers. In Chapter 3, you worked with a function called YakJuiceCalc that multiplied a couple of numbers and stored the result in a variable. The function then displayed the variable in a text box. You have to learn to work with text, numbers, variables, and other types of data if you want to write programs with *any* programming language, including Visual Basic.

This chapter is all about *data*. Here's a list of the wondrous things you'll learn in this chapter:

- [ ] What are variables?
- [ ] Understanding data types
- [ ] Working with text and numbers
- [ ] Using variables
- [ ] Passing information from one procedure to another
- [ ] How to calculate the cube root of Kant's *Critique of Pure Bull*

For the last item, you will need one ripe banana, two cups of pitted bing cherries, a short length of yellow string, a one-meter piece of barbed wire, and a clipping from the left toenail of the elusive three-footed Bnukuki snake. All three of the Bnukuki snake's legs are on one side of its body, so they only run in circles. If you see one, it shouldn't be too hard to catch. Just make sure you don't grab it at the wrong end. This is the most difficult part of the capture, because the Bnukuki snake has no head, and there isn't any way to determine which end is the right end. But we digress. Let's get down to business (I'll leave it to you to figure out which is the *left* toenail...).

What Are Variables?

Fortunately, *variables* have nothing at all to do with Bnukuki snakes. Variables in a program are just like the variables you learned about in algebra class. Variables are used as symbolic containers for information. The following code uses variables named *fred* and *x* to store two numbers. It also uses a *loop* to execute a statement 12 times. A loop structure is a special Visual Basic code construction that enables the program to execute a group of statements conditionally (such as a certain number of times):

```
Sub SomethingOrOther ()
    'First, set fred equal to 12
    fred = 12
    'That was easy enough.
    'Next, start a loop that will repeat until a counter is equal
    'to fred
    For x = 1 to fred
        'Put the value of x in a text box
        Text1.Text = x
    'Increment x by 1 and do it all again
    Next x
End Sub
```

The first line of the procedure stores the numeric value 12 in a container (a variable) named *fred*. The value of *fred* is used in the second statement as a "stopper" value. The For...Next loop executes twelve times; it starts with *x* equal to 1, then displays the value of the variable *x* in Text1. The Next x statement increments *x* by 1 and the For...Next loop repeats with a value for *x* of 2. The For...Next loop continues to repeat until *x* is equal to *fred*, or 12.

You can tell from the example that variables are just symbols that represent values. They're just like named containers for information.

Data Types

There are a lot of different types of data: numbers, text, dates and times, and currency. To further confuse the issue, there are different types of numeric data. This section will clear up some of that confusion. First, take a look at table 4.1. It shows the data types that Visual Basic supports.

Table 4.1
Visual Basic Data Types

Type name	Description	Type-declaration character	Range
Integer	2-byte integer	%	-32,768 to 32,767
Long	4-byte integer	&	-2,147,483,648 to 2,147,483,647
Single	4-byte floating-point number	!	-3.402823E38 to -1.401298E-45 (negative values) 1.401298E-45 to 3.402823E38 (positive values)
Double	8-byte floating-point number	#	-1.79769313486232D308 to -4.94065645841247D-324 (negative values) 4.94065645841247D-324 to 1.79769313486232D308 (positive values)
Currency	8-byte number with fixed decimal point	@	-922337303685477.5808 to 922337303685477.5807
String	String of alpha-numeric characters	$	0 to approximately 65,500 characters
Variant	Date/time, floating-point number, or string	(none)	Date values: January 1, 0000 to December 31, 9999; numeric values: same as **Double**; string values: same as **String**

Confused? It's really not as complex as it seems. First, consider the type of variables that deal with numbers.

Numeric Variables

It may have been a while since you had a math class, so I'll remind you that *integers* are whole numbers without a decimal fraction. The Integer and Long data types are virtually the same, except that the Long data type can store larger numbers (either positive or negative) than the Integer type. This is because the Long type uses twice as much memory as the Integer type to store its value.

The Single and Double data types also are used for numbers, but they can contain a decimal fraction, like 342.9987. Single and Double variables both store *real* numbers. A Single data type is a *single-precision* value, and a Double data type is a *double-precision* value. The Double variable can contain larger numbers and numbers with more decimal places than the Single data type because the Double type uses twice as much memory to store its value.

The Currency data type also can contain a number, but it is fixed at four decimal places. If you calculate a Currency variable using numbers with more than four decimal places, the value will be rounded to four decimal places.

Strings

A String data type contains a string of alphanumeric characters (letters, numbers, punctuation marks, and so on). Your name is a string. The text "This is a string" is a string. The characters "123 eat my shorts" make up a string.

There are a lot of ways to manipulate a string in Visual Basic. You can convert numbers in a string to a numeric variable, concatenate strings (glue a couple of strings together), trim characters out of a string, and much more. String manipulation is explained later in this chapter.

Playing with Variables

Take a moment to play with a small and useless program that displays different data types in a text box. The VARIABLE.MAK project is a program that displays a selection of buttons (see fig. 4.1). When you click on a button, a value appears in the Value text box and its data type is displayed in the Type text box.

Figure 4.1
The form for
VARIABLE.MAK.

Playing with Data Types

1. Open the project VARIABLE.MAK.

2. Run the program. Figure 4.1 shows the program's form.

3. Click on the **S**tring button. A String data type appears in the text box.

4. Click on the **I**nteger button. An Integer data type appears in the text box.

5. Click on the Sin**g**le button. A Single data type appears in the text box.

6. Click on the **D**ouble button. A Double data type appears in the text box.

7. Click on the Date/**T**ime button. The current date and time appears in the text box.

8. Click on the **C**urrency button. A Currency data type appears in the text box.

9. End the program.

The program has no problem displaying all of the different data types in the same text box because Visual Basic converts the data as necessary to display it in the text box. Run the program again and click on the buttons until you are comfortable with your understanding of the different data types. Keep the project VARIABLE.MAK open. You'll use it again in the next few sections.

Variant Data Type

The default data type is called the *Variant* data type. A Variant data type can hold a date/time value, an integer, a floating-point number, currency, or a string. If you create a variable in your program but don't explicitly specify its type, it will be created as a Variant type.

Variant data types are like chameleon variables—they can freely change type. If you create a variable and store the value 3 in it, Visual Basic represents the number as an Integer. If the variable later changes value to 3.14159, Visual Basic represents the value as a Double. The variable is still recognized as a Variant type, although Visual Basic changes the way the variable is represented internally to the Variant type.

Use VARIABLE.MAK to test the way a variant data type can change.

Working with Variant Data Types

1. Continue working with VARIABLE.MAK.

2. Run the program and click on the pi button. The Value text box displays 3 and the Type text box displays Integer. The values change to 3.14159 and Double, respectively.

3. End the program.

The procedure for the pi button sets pi to 3 and displays it in the Value text box. This causes the Type text box to display the Integer data type. The procedure changes pi to 3.14159, which causes pi's variable type to change to Double.

Because a Variant type variable can represent many different types of data, there are some potential problems you might experience when trying to manipulate and use a Variant type variable. Later in this chapter you'll read about some of those potential problems.

Declaring Variables

When you create a variable, you *declare* it. You can declare a variable *explicitly* or *implicitly*. Assume that the variable named *fredsHairyLegs* hasn't been defined yet in your program. Your program executes the following statement:

```
fredsHairyLegs = 2
```

By executing that statement, the variable *fredsHairyLegs* is created implicitly. The statement *implies* that you want to set something called *fredsHairyLegs* to 2 because you haven't explicitly declared what type of variable *fredsHairyLegs* should be. What data type is *fredsHairyLegs*? Unless you have an extremely short attention span, you'll recall that variables are created using the Variant type unless you specify otherwise. So, *fredsHairyLegs* is a Variant type variable represented internally as an Integer.

To explicitly declare a variable as a specific data type, use the Dim statement. Here's the format for the Dim statement when it's used to explicitly declare a variable:

```
Dim varname As vartype
```

Varname specifies the name of the variable and *vartype* specifies the variable's data type. Here are some examples that explicitly declare different variable types:

```
Dim fredStr As String
Dim fredInt As Integer
Dim fredSing As Single
Dim fredDoub As Double
Dim fredCurr As Currency
```

Take a few moments to experiment with declaring variables. In the following exercise, have a look at the declarations section of the code to examine the Dim statements contained in it. Then, eliminate the Dim statements and see how the program is affected.

Declaring a Variable Explicitly with Dim

1. Continue working with VARIABLE.MAK and open the Code window.

2. From the Object drop-down list, choose General.

3. From the Proc drop-down list, choose (declarations).

4. Examine the Dim statements and note that they explicitly declare a selection of the variables that are used elsewhere in the program (see fig. 4.2).

5. Turn the statements into comments by adding an apostrophe (') in front of each Dim statement.

6. Run the program and click on the six data type buttons. Note that the data types no longer match the button names—the Single, Double, and Currency buttons all generate a Double variable.

7. End the program.

Figure 4.2

Dim statements used
to declare variables.

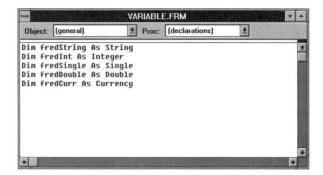

You can see that unless you explicitly declare a variable type, you don't have a lot of control over the type of variable it becomes. In some cases, implicitly declared variables inherit the expected data type. If you store a date/time in a variable, for example, it will become a date/time variable because no other variable type can store that type of data.

When should you declare a variable explicitly with the Dim statement? Whenever you want to force the variable to be treated as a specific type, declare it explicitly. Remember that the program can interpret the value 432.5234 as a Single, Double, Currency, or even String data type. If you want to make sure the variable that will contain that value is treated as a Currency data type, declare the variable explicitly as a Currency type.

How Do I Declare a Variable?

Besides using the Dim statement to declare a variable as a specific type, you can declare a variable explicitly as a specific type by using a *type-declaration character* at the end of the variable's name.

"Wha... Huh?" Just take a look at table 4.1 again and notice that there is a column titled "Type-declaration character." If you add one of the listed type-declaration characters to the end of a variable name when you create the variable, it will be created as a specific type of variable—the type associated with the type-declaration character that you use. If you use no type-declaration character, the variable is created as a Variant data type.

For example, if you want to define a variable as a String data type, add the dollar sign ($) at the end of the variable name:

```
thisOne$ = "This is a string!"
thisOtherOne$ = "45"
yetAnother$ = "3.14159"
```

An important point to note is that in the case of strings, you *must* enclose the string in quotation marks when you create it. The following statement would generate the error message "Type mismatch" when the program runs because you create a string variable and then attempt to store a number in it:

```
yetAnother$ = 365
```

Great! Now you know how to declare a variable implicitly and explicitly, either using type-declaration characters or the Dim statement. Where should the declaration *go*? That depends on how you want to use the variable, which determines the variable's *scope*.

About Scope

The *scope* of a variable refers to its visibility within the program. A variable that you create implicitly in a procedure has a scope that is limited to that procedure. Only statements within the same procedure know that the variable exists and can access it. A statement in any other procedure can't use the variable.

Sometimes you will need to use a variable with a broader scope. A variable needs to be available to all procedures in a form module or to all procedures in the application. The following list explains the types of scope that variables can have and also explains how to create variables with different scope:

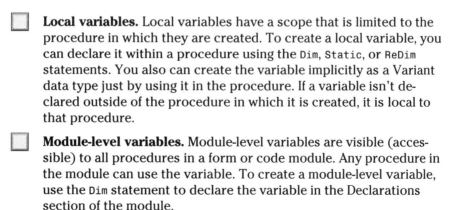

Local variables. Local variables have a scope that is limited to the procedure in which they are created. To create a local variable, you can declare it within a procedure using the Dim, Static, or ReDim statements. You also can create the variable implicitly as a Variant data type just by using it in the procedure. If a variable isn't declared outside of the procedure in which it is created, it is local to that procedure.

Module-level variables. Module-level variables are visible (accessible) to all procedures in a form or code module. Any procedure in the module can use the variable. To create a module-level variable, use the Dim statement to declare the variable in the Declarations section of the module.

☐ **Global variables.** Global variables are visible to all procedures throughout the entire program. Any procedure in the program, regardless of which module the procedure came from, can use the variable. To create a global variable, use the Global statement to declare the variable in the Declarations section of any code module.

Local Variables

A local variable is great when you need to store some temporary information, and that information doesn't have to be accessible outside of the procedure. Every procedure in your program could have a local variable named *hornyToads*, for example, and each procedure can set *hornyToads* to a different value without affecting any of the other procedures. Local variables declared implicitly or explicitly with Dim remain in existence only as long as the procedure in which they are created is executing. When the procedure ends, the variable is destroyed.

You can create local variables that live for the lifetime of the application by creating them with the Static statement. Static variables are explained shortly.

Here are three examples of statements within a procedure that create local variables:

```
Sub IHeartLocalVars ()
    Dim hornyToads as String
    uninterestedToads% = 2
    coldToads$ = "frigid frogs"
End Sub
```

For uninterestedToads% and coldToads$ to be local variables, they can't be declared with a Dim statement in the module's Declarations section. Doing so would make them module-level variables.

Module-Level Variables

Module-level variables are available to all procedures within a single code or form module. If you have a module named FUBAR.BAS that contains 20 procedures, each of those 20 procedures can access module-level variables that are defined within the module. If the project also has a module named FERGIE.BAS, none of the procedures in FERGIE.BAS can see or use the module-level variables in FUBAR.BAS.

Module-level variables are great when you want to share information between different procedures within a module. If all of the procedures for a form need to use the same variable, create the variable as a module-level variable for that form module.

Module-level variables live longer than local variables. A module-level variable remains in existence as long as the program is running. If a form is unloaded, its module-level variables still remain in existence and retain their values. This means that you can use a form's module-level variables even after the form is unloaded.

To create module-level variables, add a `Dim` statement in the Declarations section of the form or code module in which the variables will be used (see fig. 4.2):

```
Dim pinkElephants As Double
Dim redHerring
Dim greenAliens As Long
```

Global Variables

Global variables are available to every procedure in every form and code module in the program—you can use global variables *anywhere* in the program. If you want to have the user input his or her name, for example, use that name in the title of every form in the program, and create a global variable to contain the name.

To create a global variable, you must declare it in the Declarations section of a code module using the `Global` statement:

```
Global turkeyLegs As Long
Global porkButts
Global hyenaHowls As Double
```

Global variables can't be declared in a form module—they must be declared in the Declarations section of any code module. If your program uses more than one code module, it's a good idea to declare all of your program's global variables in one code module. You might even name the module GLOBAL.BAS to help you remember where your global variables are declared.

Hey! Try It Out

You might be horribly confused at this point about scope. What you need is a good example. How thoughtful it is of me to provide one for you. The sample project SCOPE.MAK illustrates variable scope. The program consists of two forms (see fig. 4.3). The **C**lear All Labels button clears the contents of all labels in both forms. The **S**et Variables button sets the value of two local variables, two module variables, and two global variables, then displays them in the top row of frames. The Co**p**y Variables button attempts to copy all of the variables to corresponding labels in the second row of frames. The **I**mport Variables button on Form2 attempts to copy all of the variables from Form1 to Form2.

Figure 4.3

The Scope forms.

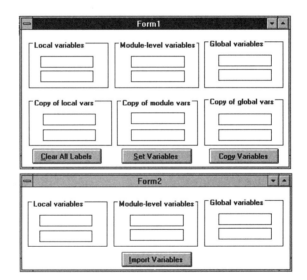

Understanding Scope

1. Open the sample project SCOPE.MAK.

2. Run the program, and click on **S**et Variables. The first row of frames should fill with values.

3. Click on the Co**p**y Variables button. The module variables and global variables appear in the second row of frames.

4. Click on the **I**mport Variables button on Form2. The global variables appear in Form2.

5. End the program.

What's going on in this program? The local variables are set within the Click event procedure for the **S**et Variables button. Because they are local variables, they aren't visible (and don't exist) outside of that procedure. When you click on the Co**p**y Variables button, the local variables aren't copied to the second row. Why? The procedure that copies the variables is a different procedure from the one that sets the local variables. Local variables can't move from one procedure to another, so the copy procedure can't copy them.

The module variables, however, *are* copied when you click on the Co**p**y Variables button. The procedure that sets the variables and the procedure that copies the variables are in the same module, so one has no problem using module-level variables set by the other.

The global variables copy, also. Hey, they're global variables. They can go *anywhere* they want to go, even without a black jacket and tie.

What about the **I**mport Variables button? When you click that button, only the global variables are imported into Form2. Why? The local variables on Form1 can't come over to play because they're from a different procedure. The module variables can't come over to play either, because Form2 and Form1 are different modules. The global variables, however, come over quite nicely.

If you're the inventive, self-motivated type, take some time on your own to wander around the code for SCOPE.MAK and figure out where and how all of the variables are declared.

Static Variables

I'm really *irritated*. I spent 10 minutes writing this section, then something went screwy with my system and I lost it. Argh! It was really witty and funny, too. Now I'll have to try again. Sigh.

Module and global variables live as long as the program that created them. You can't shake them off with a stick. When the program ends, though, the module and global variables are destroyed. Local variables, however, die as soon as the procedure ends that created the variables.

Sometimes it's necessary to make a local variable live longer than its procedure. You do this by declaring it as a *static* variable. A static variable persists as long as the program runs, just like module and global variables. Even though its value persists, however, the static variable is still a local variable and can be accessed only by the procedure in which it is contained.

Assume that you want to write a function that accumulates a total. The variable that keeps track of the running total must be static to make it persist after the function ends. Here is a sample function to accumulate a total:

```
Function Accumulate(someNumber)
    Static runningTotal
    runningTotal = runningTotal + someNumber
    Accumulate = runningTotal
End Function
```

The next time the Accumulate function executes, the previous value of *runningTotal* is increased by adding the value of *someNumber* to it. If *runningTotal* were not declared as a static variable, it would be reset to zero each time the function was executed.

TIP To make all of the variables in a procedure static variables, add the `Static` keyword in front of the Sub or Function heading:

```
Static Function EatMyShortsMan(withMustard)
```

By adding the `static` keyword in front of the procedure heading, you eliminate the need to declare variables as static within the procedure itself.

About Constants

Some things never change—deficit spending, spies in the woodwork, and toast crumbs in the butter. These things are *constant*. Guess what? You can use constants in your programs. Constants are like variables that you preset and never change.

Do you remember the VARIABLE.MAK project form earlier in this chapter? It contained a procedure that displayed a number that looked suspiciously like pi. Pi has the constant value 3.14159265 (I dropped the other twelve-zillion decimal places to conserve paper). Assume that you want to use pi in a lot of different procedures in your program. Just declare it as a constant by using the Const statement:

```
Const PI = 3.14159265
Const CAKE = "Square"
Const YES = 1
```

If you want to declare a global constant, stick the keyword "Global" in front of the Const statement:

```
Global Const SECRET_CODENAME = "Black Box"
```

Here are some rules about declaring constants:

- **Local constants.** To make a constant available only in a procedure, declare the constant within the procedure with the Const statement.

- **Module-level constants.** To make a constant available within all procedures in a form or code module, declare the constant in the Declarations section of the module with the Const statement.

- **Global constants.** To create a constant that is available to all procedures in the program, declare the constant in the Declarations section of any code module using the Global Const statement. You can't declare a global constant in a form module.

How do you use a constant? Just refer to its name as if it were a variable. To multiply a value times a constant called PI, for example, you might use this statement within a procedure:

```
circumference = PI * diameter
```

In this example, *circumference* and *diameter* are variables, and PI is a constant. When the program hits that statement, it simply replaces the PI symbolic constant with whatever value you have assigned to PI.

TIP

Dyed-in-the-wool programmers name their constants using all capitals. If you want to hobnob with these techno-nerds, name your constants using all capitals, too. It makes it easier for anyone reading your code (including you) to tell that you are using a constant and not a variable.

It's a good idea to use constants whenever you can, because constants can make it much easier to modify a program. What if the world suddenly spins off-axis and the value of pi magically changes? All you have to do is make one change to the statement that defines the constant PI, and your program will calculate correctly once again. You also eliminate the possibility that you would enter the value of pi incorrectly in a couple of procedures—it's easier to spell PI than to enter 3.14159265 each time you want to use it in a statement.

Using Variables

Now that your brain is crammed with all sorts of useful information about variables, you can start putting them to use. You may have already figured out some of the material in this section from examples in earlier chapters or in this chapter. Think of this section as a review.

Storing Stuff in a Variable

A variable isn't any good if you don't put some information in it. There are a couple of ways to store information in a variable. Often, you assign a value to a variable using the following syntax:

```
varname = value
```

To store some text in a string variable, for example, you might use statements like these:

```
janesEyes$ = "Wow!"
yourName$ = "Ferdinand Farkle"
someInterestingNumber = 37.473
```

You also can assign a value to a variable by setting it equal to the value of a control. Assume that you want to read the contents of a text box called Text1 and store the value in a variable called *fudge$*. Here is the statement you would use:

```
fudge$ = Text1.Text
```

If the text box was located in a different form module, you would add the form name in front of the control name:

```
fudge$ = Form2!Text1.Text
```

You also can set a variable equal to the value of another variable of similar type:

```
cakes$ = pies$
numOfCakesLeft% = whoAteThese%
fred = barney
```

Getting Stuff out of a Variable

If you put a value into a variable, you will want to get that value out again to use it. To place the value of a variable in a text box, for example, you might use the following statement:

```
Text1.Text = cakes$
```

There's really nothing to it. Now, take a look at ways in which you can manipulate variables.

Passing Variables Around (Arguments)

No, this section isn't about that argument you had with your spouse or significant other (or the argument you had with your spouse *about* your significant other). Arguments are expressions, constants, or variables that are passed to a procedure.

Do you remember the following function from earlier in this chapter?

```
Function Accumulate(someNumber)
    Static runningTotal
    runningTotal = runningTotal + someNumber
    Accumulate = runningTotal
End Function
```

The variable *someNumber* is an argument that is passed to the procedure. The procedure then uses that argument to perform some action. How is the argument passed to the function? It's passed by the procedure that calls the function. Here is a simple procedure that passes two numbers to the Accumulate function; one using a variable and the other a value:

```
Sub TotalIt()
    myNumber = 12
    Accumulate(myNumber)
    Accumulate (36)
End Sub
```

When you name a procedure that uses arguments, you specify the names of the arguments and their data types in the procedure heading. In the following procedure heading, a single argument named *someNumber* will be passed to the function:

```
Function Accumulate(someNumber)
```

Your procedure may require more than one argument. Here is a relatively useless function that adds three numbers together:

```
Function SumThreeNums(number1, number2, number3)
    SumThreeNums = number1 + number2 + number3
End Function
```

But wait! How do you know what the data type is for *number1, number2*, and *number3*? By default, arguments are passed as Variant data types. You can, however, specifically define the data type of an argument by declaring its type in the procedure heading. Here is a function that uses three arguments, all of different data types:

```
Sub ShootTheMoon(myName As String, myAge as Integer, myPay As
Double)
    message$ = "Your name is " & myName
    newAge% = myAge + 1
    money# = myPay * 4.5
End Sub
```

When you pass a variable to a procedure using the method in either of the previous two examples, the variable itself is passed to the procedure. The procedure could then change the value of the variable. Sometimes, that's a bad situation: changing the value of the variable could make the variable unreliable. Instead of passing the variable itself, you can pass a *copy* of the variable. This is called *passing by value*. Any changes the procedure makes affect only the copy of the variable, not the variable itself.

How do you pass a variable by value? Just add the ByVal keyword when you declare the argument in the procedure heading:

```
Function SumTwoNums(ByVal number1 As Double, ByVal number2 As
Double)
     SumTwoNums = number1 + number2
End Function
```

It's good programming practice not to modify the value of arguments within a function. You can either declare the arguments ByVal, or store the arguments in new variables, then modify the new variables.

Fiddling with Numbers

Even if you are writing a program that deals only with text, you probably will have to use numeric variables at some point in the program. For example, you may want to perform math operations.

Doing Math

You can do all sorts of math operations in a Visual Basic program. The math operators that you use are much the same as the ones you use in everyday math:

+ This operator adds together two operands. Example:
```
result = ((thisNumber + thatNumber) + 1)
```

- This operator subtracts one operand from another, and also returns the negative value of an operand. Examples:
```
result = firstNum - secondNum
negResult = -result
```

* This operator mutiplies two operands. Examples:
```
result = yaks * 2
babyYaks = ((maleYak + femaleYak) * romance)
```

/ This operator divides two operands and returns a floating-point result (a number with a decimal fraction). Example:

```
floatResult = millimeters / 2.54
```

\ This operator divides two operands and returns an integer value. The decimal fraction, if any, is truncated. Example:

```
intResult = thisNumber \ thatNumber
```

^ This operator raises an operand to a power of an exponent. Example: `result = 10 ^ 3`

Mod This operator returns the modulus, or remainder, of the division of two operands. Example:

```
justFraction = thisNumber Mod thatNumber
```

Turning Numbers into Text

Sometimes it's necessary to convert a number into a string. If you want to store the value of a numeric variable in a string variable, for example, you have to perform a conversion. The `Str$()` function converts a number to a string. The value may not look any different after the conversion, but it is recognized differently.

Here is an example of a small procedure that executes a loop ten times. In each iteration of the loop, the variable *counter* is incremented by 1. The value of *counter* is converted to text and concatenated on the end of a string:

```
For counter = 1 to 10
    countText$ = Str$(counter)
    theString$ = "I am counting..." & countText$
Next counter
```

You can simplify the procedure a little by combining the two statements inside the For...Next loop:

```
For counter = 1 to 10
    theString$ = "I am counting..." & Str$(count)
Next counter
```

NOTE You don't actually have to convert a number to a string to concatenate It to a string. The & operator automatically concatenates the number as if it were a string.

If you are converting a number to a string to display it in a label or text box, don't bother. Visual Basic will convert it for you. Just set the value property of the control equal to the numeric variable or numeric value:

```
Label1.Caption = someNumericVar
Text1.Text = 435.1957
```

If you need to convert a number to use in a calculation, however, you can use the Val() function. The following example converts the contents of the text box Text1 to a number:

```
someNumber = Val(Text1.Text)
```

If the string contains other characters besides numbers, it returns a value of zero if the first character is not a number. If the first character is a number, Visual Basic returns the value of as many numeric characters as there are at the beginning of the string. If the string is "342-Hello", for example, the Val function returns the value 342.

Fiddling with Text

In a previous example, you saw how two strings can be concatenated, or joined together. This is just one example of how you can manipulate text in a Visual Basic program. This section covers some of the most common operations you will want to perform on strings.

Gluing Together Pieces of Text

You can concatenate two strings together to form a single string. Assume that your program contains two text boxes in which the user enters his or her first and last names. You want the program to create a string that contains the text "Hello," with the user's first and last name. You can use the & operator to concatenate the strings:

```
message$ = "Hello, " & Text1.Text & Text2.Text
```

What if the first and last name are stored in variables instead of text boxes? Just specify the variable names instead:

```
message$ = "Hello, " & firstName$ & lastName$
```

What if you have a string variable and want to concatenate something to the end of it, but you don't want to create a new variable? Use a statement similar to the following:

```
listOfPeople$ = listOfPeople$ + you$
```

Trimming Unwanted Text

Visual Basic has a few functions that trim the leading and trailing spaces off of a string. When you use the Str$() function to convert a number into a string, for example, Str$() adds a leading space to the string if the number is positive. This is because the Str$ function reserves a space for the sign of the number, then omits the plus sign (it adds a minus sign if the string is negative). Go figure. You might need to remove the leading space to use the string, so you'll have to trim the leading space.

The LTrim and LTrim$ functions trim the leading spaces from a string. The difference between the two functions is that LTrim returns a Variant data type, and LTrim$ returns a String data type. Here are some examples of statements that trim the leading spaces from a variable named *boneHead*:

```
boneHead = LTrim$(boneHead)
newBoneHead = LTrim(boneHead)
someString$ = "This is a string " & LTrim$(boneHead)
```

The RTrim and RTrim$ functions perform virtually the same function as the LTrim and LTrim$ functions, except that they trim trailing spaces from the string (spaces at the end, not the beginning):

```
boneHead = RTrim$(boneHead)
newBoneHead = RTrim(boneHead)
someString$ = "This is a string " & RTrim$(boneHead)
```

What if you want to trim leading *and* trailing spaces from the string? You don't have to use both the LTrim and RTrim functions. Instead, just use either the Trim or Trim$ functions. Both functions trim the leading and trailing spaces from a string in one operation. Trim returns a Variant data type, and Trim$ returns a String type:

```
boneHead = Trim$(boneHead)
newBoneHead = Trim(boneHead)
someString$ = "This is a string " & Trim$(boneHead)
```

Will you ever have to trim the spaces from a string? Sure you will. When you start dealing with file records and random access (see Chapter 14, "Creating Your Own Files"), you're going to end up with extra spaces on strings that you store in your data files. This is because all random access records are the same length, but the strings you store in them will be different lengths. Visual Basic pads the strings with spaces to make them all the same size. The functions covered in this section will help you get rid of those added spaces.

Manipulating Strings

You might run across a situation in which you need to pull out a portion of a string. Assume that your program prompts the user to enter his or her full name in a text box and stores the name in the variable *fullName*. You then want to extract the user's first name and last name and store them in separate variables named *firstName* and *lastName*. In this situation, we'll use three functions to get the job done.

Calculating the Length of a String

The first function is the Len() function. Len() returns the number of characters in a string. We'll use Len() to determine the number of total characters in the user's first and last names, including the space between them.

Finding Some Text in a String

The second function we'll need is the InStr() function. InStr() returns the character position of the first occurrence of one string within another string. In the following example, InStr() locates the first space in the string, which marks the end of the first name and the beginning of the last name.

Pulling Out Part of a String

The other function we'll need is the Mid$() function. Mid$() returns a portion of a string based on a starting character position and ending character position that you specify.

Putting It All Together

Following is the completed procedure, with comments. Figure 4.4 shows the relationship between some of the variables used in the procedure and the string *fullName*.

Figure 4.4
What all those
variables mean.

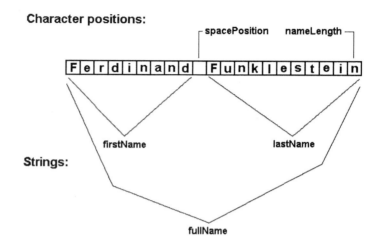

Here's the completed function:

```
Sub SplitName (fullName)
    'Determine the length of the string fullName
    nameLength = Len(fullName)
    'Locate the space between the first and last names and store
    'the character position in the variable spacePosition
    spacePosition = InStr(1, fullName, " ")
    'If spacePosition is 0, there are no spaces in the name
    If spacePosition = 0 Then 'user entered only a first name
        'Display fullName in the First name label
        Label2.Caption = fullName
        'Clear the Last name label
        Label3.Caption = ""
    Else 'Otherwise, there is a space in the name
        'Determine the length of the last name by subtracting the
        'character position of the space from the total
        'string length
        lastLength = nameLength - spacePosition
        'Determine the length of the first name by
        'subtracting the
        'length of the last name, plus 1 for the space, from the
        'total name length
        firstLength = nameLength - (lastLength + 1)
        'Pull the first name out by clipping out the
```

```
                'portion of fullName
                'from character 1 (the start) to the length of
                'the first name
                firstName = Mid(fullName, 1, firstLength)
                'Pull the last name out by clipping out
                'the portion of fullName
                'from one character to the right of the
                'space to the length of the  last name
                lastName = Mid(fullName, spacePosition + 1, lastLength)
                'Put the first and last names in their respective labels
                Label2.Caption = firstName
                Label3.Caption = lastName
        End If
        'Display the number of characters in the name
        Label9.Caption = nameLength & " characters"
    End Sub
```

Wow! That took a lot of code. Take a moment to play with a program called
STRINGY that uses this procedure. Figure 4.5 shows the form for
STRINGY.MAK.

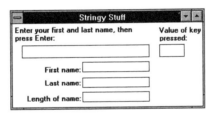

Figure 4.5

The form for
STRINGY.MAK.

Fiddling with Text

1. Open the project STRINGY.MAK.

2. Run the program, and enter your first and last names in the text box.
    Examine the information that appears in the other labels.

3. End the program.

When you press Enter, the SplitName procedure executes. The SplitName
procedure pulls the first and last name strings out of the full name and
displays them in their appropriate labels. Read the next section to find out
how the program knows that you pressed the Enter key.

Using Character Values

Without going into a long discussion about the subject, I'll tell you simply that alphanumeric characters have a numeric value associated with them. These values are called the *ASCII value*. The ASCII value of the letter "A," for example, is 65. The ASCII value of lowercase "a" is 97. A space is 32 and Enter is 13.

STRINGY.MAK is an example of a program that uses the ASCII values of characters. When you press a key, STRINGY displays in a label the ASCII value of the character you pressed. STRINGY also checks the value of each character you press to determine if you have pressed the Enter key. If you have pressed the Enter key, STRINGY calls the SplitName procedure to split your name into first and last names. All of this happens in the procedure Text1_KeyPress.

The KeyPress event occurs for a control whenever you press a key with the control active. Each time you press a key in the text box in STRINGY, a KeyPress event occurs for Text1. The ASCII value of the key that was pressed is passed to the event procedure as an Integer data type.

There are two functions in the procedure Text1_KeyPress that work with ASCII values. These functions are Asc() and Chr(). The Asc() function returns the ASCII value of the first character in a string expression. In this example, Asc() returns the ASCII value of the character you pressed.

The Chr() function creates a character string from the ASCII value specified as the argument to the function. If a program issues the statement char$ = Chr(65), for example, the variable *char$* is set to the letter "A" because ASCII 65 represents the letter "A."

Here is the complete Text1_KeyPress procedure:

```
Sub Text1_KeyPress (KeyAscii As Integer)
    'Create a character using the value KeyAscii
    'and store it in charPressed
    charPressed = Chr(KeyAscii)
    'Find the ASCII value of the character stored in charPressed
    'and store it in charVal
    charVal = Asc(charPressed)
    'Put the ASCII value of the character in Label6
    Label6.Caption = charVal
```

```
    If KeyAscii = 13 Then        'You pressed Enter...
        SplitName (Text1.Text)   '...so execute the SplitName
                                 'function
    End If
End Sub
```

Why did I go through the trouble of creating the *charPressed* and *charVal* variables in the function? The only purpose they serve is to give you an example of the Asc() and Chr() functions. If all you want to do is place in Label6 the value of the character that the user pressed, you already have the information you need—the value of KeyAscii. Therefore, this procedure performs the same function, and is much simpler:

```
Sub Text1_KeyPress (KeyAscii As Integer)
    Label6.Caption = KeyAscii
    If KeyAscii = 13 Then
        SplitName (Text1.Text)
    End If
End Sub
```

There are a lot of other ways you can manipulate text, but the functions explained in this chapter cover the most common ones.

**5
CHAPTER**

Making Decisions

Decisions, decisions. You thought it was difficult to decide which color of jellybean to pull out of the jar. Now, your *programs* have to make decisions. There's no telling what color of jellybeans *they'll* pull out.

Maybe you won't write any jellybean programs in this chapter, but you will learn about *conditional branching*. Ooh, that sounds like a real techno-geek topic! Actually, it's fairly simple. Conditional branching refers to the ways in which a program can control its execution based on certain conditions. Conditional branching is a big part of most programs, so stay awake for this chapter—you'll need it.

Here's what you'll learn about in this chapter:

- [ ] Why use conditional branching?
- [ ] What is a control structure?
- [ ] How to get out of a control structure
- [ ] How to use control and loop structures
- [ ] How to contact the Psychic Friends Network

Hey, if they're really psychic, they'll contact *you*.

Why Make Decisions?

Although events play a big role in a Visual Basic program, most programs also rely on the ability to control the execution of the program through other means. The program might need to test a string variable to determine its value, check a number to determine if it's above or below a certain value, determine if a certain file exists, or perform an action a certain number of times. *Control structures* enable the program to evaluate these types of conditions and control execution based on that evaluation.

Visual Basic has two types of control structures that enable you to control the way the program runs. *Decision structures* enable the program to make decisions on how it will operate based on test conditions. The decision structures in Visual Basic include the following:

☐ **If...Then.** Use this decision structure when you want a selection of statements to execute if some condition is true. This is like saying, "If this condition is true, do these statements."

☐ **If...Then...Else.** Use this decision structure when you want a selection of statements to execute if some condition is true, and have a different selection of statements execute if the condition is false. This is like saying, "If this condition is true, execute these statements; otherwise, execute these other statements."

☐ **Select Case.** Use this decision structure when you want to execute a specific set of statements based on one of multiple possible conditions. Using Select Case is similar to using multiple If...Then structures, but is much easier to use. This is like saying, "If the answer is 1, do this. If the answer is 2, do that. If the answer is 3, do something else. If the answer doesn't fit any of these conditions, do this other thing."

Visual Basic also provides *loop structures* that you can use to control the way the program runs. I suppose you want to know what they are. Here's a list:

☐ **Do...Loop.** A Do...Loop enables the program to execute a block of statements an indefinite number of times (loop through the statements) based on a condition. Each time the code loops, the condition is tested again. When the condition finally proves false, the loop terminates. This is like saying, "Keep executing these statements as long as this condition is true."

Visual Basic also includes a While...Wend structure that is very similar to the Do...Loop structure. The Do...Loop structure is more flexible, so that's the one we'll cover in this chapter.

For...Next. This loop structure enables the program to execute a block of statements a fixed number of times. This is like saying, "Repeat these statements 32 times."

The preceding explanations might make absolutely no sense to you at all. If that's the case, don't worry. Things will become clearer when you see some examples of these control structures.

If This Happens, Then Do That

In most programs, you need to ask, "What if?" What if this variable is equal to zero? What if the user entered an incorrect value? What if the user is trying to exit the program but hasn't saved the file? It's up to you as the programmer to plan for these situations. You can use the If...Then control structure to test a condition and base the program's execution on the result of that test.

If...Then

The If...Then decision structure enables you to execute one or more statements if a condition proves to be true. Here's the syntax of the If...Then structure:

```
If condition Then
    execute this statement...
    and this one...
    etc...
End If
```

The expression *condition* is usually a comparison of some kind, but it can be any expression that evaluates as a numeric value. To Visual Basic, the condition is either **True** or **False**. An evaluation of zero represents **False**, and any nonzero numeric value is **True**.

Have a look at an example of the If...Then structure in the following exercise. The project IF-THEN.MAK is a word-guessing game. You have to guess the secret code word. If you guess correctly, the program displays a message. Figure 5.1 shows the form for IF-THEN.MAK.

Figure 5.1

The form for IF-THEN.MAK.

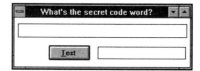

Working with If...Then

1. Open the project IF-THEN.MAK and run the program.

2. Type **frog** in the text box, and choose the **T**est button or press Enter. The word disappears—you guessed wrong.

3. Type **weasel** in the text box and press Enter. The word disappears—you guessed wrong again.

4. Type **fiddlesticks** in the text box and press Enter. Ha! You guessed right.

Here is the code for the Command1_Click event, which executes when you click the **T**est button (the button's Default property is set to True, which enables you to "push" the button by also pressing Enter):

```
Sub Command1_Click ()
    'Save the text box to a variable, then clear
    'the text box and label
    yourAnswer = Text1.Text
    Text1.Text = ""
    Label1.Caption = ""

    'If yourAnswer, coverted to uppercase, equals "FIDDLESTICKS",
    'reward the user
    If UCase(yourAnswer) = "FIDDLESTICKS" Then
        Text1.Text = "You are..."
        Label1.Caption = "Right!"
    End If

End Sub
```

The only thing that is new to you here, other than the If...Then structure, is the UCase function. The UCase function converts its argument to all uppercase letters. In this example, the UCase function is used to convert your answer to uppercase before it is tested. With the UCase function, you would have to test for a lowercase "fiddlesticks," an uppercase "FIDDLESTICKS," and a mix of uppercase and lowercase "FiDDlestICKs."

Great! Now what about that If...Then thing? This If...Then structure's condition expression is `UCase(yourAnswer)` = `"FIDDLESTICKS"`. The structure is testing to determine if your answer, converted to uppercase, is FIDDLE-STICKS. If it is, the condition proves true and the two statements within the If...Then structure are executed. If the condition evaluates as false, nothing happens—the program skips to the next statement after the `End If` statement. Since there isn't anything there, the procedure ends without executing any more statements.

If...Then...Else

This highly technical, incredibly complex program needs a little refinement. If the user enters an incorrect answer, the program should beep or make raspberry noises or something equally obnoxious. Programming for raspberry sounds is a little too complex for this book, so we'll stick with a beep and an obnoxious message. But how do we make that happen?

We need to use the If...Then...Else structure. Essentially what the program needs to do is this: "**If** the user enters the correct word, **Then** display a congratulatory message; **Else** (otherwise), beep and display an obnoxious message." It couldn't be any simpler! Figure 5.2 shows the revisions you need to make in the code.

Change the program to use the If...Then...Else structure and retest it.

Using If...Then...Else

1. Open project IF-THEN.MAK if you don't already have it open.

2. Display the code for the Command1_Click procedure.

continues

3. Change the If...Then structure to read as follows (the new stuff is in bold):

```
If UCase(yourAnswer) = "FIDDLESTICKS" Then
    Text1.Text = "You are..."
    Label1.Caption = "Right!"
Else
    Beep
    Text1.Text = "Ha! I laugh in your general direction!"
    Label1.Caption = "Wrong, Bozo!"
End If
```

4. Save the project.

5. Run the program and enter a few incorrect words.

6. Enter fiddlesticks.

7. End the program.

The statements between the If and Else statements execute if the condition proves true. The statements between the Else and End If statements execute if the condition proves false.

Figure 5.2

If...Then...Else code.

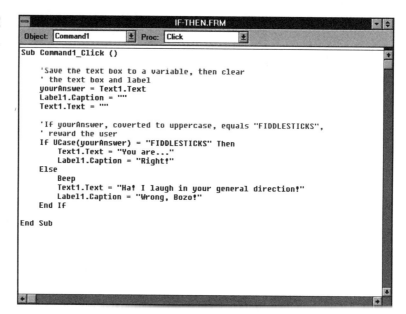

Hey, Stop Doing That!

You will often want to exit a control structure without completing it. The Exit statement makes it possible for program execution to exit a For...Next control structure, Do...Loop control structure, Sub procedure, or Function procedure. First, take a look at how you can exit a Sub or Function procedure.

Exiting a Sub or Function Procedure

To exit a Sub or Function procedure at any point in the procedure, you only have to execute the Exit Sub or Exit Function statement. Program execution jumps to the end of the Sub or Function. Any remaining statements are ignored.

In the following example, add a nested If...Then structure to the word-guessing game. This structure will display a new message if the user gets the first letter of the word correct.

Exiting a Sub Procedure

1. Open the project IF-THEN.MAK and display the Command1_Click procedure.

2. Change the If...Then control to read as follows (the new stuff is in bold):

```
If UCase(yourAnswer) = "FIDDLESTICKS" Then
    Text1.Text = "You are..."
    Label1.Caption = "Right!"
Else
    Beep
    If UCase(Mid(yourAnswer, 1, 1)) = "F" Then
        Label1.Caption = "Close, but no cigar!"
        Exit Sub
    End If
    Text1.Text = "Ha! I laugh in your general direction!"
    Label1.Caption = "Wrong, Bozo!"
End If
```

continues

3.   Run the program and enter the word **foreign** in the text box. Because your word begins with the letter F, you receive the message "Close, but no cigar!" in Label1.

4.   End the program.

5.   Save the project.

How does this new code work? If you enter the wrong answer, the Else part of the main If...Then structure executes. The program beeps. Then, the nested If...Then structure tests the following condition:

```
UCase(Mid(yourAnswer, 1, 1)) = "F"
```

The portion Mid(yourAnswer, 1, 1) uses the Mid function to return some characters from the string *yourAnswer*, starting at the first character and extending for a length of one character. In other words, it returns the first character in the string. The UCase function then converts the character to uppercase so it can be compared with "F" to determine if it is the correct first letter.

The program displays the message "Close, but no cigar!" in Label1 if the first letter is correct. The next statement, Exit Sub, causes the program to exit the procedure without executing any other statements. It doesn't display the obnoxious error messages that follow the nested If...Then structure.

To exit a Function procedure, use essentially the same technique, but change the statement to Exit Function instead of Exit Sub.

Exiting Other Control Structures

You can use the Exit statement to also exit the Do...Loop and For...Next control structures. You'll learn about these additional control structures later. For now, just understand that you use the Exit For statement to exit a For...Next structure and the Exit Do statement to exit a Do...Loop structure.

Now that you know how to get out of a control structure, take a look at a new kind of structure that enables you to test for a lot of different possible values for a condition with one structure.

Do One of the Following

You can use lots of nested For...Next loops when the condition you're testing has more than two possibilities. Here's an example:

```
If someValue = 1 Then
     'Do these statements
     Else If someValue = 2 Then
     'Do these statements
     Else If someValue = 3 Then
     'Do these statements
     Else If someValue = 4 Then
     'Do these statements
     Else If someValue = 5 Then
     'Do these statements
     Else
     'Do these statements
End If
```

Seems kind of cluttered, doesn't it? Visual Basic offers a better decision structure that is great when you need to control execution based on more than two possible conditions. It's called Select Case.

Select Case

The Select Case decision structure tests the condition just once. Then it compares the value of the condition with the values of all of the Case statements in the structure. If it finds a match, it executes the statements within that Case structure. Here's an example that tests the value of the integer stored in the variable myNumber:

```
Select Case myNumber
     Case 1
          'Do these statements
     Case 2
          'Do these statements
     Case 3
          'Do these statements
     Case 4
          'Do these statements
     Case Else
          'Do these statements
End Select
```

If myNumber equals 1, the program executes the statements under Case 1. If myNumber equals 2, the program executes the statements under Case 2, and so on. If myNumber doesn't match any of the cases, the statements following the Case Else statement are executed.

Take a few moments to play with the example in the project SEL-CASE.MAK. You probably have nothing better to do, anyway. Figure 5.3 shows the form for SEL-CASE.MAK.

Figure 5.3

The form for SEL-CASE.MAK.

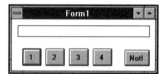

Using Select Case

1. Open the project SEL-CASE.MAK.

2. Run the program, and choose each of the five buttons. Notice the text that appears in the label.

3. End the program.

When you click a button, the event procedure for the button calls the SpitOutSomeStuff procedure and passes it a number as an argument. The SpitOutSomeStuff procedure then uses a Select Case structure to determine what action it will take. Here's the SpitOutSomeStuff procedure:

```
Sub SpitOutSomeStuff (choice As Integer)
    Select Case choice
    Case 1
        Label1.Caption = "Hi!"
    Case 2
        Label1.Caption = "Buenos dias!"
    Case 3
        Label1.Caption = "Howdy!"
    Case 4
        Label1.Caption = "What's up?"
    Case Else
        Label1.Caption = "Stop that! Don't press that button!"
    End Select
End Sub
```

The Click event procedure for button 1 (Command1) passes the value 1 to the SpitOutSomeStuff procedure. The Click event procedure for button 2 (Command2) passes the value 2 to the SpitOutSomeStuff procedure, and so on. The event for the Not! button (Command5) passes the value 41 to the SpitOutSomeStuff procedure. Because there is no Case 41 statement in the procedure, the Case Else statement is executed.

In addition to testing for numbers in the Select Case condition, you can test for any valid expression, such as a string. Here is an example of a procedure that tests the contents of a string and uses it in a Select Case structure:

```
Sub StubYourToe (scream As String)
    Select Case scream
    Case "Ouch"
        'Some statements
    Case "Oooh"
        'Some statements
    Case "Yikes"
        'Some statements
    Case "Holy smokes"
        'Some statements
    Case Else
        'Some statements
    End Select
End Sub
```

When you use a string as the condition in a Select Case structure, keep in mind that the condition is case-sensitive. If you are testing the content of the string and not its case, convert it to uppercase:

```
Select Case UCase(scream)
```

You also can test for a range of values by adding the To keyword in the condition expression. The following example executes a block of statements if the expression evaluates between 1 and 5, a different block of statements if the expression evaluates between 6 and 10, and a different block of statements if the expression does not evaluate to a value between 1 and 10:

```
Sub GuessANumber (yourNumber As Integer)
    Select Case yourNumber
    Case 1 To 5
        Label1.Caption = "You entered a number from 1 to 5"
```

```
      Case 6 To 10
          Label1.Caption = "You entered a number from 6 to 10"
      Case Else
          Label1.Caption = "Try again, bozo."
      End Select
End Sub
```

In addition to testing for a range of values, you also can test for a selection of values. The following example tests for even numbers and odd numbers:

```
Sub GuessAnEvenNumber (yourNumber As Integer)
      Select Case yourNumber
      Case 1, 3, 5, 7, 9
          Label1.Caption = "You entered an odd number"
      Case 2, 4, 6, 8, 10
          Label1.Caption = "You entered an even number"
      Case Else
          Label1.Caption = "Try again, bozo."
      End Select
End Sub
```

Another keyword you can use in addition to the To keyword is the Is keyword. The Is keyword lets you use comparison operators such as greater than (>) and less than (<) in the Select...Case structure. Here's a following code example that tests the value of the variable *choice:*

```
Select Case choice
    Case Is < 4
        Label1.Caption = "Less than four."
    Case Is = 4
        Label1.Caption = "Equal to four, Bozo."
    Case Else
        Label1.Caption = "More than four."
    End Select
```

If you omit the Is keyword and type a condition that obviously requires the Is keyword (such as **Case < 4**), Visual Basic automatically adds the Is keyword for you.

TIP In Chapter 8, "Dialog Boxes!," you'll learn about *control arrays*. A control array is an array of controls that all have the same control name, and which are referenced by their name and an array index value. The Select...Case structure is great for processing control array events. Why? You can create a Select... Case structure that contains Case statements for each array index value. The Select...Case structure can then control execution of the program based on which control in the array was selected or modified.

Do This 41 Times

Another common task in a typical program is to execute a selection of statements a specific number of times. Assume you want to add a procedure in your program that prints a user-specified range of pages. After getting the starting and ending pages from the user, your program would run through a loop of statements to print each page. If the user wanted to print 41 pages, your program would execute the print loop 41 times. This type of control structure is called a For...Next loop.

For...Next

The For...Next decision structure is really fairly simple. At the beginning of the loop, you specify a starting value and ending value for a counter. The program then executes the statements in the loop, beginning with the starting value and stopping when the counter reaches the ending value. Here's a sample For...Next structure:

```
For x = 1 To 10
    Text1.Text = "I'm counting..." & x
    'There might be other statements here...
Next x
```

How does it work? The For statement specifies the name of the counter (in this case it's x), and also specifies the starting and ending values for x. The first time through the loop, x equals 1. The statement within the loop places the text "I'm counting...1" in Text1. When execution reaches the Next x statement, the program increments the value of x by 1, making it equal to 2. Then the loop repeats, and the statement inside the loop places the text "I'm counting...2" in Text1. The process repeats 10 times.

The For...Next loop is great when you need to execute some statements a certain number of times, even when you don't know at design time how many iterations of the loop you need. Here's an example: assume you've written a program that maintains a list box with a list of file names. When the program starts, it looks at the items in the list and automatically opens each of the files. Another part of your program lets you change the items in the list, adding and deleting files. So, you have no way of knowing ahead of time how many files must be loaded when the program starts.

No problem! You can use a variable for the counter values. The following snippet of code sets a variable called numOfListItems equal to the number of items in the file name listbox named List1. It then executes a couple of statements to load the files:

```
'First, set numOfListItems equal to number of items in the list of
'files.
'If there were 6 items in the list, numOfListItems would be equal
'to 6
numOfListItems = List1.ListCount
'Start with x = 1 and execute the loop as many times as there are
'items
'in the list. If numOfListItems = 6, execute the loop 6 times.
For x = 1 To numOfListItems
     'Retrieve the name of a file from the list
     fileToGet = List1.List(x - 1)
     'Use a user-defined procedure called GetStartupFiles to load
     'the file
     GetStartupFiles fileToGet, x
Next x
```

There are some interesting things going on here that are probably new to you. First, the ListCount property of List1 is used to determine the number of items currently in the list. As the list changes (items are added or re-moved), the value of the ListCount property changes accordingly.

Next, consider the following line:

```
fileToGet = List1.List(x - 1)
```

The variable *fileToGet* is used to store the name of the file. It will later be passed to the GetStartupFiles procedure. The second portion of the line, List1.List(x - 1), retrieves the contents of the list box. A list box has an *index* that references a position in the list. The first item in a list is item 0, the second item is item 1, and so on. What's so significant about the code `List1.List(x - 1)`? Notice that `x - 1` is used as the index value. The first time through the loop, x is equal to 1. The first item in the list, however, is referenced as List1.List(0). The value of x is always 1 higher than the list box index. Therefore, 1 is subtracted from x to get the proper list index number.

Why am I confusing you with all of this? I'm doing it to illustrate that you can use the value of the For...Next counter within the loop, performing math operations on it if necessary, and to inform you that list indexes start with 0 and not with 1.

Using Step

In the previous example, x was incremented by 1 each time the loop was executed. In some situations, you may need to increment the counter in different *steps*. For example, maybe you want to increment x by 2 each time. You can do that by adding the `Step` keyword to the For...Next structure:

```
For someCounter = 1 to 100 Step 2
    'Execute some statements here...
Next someCounter
```

The first time through the loop, *someCounter* is equal to 1. The second time through the loop, *someCounter* is equal to 3. The value of *someCounter* increments by 2 each time, to 5, 7, 9, etc. How do you get only even numbers into *someCounter*? Just use a starting value of 2.

Take a few minutes to play with a little program that does absolutely nothing except spit out some numbers based on a For...Next loop. Figure 5.4 shows the form for this program. Here is the working portion of the FOR-NEXT.MAK project:

```
Sub Command1_Click ()
    'Clear the label used for program output
    Label1.Caption = ""
    'If there is no value in Text1, exit the sub without doing
    'anything
    If Text1.Text = "" Then Exit Sub
    'Set the variable startVal equal to the value of Text1.Text
    startVal = Val(Text1.Text)
    'Set the variable stopVal equal to the value of Text2.Text
```

```
        stopVal = Val(Text2.Text)
        'Set the variable stepVal equal to the value of Text3.Text
        stepVal = Val(Text3.Text)
        'Execute a For...Next loop that places the value of
        'the variable
        'counter in Label1
    For counter = startVal To stopVal Step stepVal
            Label1.Caption = Label1.Caption & " " & counter
        Next counter
    End Sub
```

Figure 5.4

The
FOR-NEXT.MAK
project form.

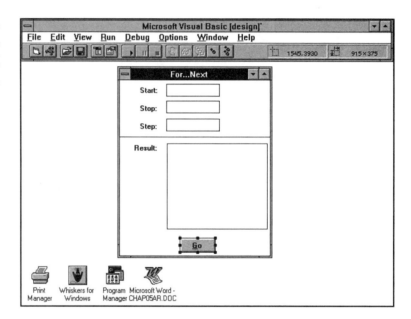

Ready to try it out? Here goes...

Using a For...Next Structure

1. Open the sample project FOR-NEXT.MAK and run the program.

2. Enter the value 1 in the Start text box.

3. Enter the value 100 in the Stop text box.

4. Enter the value 1 in the Step text box.

5. Click on the **G**o button. The values 1 through 100 appear in the Result box (which is a label control).

6. Enter the value 2 in the Step text box and click on **G**o. Odd numbers appear in the Result box.

7. Enter the value 2 in the Start text box and click on **G**o. Even numbers appear in the Result box.

8. Enter the value 100 in the Start box, 1 in the Stop box, and -1 in the Step box; choose **G**o. The program counts down from 100 to 1 in the Result box.

9. Experiment with some additional values for Start, Stop, and Step, then stop the program.

You can see from this exercise that you can decrement the counter in a For...Next structure as well as increment it. Instead of starting at 1 and going to 100, you can start at 100 and go to 1, using a negative `Step` value.

Nested Control Structures

A control structure can contain another control structure, which can contain another control structure, and so on. These are called *nested control structures*. You can nest control structures as many levels deep in a procedure as you want. Here's an example, with an If...Then structure inside of a For...Next structure:

```
Sub HowsItGoin()
    For counter = 1 to lastItem
        If someArray$(count) = "outta here" Then
            'Do something
        Else
            'Do something else
        End If
    Next counter
End Sub
```

If you create nested control structures, indent each new level of control structure one level deeper than the last structure. This will help you keep track of the logic and flow of your program.

Do This Until I Tell You To Stop

The For...Next loop is great when you want to execute some statements a certain number of times, but isn't helpful when you want to keep executing the statements until some condition proves true (or false). Instead of telling your program to "do this block of statements four million times," you might need the program to "do this until Hell freezes over." When Hell freezes over, the program should stop executing the statements in the loop and carry on with the rest of the procedure. The Do...Loop structure is exactly what you need.

Do...Loops

Assume that you want to get a string from the user, then check that string to determine how many words it contains. That sounds a lot like a word-count function for a word processor, doesn't it? Contrary to what you might think, writing a procedure to count the words in a string is easy. It's so easy that we'll add a much more wonderful and amazing feature: We'll break out the string's words and put them into a list box. Whoa! Too cool!

You've already experienced the amazing InStr() function that searches inside a string for another string (in case you're wondering where you read about InStr(), it's explained in Chapter 4). How can we break the words out of a string? Easy! Just search for spaces in the string. When you find a space, you've found the end of a word.

But wait a minute. How will your function know when to stop looking for spaces? You could use the Len() function to check the length of the string, but that wouldn't be nearly as much fun. Instead, use a Do...Loop structure.

The Do...Loop structure enables you to execute a block of statements indefinitely until a condition proves true (or false). Here's an example of the syntax for a Do...Loop structure:

```
Do While some condition is true
    'Execute these statements
Loop
```

As long as the conditional expression is True or non-zero, the program will continue to execute the statements inside the loop structure. When the conditional expression evaluates as False or zero, the program will jump to the next statement after the Loop statement. Here's an example that evaluates a variable:

```
HellStillToastyWarm = 1
Do While HellStillToastyWarm
     Print "It sure is hot down there."
Loop
```

As long as the variable *HellStillToastyWarm* is equal to any value other than zero, the program will continue to execute the loop. The program will probably be printing for a long time.

In our more practical example, we want to keep searching for spaces until there are no more spaces. Here's the Do...Loop structure we'll use:

```
Do While InStr(positionNow, fullString, " ")
     positionNow = InStr(positionNow, fullString, " ") + 1
     theWord = Mid(fullString, positionLast, positionNow -
     ➥positionLast)
     List1.AddItem theWord
     positionLast = positionNow
Loop
```

How does it work? As long the InStr function can locate another space in the string, the condition InStr(positionNow, fullString, " ") evaluates as a positive integer that identifies the location of the space inside the string. If InStr() can't find a space, which is the case when it reaches the end of the string, InStr()returns a zero. Because the condition evaluates as a zero, the condition is no longer true, and the program exits the loop.

Try experimenting with Do...Loop in the DO-LOOP.MAK project. Figure 5.5 shows the form for the DO-LOOP.MAK project.

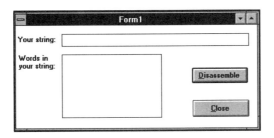

Figure 5.5
The form for the DO-LOOP.MAK project.

Using a Do...Loop Structure

1. Open the sample project DO-LOOP.MAK, and run the program.

2. In the text box, type the phrase "one two three four five," and press Enter. The first four words in the phrase appear in the list box.

3. End the program.

4. Open the Code window and view the PullOutWords procedure in the general section of the form (see fig. 5.6).

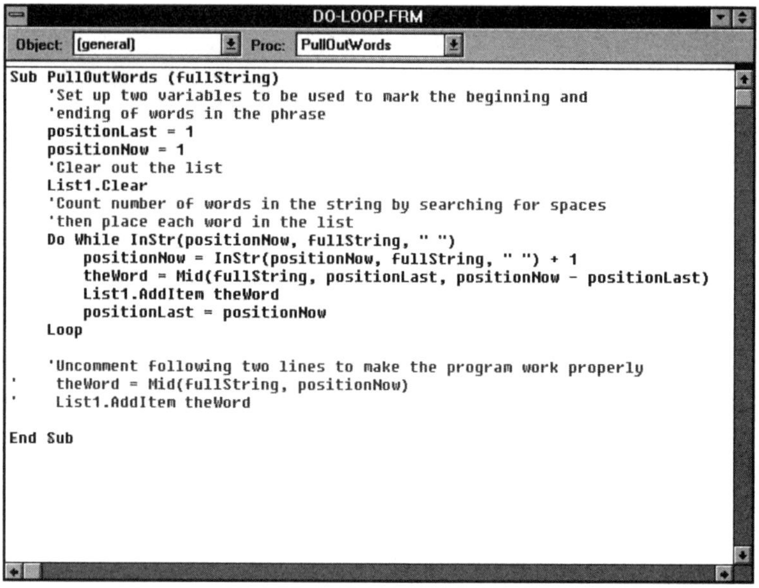

Figure 5.6

Code for the PullOutWords procedure.

```
DO-LOOP.FRM
Object: [general]          Proc: PullOutWords

Sub PullOutWords (FullString)
    'Set up two variables to be used to mark the beginning and
    'ending of words in the phrase
    positionLast = 1
    positionNow = 1
    'Clear out the list
    List1.Clear
    'Count number of words in the string by searching for spaces
    'then place each word in the list
    Do While InStr(positionNow, fullString, " ")
        positionNow = InStr(positionNow, fullString, " ") + 1
        theWord = Mid(fullString, positionLast, positionNow - positionLast)
        List1.AddItem theWord
        positionLast = positionNow
    Loop

    'Uncomment following two lines to make the program work properly
'    theWord = Mid(FullString, positionNow)
'    List1.AddItem theWord

End Sub
```

Aha! It doesn't quite work. Actually, the program *is* doing what you told it to do. The condition InStr(positionNow, fullString, " ") evaluates as a positive integer as long as the function finds a space during its search, which causes it to execute the statements inside the loop structure. When the InStr() function hits the end of the string without finding any more spaces, the condition becomes zero (False), and the loop terminates without extracting the final word in the string.

Fix the program so it will extract the last word.

Fixing Your Do...Loop

1. Open the Code window for the PullOutWords procedure in the general section of the form.

2. Uncomment the last two lines in the function (delete the apostrophe), which are as follows:

   ```
   theWord = Mid(fullString, positionNow)
   List1.AddItem theWord
   ```

3. Save the project.

4. Run the program and enter the phrase "one two three four five" in the text box. The program should now extract all of the words in the program.

Checking for a False Condition

In addition to testing for a True or non-zero condition in a Do...Loop structure, you can test for a False, or zero, condition. This enables you to continue to execute a block of statements while the condition is False, rather than executing the statements while the condition is True. When the condition becomes True, the loop ends.

Instead of using Do While to test for a False condition, use the Do Until variation of the Do...Loop structure. Here's an example:

```
HellFreezesOver = 0
Do Until HellFreezesOver
    If temperature < -40
        Print "It's cold!"
        HellFreezesOver = 1
    Else
        Print "Still too hot!"
    End if
Loop
```

The loop continues to execute as long as the variable *HellFreezesOver* is equal to 0. When *HellFreezesOver* becomes equal to 1, the loop terminates.

Testing the Condition at the End of the Loop

In the DO-LOOP.MAK project, the condition is tested at the beginning of the loop. In this type of Do...Loop structure, the statements inside the loop are not executed at all if the condition is initially False. To force the statements to execute at least one time, even when the condition is False, test the condition at the end of the Do...Loop structure instead of at the beginning:

```
Do
        'Do these statements until the condition is false
Loop While condition
```

In this type of Do...Loop structure, the statements are executed at least once—they execute the first time through the loop. If, at the end of the loop structure, the *condition* evaluates as False or zero, the loop terminates.

Take a look at an example. I'll modify the loop from the previous example:

```
HellFreezesOver = 0
DO
    If Temperature < -40
        Print Its Cold!
        HellFreezesOver = 1
    Else
        Print "Still too hot!"
    End If
Loop Until HellFreezesOver
```

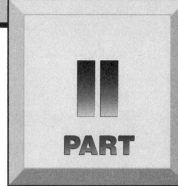

PART

Doing Something Useful

By now you should be fairly comfortable working with Visual Basic. If you didn't get impatient and skip the earlier chapters, you should now have a good understanding of forms, controls, properties, methods, variables, and control structures. In fact, you have enough information already to write some pretty useful little programs, but you're probably wanting *more*!

- **6: Doing Simple File Stuff.** Hey, it's easy to work with files in Visual Basic. This chapter teaches you how to use drive, directory, and file list boxes. You also learn to erase, copy, move, and rename files in a Visual Basic program.

- **7: Duck with Plum Sauce (Menus).** This chapter explains how to add menus to a program and write code to make them work.

- **8: Dialog Boxes!** Chapter 8 introduces you to some of the concepts and controls you'll use to create dialog boxes for your programs.

- **9: Even More Dialog Boxes!** Dialog boxes are a big topic, so they take two chapters. Chapter 9 shows you how to do some really cool stuff, like use standard dialog boxes that are provided by Windows.

- **10: Working with Pictures.** Chapter 10 slips into graphics mode, teaching you how to use picture boxes and image boxes.

- **11: Printing Stuff.** You're sure to want to print stuff from at least one program you write, so Chapter 11 will lay the groundwork on printing. You'll learn how to set printer options and send data to the printer.

Doing Simple File Stuff

You probably work with files quite a bit. Until a better method of organizing information comes along, the file and directory structures that have been around since the first version of DOS will haunt us still. This chapter explains how you can add file controls to your Visual Basic programs and write procedures that perform various file actions. Here's a list of the nuggets of wisdom you'll glean from this chapter:

- Understanding the file controls
- Synchronizing file controls
- Finding, erasing, copying, moving, and renaming files
- Executing a program file

A Look at the File Controls

Visual Basic makes it very easy for you to add file controls to programs you write. If you need to create a dialog box that displays a list of files, for example, you have to do little more than draw the control on the form and add a couple of lines of program code to your event procedures. This section of the chapter examines the drive, directory list box, and file list box controls. Figure 6.1 shows these three controls on a form.

Figure 6.1

The drive, directory
list box, and file list
box controls.

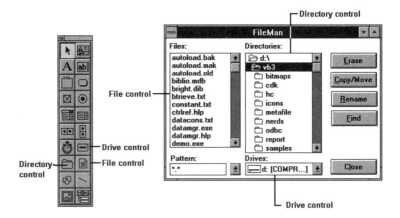

The Drive Control

The drive control is a drop-down list control that contains a list of all of the
drives currently connected to the system, either locally or by redirection
across the network. At run time, you can click on the drive control and
select a drive. The icons in the drive control list automatically identify the
type of drive as a floppy drive, hard disk, remote network drive, or CD-ROM
drive. Figure 6.2 shows a drive control in action, with different types of
drives displayed in the list.

Figure 6.2

Various types of
drives in a drive
control.

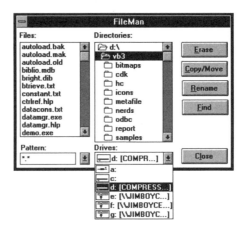

You don't have to write any code for the drive control to enable the user to
select a drive from the list. That function is handled automatically by the
control. You do, however, have to add code to coordinate a directory list box

control with the drive control, or to have the program perform some action when the user selects a drive from the list. You'll learn how to do that a little later.

In addition to design time properties, Drive controls also have properties that are available only at run time. The Drive property is an example of a run time only property. The Drive property specifies the currently selected drive. When the user selects a drive, the Drive property of the Drive control changes. You can use the Drive property to set the Path property (explained next) of a Dir control.

The Directory List Box Control

The directory list box control displays a list of directories on the current drive. You can use a directory list box to enable users of your program to select a directory. Like the drive control, the directory list box functions on its own to a limited degree without any code from you. At run time, you can select various directories using the control, moving up or down in the directory structure. To make the directory list box change when the user selects a different drive, or to make a file list change when the user selects a different directory, you must add a couple of lines of code to your program.

The Path property of a Dir control is available only at run time. When the user selects a directory in the Dir control, the Path property changes. You then can use the Path property of the Dir control to set the Path property of a File control, which is explained next.

The File List Box Control

The file list box control displays a list of files in the current directory. By default, you can select only one file from the file list, but you can set the file list box control's properties to enable your users to select multiple files from the list.

As with the other two file controls, the file list box control works to a limited degree on its own. To make the file list change when the drive or directory box changes, you have to add a couple of lines of code to the program.

Are you tired of reading that you have to add some code to the file controls to make them useful? Good! Start writing some code. To provide a little more experience with drawing controls and writing code, the first few exercises in this chapter require you to do a little more work than those in previous chapters.

Making File Controls Work Together

When you use file controls in a program, it's likely that you will want to use all three controls together (drive, directory, and file). Synchronizing the three controls so they work together is surprisingly simple. First, start a new project and draw the three controls on Form1. Figure 6.3 shows the three file controls added to the form.

Figure 6.3

File controls added to the form.

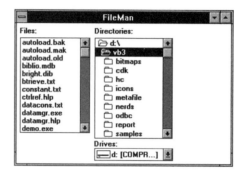

NOTE

Your *Understanding Visual Basic Disk* includes a project called FILES.MAK. If you prefer, you can skip steps 1 through 4 in the following exercise and simply load FILES.MAK instead. If you create your own FILES.MAK, you overwrite the existing FILES.MAK project with your own.

Drawing File Controls

1. Start Visual Basic, which begins a new project and displays a new Form1.

2. From the Toolbox, click on the drive control and add the drive control to the form as shown in figure 6.3. The default name for the drive control is Drive1.

3. From the Toolbox, click on the directory list box control, and draw the control on the form as shown in figure 6.3. The default name for the directory list box control is Dir1.

4. From the Toolbox, click on the file list box control, and draw the control on the form as shown in figure 6.3. The default name for the file list box control is File1.

5. Run the program.

6. Choose a drive from the drive control. The directory and file lists do not change.

7. Choose a directory from the directory list. The file list does not change to show the files in the newly selected directory.

8. Double-click on a file in the file list. Nothing happens.

9. End the program.

10. Choose Save Project As to save the project. Visual Basic will prompt you for a name by which to store the form. Enter FILES.FRM as the file name for the form. When prompted for a project file name, enter FILES.MAK.

That was easy enough. Now you need to add a few statements to the program to make the file controls work together. Here is a description of the procedures you need to create for two of the controls:

☐ **Drive1.** Create a procedure for the Change event of this control. The Drive1_Change() procedure will be executed when the user changes the drive selection in the list (selects a drive). This procedure will set the directory list box's path to match the newly selected drive.

☐ **Dir1.** Create a procedure for the Change event of this procedure. The Dir1_Change() procedure will set the path of the File1 control to match the path of the Dir1 control.

What about the File1 control? By adding the two procedures described here, all three file controls will be synchronized with one another. To perform an action on a selected file, however, you will have to write some additional procedures. Those procedures will be explained later. For now, add the code to Drive1 and Dir1.

Synchronizing the File Controls

1. Double-click on the drive control to open the Code window. The Code window displays the default event procedure for the control, which is the Change procedure.

continues

2. Change the Drive1_Change() procedure to read as follows:

```
Sub Drive1_Change()
    Dir1.Path = Drive1.Drive
End Sub
```

This procedure sets the Path property of the Dir1 control to match the Drive property of the Drive1 control. When the user selects a different drive, the path is changed in the Dir1 control.

3. From the Object drop-down list in the Code window, choose the Dir1 control to display the Dir1_Change event. Change is the default event for a directory list box control.

4. Change the Dir1_Change() procedure to read as follows:

```
Sub Dir1_Change()
    File1.Path = Dir1.Path
End Sub
```

This procedure sets the Path property of the File1 control to match the Path property of the Dir1 control.

5. Run the program and select a drive from the drive control. The directory in the directory list box control should change to match the newly selected drive, and the file list should change to display the files in the new directory.

6. Select a different directory. The file list should change to show the files in the newly selected directory.

7. Without a disk in drive A, select a: from the drive list. This will cause an error, and Visual Basic will display an error message informing you that the device is unavailable.

8. End the program.

You can see that it's an extremely simple task to synchronize the file controls. You need to add a few lines of code, however, to handle the possibility that there will be no disk in the floppy drive or that a local or remote network disk will suddenly be unavailable. Error handling is explained in more detail in Chapter 12. For now, just add a simple error handler to the Drive1_Change() procedure.

Handling "Device Not Available" Errors

1. Continue working with FILES.MAK.

2. Display the Code window for the Drive1_Change() procedure.

3. Modify the procedure to read as follows (the new code is shown in bold):

```
Sub Drive1_Change ()
      On Error Resume Next
      Dir1.Path = Drive1.Drive
End Sub
```

4. Save the project.

5. Run the program. With no disk in drive A:, select a: from the drive list. The drive list will change, but the directory and file list do not change to match the drive, and no error is generated.

6. End the program.

Great! Now you have the file controls synchronized, and you've planned for the possibility that a selected drive might not be available. You could use the program just as it is to view the files on a drive. With only three lines of code in the program, though, the program isn't very functional. It's time to make your program do something useful. For example, wouldn't it be nice to be able to erase a file using your new program?

Doing Things with Files

Setting up file controls and enabling the user of your program to view a file list and select a file is just one small part of enabling the user to access files. To make the program more useful, you need to add some procedures that perform actions such as erase or copy on the selected file. First, let's have a look at how you can zap a file out of existence.

Erasing a File

Erasing a file from a VB program is simple: you simply issue the Kill statement and provide it with the path and name of the file to erase. VB handles the process of deleting the file. What you need to worry about is verifying that the user *really* wants to erase the selected file and design the code to handle possible errors that might occur during the erase process. There is no equivalent of the manslaughter charge when it comes to erasing a file (*fileslaughter*, maybe?). If you kill a file, you have to mean it.

Add an **E**rase button to your FILES.MAK form. The Click event procedure for the button will contain some code that erases the selected file. Figure 6.4 shows the **E**rase button added to the form.

Figure 6.4

The **E**rase button added to the form.

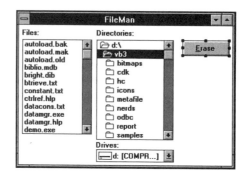

Adding an Erase Feature

1. Open (or continue with) the project FILES.MAK.

2. Display the form, choose the Command button tool from the Toolbox and draw a command button on the form (see fig. 6.4).

3. Change the Caption property of the button to &Erase.

4. Change the Name property of the button from Command1 to cmdErase.

5. Double-click on the cmdErase button to display the Code window for its Click procedure.

6. Write the following cmdErase_Click() procedure:

```
Sub cmdErase_Click ()
    If Right(File1.Path, 1) = "\" Then
        fileToErase = File1.Path & File1.FileName
    Else
        fileToErase = File1.Path & "\" & File1.FileName
    End If
```

```
       retval = MsgBox("Erase " & fileToErase & "?", 52,
       ➥"Are you sure?")
       If retval = 6 Then
             On Error GoTo cmdEraseError
             Kill fileToErase
              File1.Refresh
       End If
       Exit Sub

   cmdEraseError:
        MsgBox "Sorry, can't erase the file."
        Resume Next

   End Sub
```

7. Save the project.

Let's take a look at how the procedure works by first examining the If...Then structure at the beginning of the procedure:

```
If Right(File1.Path, 1) = "\" Then
     'If the right-most character in the path is "\", the
     'path already contains a backslash character. So, just
     'concatenate the Path property and the FileName property to
     'derive the full path and file name for the selected file,
     'then store the result in the
     'variable fileToErase
     fileToErase = File1.Path & File1.FileName
Else 'Otherwise, stick a backslash (\) between the Path
     'and FileName
     'properties to separate them
     fileToErase = File1.Path & "\" & File1.FileName
End If
```

If you don't add this bit of conditional testing, and simply concatenate the Path and FileName properties to derive the file name, the file name will be correct only when the file resides in the root directory. This is because the Path already has a backslash character in it (such as B:\) to separate it from the FileName. If you select a file from a subdirectory, the Path property does not include an ending backslash; you must add one to it to separate it from the FileName property.

Next, have a look at the business end of this procedure:

```
'Display a message box containing Yes and No buttons that prompts
'the user to verify whether he/she wants to erase the file, and
'store the result (representing the button that was selected in the
'message box), in the variable retval
retval = MsgBox("Erase " & fileToErase & "?", 52, "Are you sure?")
If retval = 6 Then 'The user pressed the Yes button
        'If an error occurs, go to the label named cmdEraseError
        On Error GoTo cmdEraseError
        'Use the Kill statement to erase the file represented by the
        'file name stored in fileToErase
        Kill fileToErase
        'Refresh the file list to make the erased file disappear from
        'the list
        File1.Refresh
End If
'Get out of the sub without executing the statements that follow in
'the cmdEraseError block
Exit Sub

cmdEraseError:
        'If an error occurs during the erase, display a message box,
        'then resume execution with the next statement, which is
        'End Sub
        MsgBox "Sorry, can't erase the file."
        Resume Next
End Sub
```

You might be puzzling over the use of MsgBox in this procedure. The MsgBox statement and MsgBox() function are explained in Chapter 8, "Dialog Boxes!" For now, a brief explanation will do.

The MsgBox statement displays a message in a dialog box (see fig. 6.5). The MsgBox() function performs the same task, but also returns an integer that identifies the button that the user selected in the dialog box. Here's the syntax for MsgBox statement and function:

```
MsgBox <message string>, <buttons>, <dialog title>
```

or

```
retval = MsgBox(<message string>, <buttons>, <dialog title>)
```

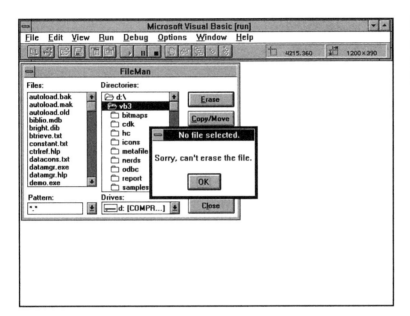

Figure 6.5

A message box generated with MsgBox.

The value specified by the *message string* parameter is the actual text of the message that will appear in the message box. You can use a literal string in quotes, a variable, or concatenate literal strings and variables to derive the message.

The *buttons* parameter determines the buttons and icon that are displayed in the dialog box (OK, Cancel, Yes, No, information icon, question mark icon, and so on). You'll learn in Chapter 8 about the values you can use to specify which buttons and icon will display in the dialog box. For now, just believe me when I tell you that 52 gives you an exclamation icon and Yes and No buttons.

The last parameter, *dialog title*, is a string that specifies the title that appears in the title bar of the dialog box. As with the message, you can use a literal string, a variable, or a combination.

The function form of MsgBox is used to prompt the user to verify the file deletion because the program can then test the value of the *retval* variable to determine which button the user pushed. If the user pushed the Yes button, the MsgBox function returns the value 6. Pushing any other button returns a different value (explained in Chapter 8).

Even More File Stuff

Instead of making you draw a bunch of controls and type a lot of code for the rest of the exercises in this chapter, I've generously (no applause necessary) done most of the work for you. Open the project FILEMAN.MAK. This new project contains the same functions that you have already added to FILES.MAK, but its interface is finished to save you some time. FILEMAN.MAK also contains most of the program code you will need so you can follow along rather than spend a lot of time typing.

Another difference between FILES.MAK and FILEMAN.MAK is that FILEMAN.MAK contains three forms. The first form is named frmFileMan, which is the startup form. The second form is named frmCopyMove. You'll use this second form for copying and moving files. The third form is named frmFindFile. You'll use this form for finding files. Also, the FILEMAN.MAK project includes a module file called FILEMAN.BAS that defines a few global variables.

Now, let's starting fiddling with files.

Copying or Moving a File

The kind folks who developed Visual Basic thoughtfully provided a statement called FileCopy that enables you to copy a file. Here's the syntax of the FileCopy statement:

```
FileCopy <source>, <destination>
```

The *source* parameter specifies the name of the file to be copied. The *destination* parameter specifies the location where the new copy of the file will be stored. If you include a new file name as part of the *destination* parameter, the file will be renamed during the copy operation.

The FileMan program (FILEMAN.MAK) contains a form named frmCopyMove that is used when copying a file. When you select a file in the main form and choose the Copy/Move button, the program first verifies that a file is selected by checking the FileName property of the File1 control. If the FileName property is blank, no file is selected and the program displays an error message and exits the procedure. If a file is selected, the program appends a backslash to the path, if necessary (if the path is the root). The program then sets up the controls on frmCopyMove and shows the form.

In the following exercise, take a look at how the program's Copy/Move function works. Figure 6.6 shows the main form and the Copy/Move form (frmFileMan and frmCopyMove).

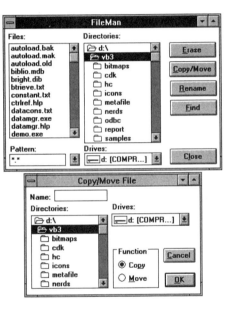

Figure 6.6

The main form and Copy/Move form.

Copying and Moving Files

1. Open the project FILEMAN.MAK and display frmFileMan and frmCopyMove (see fig. 6.6).

2. Double-click on the **C**opy/Move button to display the Code window and view the cmdCopy_Click() procedure.

3. Examine the code for the cmdCopy_Click() procedure. The last four lines of the procedure set up and display the frmCopyMove form.

```
Sub cmdCopy_Click ()
    If File1.FileName = "" Then
```

continues

```
                    MsgBox "Please choose a file.", 0, "No file selected."
                    Exit Sub
              End If
              If Right(File1.Path, 1) = "\" Then
                    fileSource = File1.Path & File1.FileName
              Else
                    fileSource = File1.Path & "\" & File1.FileName
              End If
              frmCopyMove!Text1.Text = File1.FileName
              frmCopyMove!Drive1.Drive = Drive1.Drive
              frmCopyMove!Dir1.Path = Dir1.Path
              frmCopyMove.Show 1
        End Sub
```

4. Close the Code window and examine the Copy/Move form (frmCopyMove).

5. Double-click on the OK button on the frmCopyMove form to display the Code window and view the cmdCopyMoveOK_Click() procedure. Here is the business end of this procedure:

```
    'Set up an error handler in case an error occurs
    On Error GoTo cantDoIt
    'Copy the file
    FileCopy fileSource, fileDestination
    'If the optMove button is selected, erase the source file
    'after the copy is completed
    If optMove Then
          Kill fileSource
    End If
```

The FileCopy statement is used to copy the file. If the optMove button is selected, the procedure also erases the source file after the copy is completed.

6. Run the program.

7. Select a file, and choose the Copy/Move button.

8. In the Copy/Move dialog box, select a different directory or change the file name, and choose OK. The file will be copied as you have specified.

9. End the program

The key to this procedure is the `FileCopy` statement. The `FileCopy` statement copies the file for you. The other important point to understand about this procedure is that moving a file is not very different from copying a file. The only difference is that after copying the file to the new destination file, the source file is erased. To move a file, therefore, you must use a combination of two Visual Basic statements: `FileCopy` to create a copy of the file and `Kill` to erase the source file.

Renaming a File

Renaming a file is a simple process in a Visual Basic program. You simply use the `Name` statement. Here's the syntax for the statement:

```
Name <oldname> As <newname>
```

The FileMan program uses this method to rename a file. Take a look at the `cmdRename_Click()` procedure in the following exercise.

Renaming a File

1. Open (or continue with) the project FILEMAN.MAK.

2. Display the frmFileMan form (the main form) and double-click on the **R**ename button to display the Code window for the `cmdRename_Click()` procedure. This procedure checks the length of the new file name to see if it is longer than 12 characters. If so, the procedure aborts because the file name is not valid. Otherwise, the procedure uses the following code to rename the file:

```
'If an error occurs (like a bad file name), go to the
'error handler
On Error GoTo cmdRenameError
'Create the new file name by appending the path and the new name
fileNewName = filePath & retval
'Rename the file
Name fileOldName As fileNewName
'Refresh the directory list to show the new name (assuming the
'file hasn't been moved to a different directory by renaming it).
File1.Refresh
Exit Sub
```

continues

3. Run the program and rename a file. (Make sure to choose a file that you no longer need, or rename the file a second time to restore its original name.) Figure 6.7 shows the input box that FileMan displays to prompt you for a new file name.

4. End the program.

Figure 6.7

An input box that prompts for a new file name.

You can see that renaming a file is a fairly simple process. Most of the procedure is taken up by code that checks the path string, checks the file name, and so on. The code that actually renames the file consists of a single statement.

Finding a File

The FileMan program includes a **F**ind button that provides access to the frmFind form, which enables you to search through a directory and all of its subdirectory files that match a file pattern that you specify. The names of any matching files are placed in a list box, and the total number of matching files found is reported in a label above the list box.

Adding the capability to search for files is a little more difficult to implement than copying and erasing files. To create a procedure that searches for files, you can use the Dir() function. The Dir() function returns the name of a file that matches a search pattern. The syntax of the Dir() function is as follows:

```
Dir (filePattern, attributeMask)
```

The *filePattern* parameter specifies the search string, such as *.DOC, MONKEY.EAT, BANANA.OLD, and so on. The *filePattern* parameter can include any valid wild card combination. The *attributeMask* parameter, which is optional, specifies file attributes. FileMan doesn't search by file attributes, but you could modify it to do so (find only hidden files that match the pattern, for example). If you're interested in the *attributeMask* parameter, check the Visual Basic Help file for the Dir function—the Help file explains the attribute mask values.

The first time you issue the `Dir()` function, you must include a *filePattern* parameter. If you don't, an error occurs. To find additional files that match the *filePattern* parameter, issue the `Dir` function without a *filePattern* argument. Following is the portion of the procedure that searches for matching files. The *fileFound* variable is used to store the name of any matching files that the procedure finds. The *dirsWhereFilesFound* variable is used to keep count of the number of directories in which matching files were found. This variable is later subtracted from the total items in the list to determine how many matching files were found.

Here's a fragment of the procedure, with comments:

```
'Issue the Dir() function the first time to see if there are any
'matching files. If so, store the name in the fileFound variable.
fileFound = Dir(pathToSearch)
'If fileFound is empty, there were no matching files.
If fileFound <> "" Then     'fileFound is not empty, so matching
'files were found
     'Add the name of the directory to the list, but preface it
     'with a little arrow symbol made from an equals sign
     'and a chevron.
     List1.AddItem "=> " & Dir2.Path
     'Add 1 to the number of directories where matching files
     'were found
     dirsWhereFilesFound = dirsWhereFilesFound + 1
End If
Do While fileFound <> ""  'Keep doing the loop as long as there are
     'matching files
     'Add the name of the file to the list
     List1.AddItem "   " & fileFound
     'Issue the Dir() function again to find any more matching
     'file names
     fileFound = Dir
Loop
'The loop terminates when there are no more matching files in the
'current directory, because the Dir() function returns and empty
'value "" when there is no file found.
```

Rather than have you run through exercises to look at the code, I'll let you examine the code for the search procedures on your own. The code contains liberal comments that should help you understand how the procedures work. Look at the procedures cmdFind_Click() and Dir2_Change() on frmFind to learn how the search procedures work. If you can't figure out how it works, and you want to add the feature to your own program, just copy the code to your program from FileMan.

Executing a Program File

Another common operation your programs might need to perform is starting other programs. If you double-click on a file in the FileMan file list, for example, you could have the program execute the file. Adding that capability to your FileMan is fairly simple—you only need to use the Visual Basic Shell() function. Here's the syntax of the Shell() function:

```
Shell (commandString, windowStyle)
```

The *commandString* parameter specifies the name of the file to execute, including any command line parameters (like NOTEPAD.EXE MYFILE.TXT, for example). The file specified in the *commandString* parameter must be an EXE, COM, PIF, or BAT file located in any of the following places:

- The current directory
- The Windows directory
- The Windows System directory
- Directories on the system PATH

If the Shell() function can't find the file, or the file specified is not one of the four allowable file types, an error occurs. If you don't handle the error in your procedure, the program that is trying to execute the Shell() function will bomb.

The *windowStyle* parameter determines the mode in which the program will start. Table 6.1 shows a list of the values for *windowStyle* and the effect they have.

Table 6.1
Values for the windowStyle Property

Value	Window mode
1, 5, or 9	Normal window with focus
2	Minimized as an icon with focus (the default)
3	Maximized with focus
4, 8	Normal window without focus
6, 7	Minimized as icon without focus

If you want to start a program in normal window mode, for example, you can use a value of 1, 5, or 9 to start the program in a window with focus. *Focus* means the window is active. You also can start the program in a window without focus by using the values 4 or 8 (the program window will not become active on startup).

The important point of adding program-starting capability to FileMan is that you must create a simple error handler that will keep FileMan from crashing if the user tries to start any type of file other than EXE, COM, BAT, or PIF files.

NOTE It's possible to start a program by double-clicking on a document file, but you can't add that capability with the shell() function. Instead, you have to use a Windows API call that uses the Registration Database to start the application and load the file. Sorry, but that's not within the scope of this book. At least you know in general how to do it, and you'll sound really intelligent when you mention it the next time you're at a party.

Okay, let's add program-starting capability to your FileMan program! You can draw your own Run dialog box, but I've thoughtfully provided one for you (see fig. 6.8). All you have to do is add it to your FileMan project.

Figure 6.8

A Run dialog box for
your FileMan.

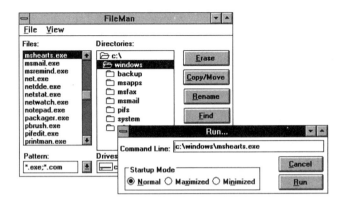

Modifying FileMan To Start Programs

1. Open the project FILEMAN.MAK.

2. Choose **F**ile, A**d**d File. This displays the Add File dialog box.

3. From the Add File dialog box, locate the file RUN.FRM that is included
   with your *Understanding Visual Basic* sample files, and select the file and
   choose OK. This adds the form to your project.

4. In the Project window, choose the RUN.FRM file, and choose the View
   Form button to display the form (see fig. 6.8).

5. Double-click on the Cancel button to open the Code window and display
   the Click procedure for cmdCancel (the name of the Cancel button). Make
   sure the procedure looks like this:

   ```
   Sub cmdCancel_Click ()
        Unload frmStartProgram
   End Sub
   ```

6. From the Object drop-down list, choose cmdRun, and add the following
   code to the cmdRun_Click() procedure:

   ```
   Sub cmdRun_Click ()
        On Error GoTo cmdRunError
        If optNormal Then retval = Shell(Text1.Text, 1)
        If optMinimized Then retval = Shell(Text1.Text, 2)
        If optMaximized Then retval = Shell(Text1.Text, 3)
        frmStartProgram.Hide
        Exit Sub
   ```

```
cmdRunError:
    MsgBox "Can't run that file."
    Resume Next
End Sub
```

That takes care of the code that actually executes the file specified in the Text1 control in frmStartProgram. Now, how do you make the Run dialog box appear when you double-click on a file name in the file list box? It's simple—just add some code for the DblClick procedure of the File1 control.

Adding Double-Click to the File List

1. Display the frmFileMan form, and double-click on the File1 control to display the Code window for the File1 control.

2. From the Proc drop-down list, choose the DblClick event to display a new procedure named `File1_DblClick()`.

3. Modify the File1_DblClick() event procedure to look like the following:

```
Sub File1_DblClick ()
    If Right(Dir1.Path, 1) <> "\" Then
    fileToRun = Dir1.Path & "\" & File1.FileName
    Else
    fileToRun = Dir1.Path & File1.FileName
    End If
    frmStartProgram!Text1.Text = fileToRun
    frmStartProgram.Show 1
End Sub
```

4. Save the project.

5. Run the program to test it.

6. If you had no errors in step 5, choose File, Make EXE File and create an EXE file for your new FileMan program.

Duck with Plum Sauce (Menus)

I'll have the duck with plum sauce, fried rice, egg-drop soup, and a bowl of bean embryos. Oh, sorry... they aren't that kind of menus. This chapter is about adding menus to your programs. It's so easy to do that you could probably do it in your sleep without reading this chapter. But I put this chapter in the outline and the publisher bought it, so now I have to come through.

Take heart! You'll learn all manner of strange things in this chapter, including the following:

- Planning your menu
- Setting up menu names and menu captions
- Adding menus to a program
- Using menu separators
- Creating a toggle menu item
- Enabling and disabling menu items

As with all other aspects of interface design, you need to put some planning into your menu.

Planning Your Menu

Stop, put this book down, and take five minutes to look at some of the menus in your average Windows programs. Go ahead—I'll wait... (you might want to have a look at figure 7.1 before you go).

Figure 7.1

Samples of Windows program menus.

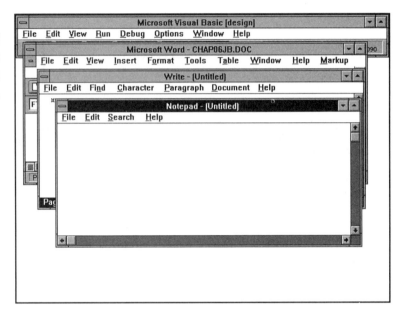

Ah, you're back! Did you notice that the menus all are arranged in basically the same fashion (see fig. 7.1)? File is always first, Edit is always second, and Help is always last. That consistency is a major aspect of the Windows environment. Developers make their programs as similar to other Windows programs as possible to ensure that it will be easy for a new user to learn to use their program.

Do developers steal each other's program designs? No, but they do all follow the same standards. When you are designing a menu for your own program, look at the typical menu arrangement in other Windows programs. Not only should you place your menus in the same locations (File first, for example), but the location of menu *items* in each menu should also be the same. If you add an Edit menu to your program, for example, the Cut, Copy, and Paste items, as well as any other standard Edit menu items, should be arranged in the same order within the menu as they are in other Windows programs.

Standardizing your menu also should include adding standard shortcut keys and access keys. Access keys are the underlined characters that appear in a menu; they provide a means for the user to select a menu item by using the keyboard. The **t** in the Cu**t** item, the **C** in the **C**opy item, and the **P** in the **P**aste item all are access keys (also called *hot keys*).

Shortcut keys are key combinations the user can press to activate a function. The shortcut key for the **C**opy command, for example, is Ctrl+C. The shortcut key for the **P**aste command is Ctrl+V. When you design your menu, check other Windows applications and, as often as possible, use the same access keys and shortcut keys that these other programs use.

Using the Menu Design Window

Remember from the beginning of the chapter when I told you that designing a menu was so easy you could do it in your sleep? I lied. You have to be a quantum physicist to understand it—you actually have to click a few buttons and type a few words to create a menu. That has to be difficult, doesn't it? Look at figure 7.2 and see for yourself.

Figure 7.2

The Menu
Design Window.

The Menu Design Window enables you to quickly create (I lied again) a menu. The following list describes the controls in the Menu Design Window:

Ca**p**tion. Use this edit box to specify the caption (text) that will appear in the menu bar (for a menu) or within a menu (for a menu item).

☐ Na**m**e. This is the name of the menu control. Each menu and menu item must have a name, just like command buttons, text boxes, and other controls. The standard prefix for menu names is *mnu*.

☐ Inde**x**. This is a numeric value assigned to the menu item if it is part of a control array. Control arrays are explained in Chapter 8, "Dialog Boxes!"

☐ **S**hortcut. This list box lets you select from a wide range of pre-defined shortcut key combinations.

☐ **W**indowList. If this check box is checked, and you're using an MDI (Multiple Document Interface), the associated menu item will display a list of open child windows.

☐ HelpContextID. This is an optional numeric value that you can use to call a topic page in the Help file for the menu item. It enables context-sensitive help for the menu item. If the item is selected and the user presses F1, this numeric value, which you associate in the Help file with a topic page for the menu item, is used to locate and display the Help topic.

☐ **C**hecked. If this check box is checked, the menu item will start out with a check beside it. You can set this property of a menu item at run time, enabling you to check and uncheck a menu item.

☐ **E**nabled. If this check box is checked, the menu item is enabled, which means the user can access it. If this check box is not checked, the menu item is dimmed (disabled). You can enable and disable menu items at run time. If you disable a menu at design time, it will remain disabled unless your program code enables it.

☐ **V**isible. This property determines whether or not the menu item is displayed on the menu. If this property is set to False (the check box is cleared), the item does not appear on the menu and the items below it shift up to take its place.

☐ Arrow buttons. The four arrow buttons on the dialog box enable you to change the indention level of the menu items. Topmost-level items appear on the menu bar. Second-level items appear within the parent menu. Third-level items are cascading menu items of their parent item. Cascading menus are multilevel menus, and they're explained later in this chapter.

☐ **N**ext. Selects the next menu item in the list.

☐ **I**nsert. Inserts a new menu item at the selected location.

☐ Dele**t**e. Deletes a menu item.

You'll use most of these controls in this chapter to create a menu item. Because *Understanding Visual Basic* doesn't cover the Windows Help Compiler, you won't assign HelpContextIDs to the menu items.

Creating a menu item is really no more difficult than specifying a caption and menu control name, then setting a few properties. First, think about your menu captions and menu item names.

Menu Captions and Menu Names

Use the Caption edit box to specify the caption for a menu item. The caption is the text that appears in the menu bar for top-level items in the list, or is the name of the menu item as it appears on its menu. As with other captions, adding an ampersand character (&) to a menu caption causes the letter following it to be underlined. This underlined character is the access key discussed earlier in this chapter. When the menu item is displayed, the user can press Alt and the access key to activate the associated menu item.

Use the Name edit box to specify the name for the control. Unlike other controls, menus are not assigned control names automatically; you must assign a name. The recommended standard is to use the prefix *mnu* to identify the control as a menu, and use the name of the menu as the remainder of the control name. The Open item on a File menu, for example, might have the name *mnuFileOpen*.

Adding Items to a Menu

Now it's time to start creating a menu. You already have a working FileMan program, so let's add a menu to it. The menu items will duplicate the functions of the control buttons on FileMan's main form.

Creating a Menu

1. Open the project FILEMAN.MAK, choose frmFileMan from the Project window, and click on the View Form button.

2. With the frmFileMan form displayed, choose **W**indow and **M**enu Design to display the Menu Design Window.

3. In the Caption edit box, type **&File**.

continues

4. In the Name edit box, type **mnuFile**. Press Enter to create the item and clear the Caption and Name edit boxes.

5. In the Caption edit box, type **&View**.

6. In the Name edit box, type **mnuView** and press Enter.

7. Click on &View in the menu list box in the bottom portion of the Menu Design Window, and choose the Insert button. This inserts a new menu item between the File and View menu items.

8. In the Caption edit box, type **&Duplicate....**

9. In the Name edit box, type **mnuFileDuplicate**.

10. Click on the right-arrow button to indent the Duplicate menu item by one level, and choose OK to close the dialog box.

11. Notice that your FileMan main form now has a menu bar (see fig. 7.3). Click on FileMan's File menu to display the menu items in the File menu (there is only one—Duplicate).

12. Run the program and choose File, Duplicate. Nothing happens.

13. End the program.

Figure 7.3

Menu added to
FileMan's
main form
(frmFileMan).

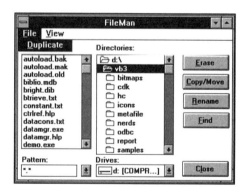

Now you have a couple of menu items in your FileMan program. As you can see from the last step in the exercise, you can select menu items when the program is running, but they don't do anything. Why? You haven't written any code for the Click event procedures of the menus. Before you do that, however, add a few more of the menu items you will need for the FileMan program.

Adding More Menu Items

1. Continue working with FILEMAN.MAK.

2. Select the frmFileMan form and choose **W**indow, **M**enu Design.

3. Click on &View in the menu item list, and click on the **I**nsert button twice to insert two blank menu items.

4. In the Ca**p**tion edit box, type **De&lete**.

5. In the Na**m**e edit box, type **mnuFileDelete**, and press Enter.

6. In the Ca**p**tion edit box, type **&Rename**.

7. In the Na**m**e edit box, type **mnuFileRename**, and press Enter.

8. Choose the mnuFileDelete item in the list, and click on the right arrow to shift the De**l**ete menu under the **E**dit menu.

9. Choose the mnuFileRename item in the list, and click on the right arrow to shift the **R**ename menu under the **E**dit menu.

Hey, we're really cookin' now! You can see that it's really easy to create menus. Before you finish adding all of the menu items for the program, though, make a few of the menu items work.

Creating Code for a Menu Item

Adding code for a menu item is essentially the same as adding code for any Visual Basic control. The easiest way to add code for a specific menu item is to select the menu item at design time. Visual Basic then opens a Code window showing the Click event procedure for the selected menu item.

If your program already contains the code you want executed when the menu item is selected, the Click event procedure for the menu item can be very simple. In the FileMan program, for example, the procedure for erasing a file is already written—it's contained in the cmdErase_Click() procedure. How can you quickly make the De**l**ete item in the **F**ile menu work? Just add some code to the Click event for mnuFileDelete that "clicks" the **E**rase button.

Coding the Delete Menu Item

1. Continue working with the FILEMAN.MAK project.

2. From the frmFileMan form, choose File, Delete to open the Code window for the `mnuFileDelete_Click()` event procedure.

3. Modify the `mnuFileDelete_Click()` procedure to read as follows:

```
Sub mnuFileDelete_Click ()
    cmdErase_Click
End Sub
```

4. From the Object drop-down list, choose `mnuFileRename` to display the `mnuFileRename_Click()` event procedure.

5. Modify the `mnuFileRename_Click()` procedure to read as follows:

```
Sub mnuFileRename_Click ()
    cmdRename_Click
End Sub
```

6. Run the program and test the Delete and **R**ename options in FileMan's **F**ile menu to make sure they work.

7. Save the project.

You can see that adding functionality to a menu item is often as simple as issuing a Click event for an existing control, such as a command button. In other situations, you might need to generate other events, such as setting a radio button, filling a text box, and so on. If the code you need does not exist in your program, however, you can add it to the Click event procedure of the selected menu item. In our FileMan program, for example, you could have added the code to erase a file to the `mnuFileDelete_Click()` procedure instead of the `cmdErase_Click()` procedure.

Completing the FileMan Menu

At this point you have a functioning menu system, although some of the menu items don't have any code associated with them, and therefore don't actually do anything. In this section you'll learn some useful things about menus and complete your FileMan menu structure.

Assigning Shortcut Keys

Every good menu deserves a few shortcut keys. Adding shortcut keys to a menu item is simple. The main point to remember is that your shortcut keys should follow the Windows standard whenever possible. In our FileMan program, we'll use the same shortcut keys that the Windows File Manager uses.

To assign a shortcut key to a menu, select the menu item in the Menu Design window, and select the desired shortcut key from the <u>S</u>hortcut drop-down list.

Assigning Shortcut Keys

1. Continue working with FILEMAN.MAK and reopen the Menu Design window.

2. Select the De&lete item from the menu item list, and choose Del from the <u>S</u>hortcut drop-down list. The designation "Del" should appear in the menu item list to the right of the De&lete item.

3. Choose OK.

That's all there is to it. Later in this chapter you'll add shortcut keys to some of the other menu items. Next, add a menu separator to the menu.

Putting a Separator on a Menu

Many menus include *menu separators*. A menu separator is a horizontal line on the menu that separates one group of items from another. In most programs, for example, the opening/saving items in the <u>F</u>ile menu are separated from the printing items by a menu separator. A menu separator gives you a means of grouping menu items together by logical function.

To place a separator on a menu, enter a single dash (-) as the caption. Visual Basic takes care of creating the separator for you. All controls must have a name, however, so you have to give each menu separator a unique name. Separators in the <u>F</u>ile menu might be mnuFileSep1, mnuFileSep2, or other similar names.

Add some separators and additional menu items to your <u>F</u>ile menu.

Adding Separators to the File Menu

1. Continue working with FILEMAN.MAK and display the Menu Design Window for the frmFileMan form.

2. Select the &View item in the menu item list, and choose the Insert button to insert a new blank item between the Rename and View items.

3. In the Caption edit box, type - (a single dash).

4. In the Name edit box, type mnuFileSep1.

5. Click the right-arrow button to indent the separator item one level to the right, making it part of the File menu. Press Enter to select the next menu item (&View).

6. With the &View item selected, choose the Insert button to insert a new blank item between the separator and the View menu item.

7. In the Caption edit box, type **Ru&n**.

8. In the Name edit box, type **mnuFileRun**.

9. Click the right-arrow button to indent the menu item under the File menu, and choose OK to close the Menu Design Window.

10. Run the program and test the menus. You should see a separator between the Rename and Run items in the File menu.

11. End the program and save the project.

When you pull down the File menu now, you should see a separator between the Run menu item and the other items on the File menu (see fig. 7.4).

Figure 7.4

A separator on the File menu.

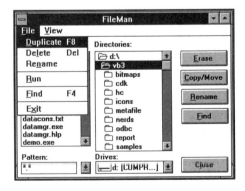

Adding More Menu Items

Next, add some additional menu items to FileMan's menus. The code for each menu is given later in the chapter. If you don't want to go through the hassle of adding the menus, you can load the project MENUS.MAK. The MENUS.MAK project is identical to the FILEMAN.MAK project, with the exception that the menus have been created for you. You won't get any practice creating menu items, however, and anyone looking over your shoulder might get the impression that you're lazy if you don't complete the next exercise.

Completing the FileMan Menu

1. Continue working with FILEMAN.MAK.

2. Add the menu items shown in table 7.1. Figure 7.5 shows how the Menu Design Window should look when you finish.

Table 7.1
Menu Items for FileMan

Parent menu	Menu caption	Menu name	Shortcut key
File	&Duplicate	mnuFileDuplicate	F8
File	De&lete	mnuFileDelete	Del
File	Re&name	mnuFileRename	
File	-	mnuFileSep1	
File	&Run	mnuFileRun	
File	-	mnuFileSep2	
File	&Find	mnuFileFind	F4
File	-	mnuFileSep3	
File	E&xit	mnuFileExit	
View	&All files	mnuViewAll	

continues

Table 7.1
Continued

Parent menu	Menu caption	Menu name	Shortcut key
View	&Program files	mnuViewProgs	
View	&Doc/Text files	mnuViewDocs	
View	&INI files	mnuViewIni	
View	-	mnuViewSep1	
View	&Refresh	mnuViewRefresh	F5

Figure 7.5
The Menu
Design Window
after completing
the menu.

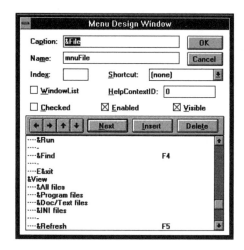

Now that you have the menu structure completed, you need to add some code for the new items. To add code for a particular menu, just select that menu item from the form. Visual Basic will automatically display the Code window with the Click event procedure of the item. Or, you can select the menu item by name from the Object drop-down list in the Code window.

Add the following code for the **D**uplicate item in the **F**ile menu:

```
Sub mnuFileDuplicate_Click()
    cmdCopy_Click
End Sub
```

Add the following code for the De**l**ete item in the **F**ile menu:

```
Sub mnuFileDelete_Click()
     cmdErase_Click
End Sub
```

Add the following code for the Re**n**ame item in the **F**ile menu:

```
Sub mnuFileRename_Click()
     cmdRename_Click
End Sub
```

Add the following code for the **R**un item in the **F**ile menu:

```
Sub mnuFileRun_Click()
     File1_DblClick
End Sub
```

Add the following code for the **F**ind item in the **F**ile menu:

```
Sub mnuFileFind_Click()
     cmdFind_Click
End Sub
```

Add the following code for the E**x**it item in the **F**ile menu:

```
Sub mnuFileExit_Click()
     End
End Sub
```

Add the following code for the **A**ll files item in the **V**iew menu:

```
Sub mnuViewAll_Click()
     File1.Pattern = "*.*"
End Sub
```

Add the following code for the **P**rogram files item in the **V**iew menu:

```
Sub mnuViewProgs_Click()
     File1.Pattern = "*.exe;*.com;*.bat;*.pif"
End Sub
```

Add the following code for the **D**oc/Text files item in the **V**iew menu:

```
Sub mnuViewDocs_Click()
    File1.Pattern = "*.doc;*.txt"
End Sub
```

Add the following code for the **I**NI files item in the **V**iew menu:

```
Sub mnuViewIni_Click()
    File1.Pattern = "*.ini"
End Sub
```

Add the following code for the **R**efresh item in the **V**iew menu:

```
Sub mnuViewRefresh_Click()
    File1.Refresh
End Sub
```

That's it! Your menu is finished. Save the project, and run the program to test it. Check each menu item to make sure it works properly. If you have any problems, check the procedures against the code provided previously.

Even More Amazing Menu Stuff!

There are a couple of interesting things you can do with menus that you haven't covered yet. Some programs, for example, use checks beside menu items to indicate that that particular menu item is selected. Sometimes these checked menu items are called *toggles*.

Creating a Toggle Item

The **C**hecked check box in the Menu Design Window enables you to set the Checked property of a menu item. If the Checked property is True, the menu item has a check beside it (see fig. 7.6). If the Checked property is False, there is no check beside the item.

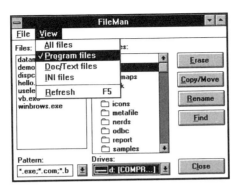

Figure 7.6
A checked
menu item.

Unless you want the menu item to be initially checked, you should set the Checked property at run time rather than at design time. The following two statements set the Checked property of a menu item. The first statement places a check beside the menu item, and the second statement removes the check from a menu item:

```
menuControlName.Checked = True
menuControlName.Checked = False
```

One of the problems in handling checked menu items is determining the state of the item. If an item is checked, for example, and the user clicks on the menu item, your program code should remove the check (toggle the state of the item). Although you can use an If...Then structure to test the value of the Checked property and then set it accordingly, there is an easier method that requires only a single line of code. Here's an example using the menu control mnuViewAll as an example:

```
mnuViewAll.Checked = Not (mnuViewAll.Checked)
```

The Not operator in this situation reverses the value of the property. If the value is True, the Not operator makes it False. If the value is False, the Not operator makes it True. Just substitute the appropriate menu control name in place of mnuViewAll in the previous example.

Usually, you are doing more than just toggling a menu item on and off. Often you must set other control properties or execute statements based on the new state of the menu item. In addition to toggling the state of the menu, you often must use a conditional structure such as If...Then to perform some action based on the current state of the menu item. In our FileMan program, for example, let's add checks to the first four items in the **V**iew menu. When one is checked, the others must all be unchecked. Start with the **A**ll files item.

Adding Checks to a Menu

1. Continue working with FILEMAN.MAK (or MENUS.MAK if you're being lazy).

2. Open the code window for the mnuViewAll_Click() procedure.

3. Modify the procedure to read as follows:

```
Sub mnuViewAll_Click ()
        mnuViewAll.Checked = Not (mnuViewAll.Checked)
        If mnuViewAll.Checked Then
                File1.Pattern = "*.*"
                mnuViewProgs.Checked = False
                mnuViewDocs.Checked = False
                mnuViewIni.Checked = False
        Else
                mnuViewAll.Checked = True
        End If
End Sub
```

The first statement toggles the state of the menu item. The If...Then structure tests the state of the menu item. If it is checked, the statements within the If...Then structure set the Pattern property of File1 and remove the checks from the other three menu items. If the item is not checked, the Else portion of the If...Then structure turns it back on. Therefore, if the **A**ll files item is checked and the user clicks on it, nothing really changes. The only way to remove the check is to select one of the other three items in the **V**iew menu.

Next, change the code for the mnuViewDocs_Click() procedure.

Changing the Doc/Text Files Item

1. From the Object drop-down list in the Code window, choose mnuViewDocs.

2. Modify the procedure to read as follows:

```
Sub mnuViewDocs_Click ()
      mnuViewDocs.Checked = Not (mnuViewDocs.Checked)
      If mnuViewDocs.Checked Then
            File1.Pattern = "*.doc;*.txt"
            Combo1.Text = "*.doc;*.txt"
            mnuViewAll.Checked = False
            mnuViewProgs.Checked = False
            mnuViewIni.Checked = False
      Else
            File1.Pattern = "*.*"
            mnuViewAll.Checked = True
            Combo1.Text = "*.*"
      End If
End Sub
```

3. Save the project.

The first statement in this procedure toggles the state of the menu item. If the menu item is checked, the Pattern property of File1 is set to "*.doc;*.txt" to display these two types of files. Then, each of the other three view items are cleared (unchecked).

Next, change the procedures for the remaining two view options.

Completing the Changes

1. From the Object drop-down list, choose mnuViewIni.

2. Modify the mnuViewIni_Click() procedure to read as follows:

```
Sub mnuViewIni_Click ()
      mnuViewIni.Checked = Not (mnuViewIni.Checked)
      If mnuViewIni.Checked Then
            File1.Pattern = "*.ini"
            Combo1.Text = "*.ini"
            mnuViewAll.Checked = False
            mnuViewProgs.Checked = False
            mnuViewDocs.Checked = False
```

continues

```
        Else
             File1.Pattern = "*.*"
             mnuViewAll.Checked = True
               Combo1.Text = "*.*"
        End If
    End Sub
```

3. Choose `mnuViewProgs` from the Object drop-down list.

4. Modify the `mnuViewProgs_Click()` procedure to read as follows:

```
Sub mnuViewProgs_Click ()
    mnuViewProgs.Checked = Not (mnuViewProgs.Checked)
    If mnuViewProgs.Checked Then
        File1.Pattern = "*.exe;*.com;*.bat;*.pif"
        Combo1.Text = "*.exe;*.com;*.bat;*.pif"
        mnuViewDocs.Checked = False
        mnuViewIni.Checked = False
        mnuViewAll.Checked = False
    Else
        File1.Pattern = "*.*"
         mnuViewAll.Checked = True
        Combo1.Text = "*.*"
    End If
End Sub
```

5. Save the project.

6. Run the program and test each menu item. If an error occurs or the items don't work as they should, check your code and retest.

With this exercise completed, your menus should be fully functional. If you choose the **P**rogram files, **D**oc/Text files, or **I**NI files items from the menu, and the item is not checked, the program will check the item and clear the checks from the other items. It also will set the `Pattern` property of File1 accordingly.

Enabling and Disabling Menu Items

The FileMan program has no menus that need to be disabled or enabled when the program is running. However, the availability of the menu items in many other types of programs often changes while the program is running. If there is nothing on the Clipboard, for example, the **P**aste item in the **E**dit menu should be dimmed.

If you need to enable or disable a menu item at run time, just set the `Enabled` property accordingly. Setting the `Enabled` property to False dims the menu item. If you need to disable the item, set its `Enabled` property to False. To enable a menu item, set its `Enabled` property to True. Here are two examples using the control `mnuFileExit` as an example:

```
mnuFileExit.Enabled = True
mnuFileExit.Enabled = False
```

You also can change the `Visible` property of a menu item. Instead of dimming the item, making a menu item invisible removes it from the menu altogether. The remaining menu items, if any, shift up to "close the gap." Setting the `Visible` property to False makes the item disappear; setting the `Visible` property to True makes it reappear.

TIP If you want to toggle the `Enabled` or `Visible` properties of a menu item, use the `Not` operator. Here's an example:

```
mnuViewAll.Enabled = Not (mnuViewAll.Enabled)
mnuViewAll.Visible = Not (mnuViewAll.Visible)
```

In the first statement, if the menu item is enabled, it will be disabled. If it is disabled, it will be enabled. In the second statement, if the menu item is visible, it will be made invisible. If it is invisible, it will be made visible.

Creating Cascading Menu Items

The last little bit of useful knowledge I'll throw at you in this chapter is how to create a cascading menu item. Cascading menu items provide multiple levels of menus. Choosing a cascading menu item opens another menu of choices associated with the item. Figure 7.7 shows a cascading menu item.

Figure 7.7

A cascading
menu item.

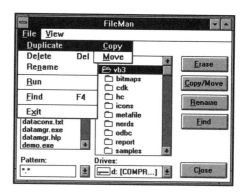

Creating a cascading menu is easy; just create another level of indented menu items to serve as the cascading menu.

In FileMan, the **D**uplicate item in the **F**ile menu could easily be converted to a cascading menu that includes the items **C**opy and **M**ove. Both of these new items will display the same Copy/Move dialog box, but you can modify the program such that selecting the **C**opy item displays the Copy/Move dialog box with the Copy radio button selected. Selecting the **M**ove item will display the Copy/Move dialog box with the Move radio button selected.

The changes you need to make are very minor. Just modify the menu to include the two new items, and add two lines of code to each of the procedures for the new menu items.

Adding Cascading Menu Items

1. Continue working with FILEMAN.MAK (or MENUS.MAK).

2. Open the Menu Design Window and click on De&lete in the menu item list.

3. Click on the **I**nsert button to insert a new menu item between &Duplicate and De&lete.

4. In the Ca**p**tion edit box, type **&Copy**.

5. In the Na**m**e edit box, type **mnuFileDupCopy**.

6. Click the right-arrow button to indent the &Copy item underneath the &Duplicate item, and press Enter to move to the De&lete menu item.

7. Click on the **I**nsert button to insert a new menu item between &Copy and De&lete.

8. In the Caption edit box, type **&Move**.

9. In the Name edit box, type **mnuFileDupMove**.

10. Click the right-arrow button to indent the &Move item underneath the &Duplicate item.

11. Choose OK. Visual Basic displays an error message telling you that you can assign a shortcut key to a menu name. Because you have added items to the &Duplicate item, it is now a menu name and not a menu item.

12. Choose OK to clear the error dialog box, and set the Shortcut key for the &Duplicate item to (none).

13. Choose OK to close the Menu Design window.

If you click on the File menu in frmFileMan, and then click on the Duplicate item, you'll see that you now have a cascading menu. All that is left is to change one procedure and add two new ones.

Completing FileMan!

1. Open the Code window and choose `mnuFileDuplicate` from the Object drop-down list.

2. Place an apostrophe at the beginning of the second statement to turn it into a comment. The procedure should read as follows:

```
Sub mnuFileDuplicate_Click ()
    cmdCopy_Click
End Sub
```

Alternatively, you could delete the second line altogether, or delete the entire procedure. Because this menu now displays a cascading menu, you don't need a procedure associated with it.

3. From the Object drop-down list, choose `mnuFileDupCopy`.

4. Modify the Click event procedure for `mnuFileDupCopy` to read as follows:

```
Sub mnuFileDupCopy_Click ()
    frmCopyMove!optCopy = True
    frmCopyMove.Show
End Sub
```

continues

5. From the Object drop-down list, choose mnuFileDupMove.

6. Modify the Click event procedure for mnuFileDupCopy to read as follows:

```
Sub mnuFileDupMove_Click ()
    frmCopyMove!optMove = True
    frmCopyMove.Show
End Sub
```

7. Save the project.

8. Run the program to test it. If everything works properly, make any additions or changes to the program that your heart desires, and compile it.

You can see that adding a cascading menu is easy. Just remember that when you create a cascading menu, the original item becomes a menu name, not a menu item. Therefore, you can't assign a shortcut key to it.

Dialog Boxes!

Dialog boxes are everywhere. You can't swing a dead cat without hitting a dialog box (wear gloves if you decide to try that). This chapter introduces a topic—dialog boxes—with which you're already familiar, although you may not realize it. In a Visual Basic program, most dialog boxes are nothing more than forms. If you completed Chapters 6 and 7, you've already worked with some dialog box forms. This chapter offers some tips on creating dialog boxes and working with specific types of controls. If you're not careful, you might learn something about the following topics:

- Creating dialog boxes
- Working with specific types of controls
- Moving information in and out of a dialog box

Dialog Boxes Are Just Forms

In a Visual Basic program, there is no difference between a dialog box and any other type of form. The dialog box might have a different border style or other properties, but it's still just a form that contains controls. Figure 8.1 shows a form used as a dialog box.

Figure 8.1

A form used as a dialog box.

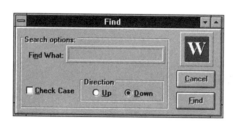 

You already know how to create forms and add controls to a form. Nevertheless, there are some issues to remember when you're creating forms to use as dialog boxes.

Creating a Dialog Box

Before you create a dialog box for your program, decide whether or not the dialog box is really necessary. Visual Basic provides a Common Dialog control that you can use to add common File, Print, Font, and Color dialog boxes to your program. Figure 8.2 shows a common File dialog box.

Figure 8.2

A common File dialog box.

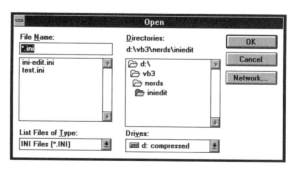

Chapter 9 discusses the advantages of using common dialog boxes. If your program requires a dialog box for opening and saving files, printing, selecting fonts, or setting colors, read Chapter 9 to determine if the Common Dialog control can help you save some development time and improve your program's appearance.

If you need to create custom dialog boxes for your program, spend some time analyzing similar dialog boxes in other programs. This will help you decide how the controls on your dialog boxes should be arranged. When you're ready to create the dialog box, simply create a form for it and place the controls on the form.

BorderStyle, Control Menus, and Buttons

Although dialog boxes are forms like any other program form, you will often set a few properties differently for dialog box forms than for other forms. The BorderStyle property is a good example of a property you need to consider for dialog boxes.

Most dialog boxes use a fixed-double border. Figure 8.3 shows two dialog boxes; one with a fixed-double border and another with a fixed-single border.

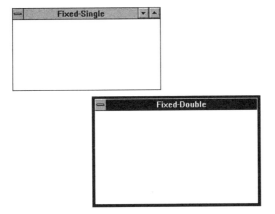

Figure 8.3

Fixed-double and fixed-single borders.

In most cases, there is no reason to make a dialog box resizeable. The controls are in a fixed location, and resizing the dialog box simply results in lots of empty space around the controls. In some situations, however, you might want the dialog box to expand to display other controls that are hidden. You can accomplish this with fixed border dialog boxes. Chapter 9 explains how to expand a dialog box in this way.

In addition to specifying a fixed border, you also should eliminate the Minimize and Maximize options from the dialog box. If you set the BorderStyle property to either fixed-double or fixed-single border style, but do not set the MinButton and MaxButton properties to False, the dialog box will not display minimize or maximize buttons. The control menu, however, still will contain Minimize and Maximize items. To elminate the Minimize and Maximize items from the control menu, set the MinButton and MaxButton properties of the form to False.

If you set the ControlBox property of a dialog box form to False, the dialog box will not display a control menu. This is generally not a good idea, however, because the user has no way of closing the dialog box unless you specifically include a button or other control to do so. By setting the ControlBox property to True, you give your users an easy way to close the dialog box.

Moving from One Control to Another

When you're working with a dialog box, you can cycle through the controls in it by using the Tab key. If you press the Tab key, another control *receives focus*, which means it becomes active. The order in which the controls are activated when you press the Tab key is called the *tab order*.

Is tab order important? Sure it is! By organizing the tab order for your controls, you can help the user move through the form or dialog box controls in a logical order. If you're having the user enter text in five different text boxes, for example, set the tab order to move through the text boxes from top to bottom.

To set the tab order of a control, you can set its TabIndex property. It's difficult to set the TabIndex for more than one control and have them all "stick," however, because changing the TabIndex property for a control forces a change to the TabIndex property of another control. The easiest way to set TabIndex properties for controls is to create the controls in the order you want their TabIndex properties set. The first control will have its TabIndex set to 0, the second control will be 1, the third control will be 2, and so on. This method requires a little planning on your part, but you should plan your dialog layout and controls ahead of time, anyway.

Loading and Showing the Dialog Box

Dialog boxes, like other forms, must be loaded before you can use them. You can load a dialog box explicitly by loading its form, or you can load it implictly by showing it. You'll probably remember from Chapter 2 that you can load a form using the Load statement:

```
Load frmDlgRun
```

The Load statement places the form in memory, but doesn't display it. To display a form that has been loaded, or to implicitly load and show a form, use the Show method:

```
frmDlgRun.Show
```

But wait a minute! What if you don't want the user to be able to switch away from the dialog box without taking some kind of action, such as clicking an OK button or canceling the dialog box? This type of dialog box is *modal*. When a modal form is displayed, no other input can occur in any of the program's other forms until the modal form is hidden or unloaded. Other running programs, however, are not affected.

To display a modal form, you can specify a *style* parameter with the Show method:

```
frmDlgRun.Show 1
```

A value of 1 for the *style* parameter causes the form to be displayed modally. A value of 0, or omitting the parameter, causes the form to be displayed *modelessly*. The user can switch from a modeless form to any other form displayed by the program.

NOTE   When you show a modal form, none of the statements following the Show statement are executed until the modal form is hidden or unloaded (by a user action in the modal form). If you show a modeless form, execution continues after the Show statement, even if the user takes no action in the dialog box.

You should use a modal dialog box any time you are prompting the user for information that is required before the program can continue. The modal dialog box forces the user to either enter the required information or abort the process.

TIP The Copy/Move and Run dialog boxes in FileMan are displayed modally. Check the code for the `cmdCopy_Click()` procedure on frmFileMan to find an example of a Show statement that shows a form modally.

In addition to showing a dialog box, you also need to decide how to hide or unload the dialog box when the user has finished with it. A user action such as clicking an OK button doesn't hide a modal form by itself. Instead, you must add a statement to the Click event procedure for the button (or which-ever control is appropriate) to hide or unload the form. Either of the two following statements result in the dialog box being removed from the display:

```
frmCopyMove.Hide
Unload frmCopyMove
```

The primary difference between Hide and Unload is that hiding a form doesn't remove it from memory. If the dialog box is relatively simple, you can leave it in memory and hide it instead of unloading it. Your program will be able to display the dialog box more quickly the next time it is needed. If the dialog box is complex or you want to conserve memory as much as possible, unload the dialog box. Remember, however, that you can't access controls on the dialog box if it has been unloaded.

Putting Stuff in the Dialog Box

You can preset the properties of controls on a dialog box at design time, but it's often a good idea to set control properties at run time to ensure that the correct settings are displayed in the dialog box. In some cases, you *must* set the properties of controls in the dialog box at run time because the settings are based on conditional decisions in the program. When you added a cascading menu to FileMan in Chapter 9, for example, you preset the optCopy and optMove controls according to whether the Copy or Move menu items were selected.

For lack of a better term, let's call presetting dialog box control properties *putting stuff in a dialog box* (okay, the techno-geek term is *initializing the dialog box*). Putting stuff in a dialog box consists of setting properties for the controls on the dialog box. If you need to place some text in a text box, for example, just set the Text property of the control. You can set the property even if the dialog box is hidden. Just remember that you need to specify the name of the form in addition to the name of the control if the control is on a different form from the one containing the procedure that is setting the control:

```
frmCopyMove!optCopy.Value = True
```

Just specify the form name, an exclamation mark, the control name, the property, and its value.

TIP Each control has a default property. If you omit the property name, VB attempts to set the default property for the control. The default property for a radio button is Value. In the previous example, the Value property could be omitted and the statement shortened to the following:

```
frmCopyMove!optCopy = True
```

If you need to set properties of controls on a dialog box when you show the dialog box, it's a good idea to set the properties before you show the form. It's like putting on your clothes—you have to have them on to go outside (usually), and you could put them on *after* you get outside, but wouldn't you really rather put them on *before* you go outside? By initializing the dialog box's controls, you ensure that the dialog box contains all of the correct information as soon as it appears. Include the necessary statements to initialize the dialog box controls in the procedure that calls the form.

Getting Stuff out of the Dialog Box

Retrieving information from a dialog box consists of reading the values of properties in the dialog box. In many situations, your dialog box form need have few procedures associated with it, particularly if you are using the dialog box to set program options. Assume, for example, that the only procedure in your dialog box form is associated with an OK button on the form. All the OK button does is hide the form. You can preset the values for the dialog box (put stuff in it), show the dialog box, and let the user change values to his/her heart's content. When the user clicks on OK, the dialog box disappears. Because you have only hidden the form and not unloaded it, you still can access the control properties on the form. Your program can read the properties and take whatever action is necessary based on the user's selections in the dialog box.

Putting It All Together

Now that you have some background information on creating and using dialog boxes, you should try out what you know. In the following exercises, set up a dialog box to control a few features of a simple text editor. Because the dialog box is a modal box, we'll preset its values, then read the values after the dialog box is closed. The values of the dialog box's controls will be used to set a few characteristics of the editor's main program window. Figure 8.4 shows the main editor and the Settings dialog box.

Figure 8.4

The Editor and the Settings dialog box.

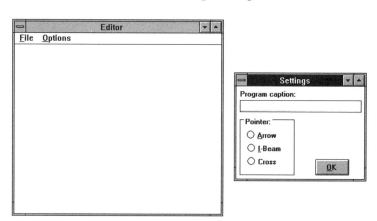

Here is a list of the controls in the Settings dialog box:

    optPointerArrow. This radio button controls the option to use an arrow pointer in the text box on frmEditor.

    optPointerIbeam. This radio button controls the option to use an I-beam cursor in the text box on frmEditor.

optPointerCross. This radio button controls the option to use a cross pointer in the text box on frmEditor.

Text1. This text box is used to specify the caption in the title bar of frmEditor.

Most dialog boxes have many more controls than this one, but these are enough to give you a good idea of how you can stuff values in a dialog box and read your users' changes to the dialog box.

The EDITOR.MAK project contains the forms and controls for this simple editor. The forms and controls are already created for you, but frmEditor contains very little code. Enough code has been added to make the File, Exit menu item work (it issues the End statement), and the frmEditor form's Resize event procedure contains a couple of lines of code that resize the text box to fit the window size when frmEditor is resized. It's up to you to add the code to display the Settings dialog box and to set program options based on settings in the dialog box.

First, add some code to the mnuOptSettings_Click( ) event to display the Settings dialog box when the user chooses **O**ptions, then **S**ettings.

Showing the Settings Dialog Box

1. Open the project EDITOR.MAK that is included on your *Understanding Visual Basic Disk*.

2. Display the frmEditor form, click on the **O**ptions menu, and click on the **S**ettings item to display the Click event procedure for mnuOptSettings.

3. Add a line of code to the procedure to display the Settings dialog box as a modal form:

```
Sub mnuOptSettings_Click ()
    dlgSettings.Show 1
End Sub
```

4. From the Project window, select the dlgSettings form, and choose the View Form button to display the form.

continues

5. Double-click on the OK button on the Settings dialog box (dlgSettings) to open the Code window for the Click event procedure of the OK button (cmdOK).

6. Add the following code to the cmdOK_Click() event procedure, which will cause the dialog box to be closed when the user chooses the OK button:

```
Sub cmdOK_Click ()
      dlgSettings.Hide
End Sub
```

7. Save the project.

8. Run the program and choose **O**ptions, **S**ettings. The Settings dialog box should display.

9. Try to click on the frmEditor form. You should be rewarded with a beep, and should be prevented from switching away from the Settings dialog box.

10. Choose the OK button to close the dialog box.

11. End the program.

That's all the code you need to display and close the dialog box. Next, you need to add some code that presets the dialog box values based on the current state of the frmEditor program window.

Remember that displaying a modal form causes execution to halt until an action occurs to close the modal form. In this case, none of the statements following the Show statement will execute until the user chooses the OK button in the dialog box or chooses the **C**lose item from the dialog box's control menu. Therefore, the statements that preset the dialog box values should go before the Show statement, and the statements that alter the form's settings should go after the Show statement.

Stuffing the Dialog Box

1. Open the Code window for frmEditor and display the mnuOptSettings_Click() procedure.

2. Modify the procedure to read as follows:

```
Sub mnuOptSettings_Click ()
      'Set the pointer radio button to match the current
      'MousePointer property of the text box
      Select Case frmEditor.Text1.MousePointer
            Case 1  'Arrow pointer
                  dlgSettings!optPointerArrow = True
            Case 2  'Pointer is Cross (bad hair day)
                   dlgSettings!optPointerCross = True
            Case 0, 3  'Pointer is I-Beam
                  dlgSettings!optPointerIbeam = True
      End Select
      'Place the form's caption in the dialog's text box
      dlgSettings!Text1.Text = frmEditor.Caption
      'Show the form as a modal form
      dlgSettings.Show 1
End Sub
```

3. Run the program and choose <u>O</u>ptions, <u>S</u>ettings to display the Settings dialog box. The I-Beam option button should be selected, and the caption Editor should appear in the text box.

4. End the program and save the project.

At this point, the dialog box is being stuffed with the current settings. The Select Case structure tests the MousePointer property of the editor's text box and sets the appropriate radio button to match.

Even though the dialog box displays the current settings, it still isn't functional. Changing a setting in the dialog box has no effect. So, you need to add some code to set the program's properties based on the settings in the dialog box after the user closes it.

Modifying Settings Based on the Dialog Box

1. Continue working with EDITOR.MAK and display the Code window for the mnuOptSettings_Click() procedure.

2. Add the following statement at the end of the procedure, after the Show statement (the Show statement is shown here in italic for reference—do not add it a second time to the procedure):

continues

```
        dlgSettings.Show
        setOptions
    End Sub
```

Next, create a procedure called setOptions in the General section of
frmEditor. This new procedure will contain the statements that set the
program's properties based on the dialog box settings.

3. In the Code window for frmEditor, choose General from the Object drop-
   down list.

4. From Visual Basic's menu, choose <u>V</u>iew, then <u>N</u>ew Procedure.

5. In the New Procedure dialog box, choose the <u>S</u>ub radio button, type
   setOptions in the <u>N</u>ame edit box, then choose OK.

6. Make the setOptions() procedure read as follows:

```
Sub setOptions ()
    'Set title bar caption
    frmEditor.Caption = dlgSettings!Text1.Text
    'Set the mouse pointer
    If dlgSettings!optPointerArrow Then
frmEditor.Text1.MousePointer = 1
    If dlgSettings!optPointerCross Then
frmEditor.Text1.MousePointer = 2
    If dlgSettings!optPointerIbeam Then
frmEditor.Text1.MousePointer = 3
End Sub
```

7. Save the project.

8. Run the program, then test the function of the Settings dialog box. Choosing one of the Pointer radio buttons should change the style of pointer
   used for the text box on the main form. Changing the text in the Settings
   dialog text box should change the caption of the main form.

9. End the program.

You could have added the statements to set the program properties at the
end of the mnuOptSettings_Click() procedure instead of creating a new
procedure. I had you create a new procedure (setOptions) to give you some
more practice creating procedures. Also, you'll modify the setOptions
procedure later in the chapter to incorporate a *control array* and simplify the
procedure.

Tips for Specific Controls

If you've worked through the previous chapters, you already have some experience with dialog boxes. This section offers some tips on using specific types of controls in dialog boxes.

Labels and Text Boxes

You've worked with labels and text boxes a lot in previous chapters. Labels are fine when you need to label a control or other feature on a form, but either type of control will work when you need to display information in a dialog box. You should use a text box, however, only when you want the user to be able to modify the contents of the text box. If you simply want to display some information in a box, use a label control with a BorderStyle property of 1 - Fixed Single. This will make the label control look just like a text box, but the user won't be able to change the contents of the label.

The default property for a text box is the Text property. To set the Text property, you can omit the property name. The following two statements have the same effect:

```
Text1 = "Oh frabjous day!"
Text1.Text = "Oh frabjous day!"
```

The default property for a label is the Caption property. As with the text box control, you can omit the property name when setting the caption of a label. The following two statements have the same effect:

```
Label1 = "I'm hungry - peel me a frog!"
Label1.Caption = "I'm hungry - peel me a frog!"
```

If your form uses a background color other than white, and you want labels to stand out, set the BackColor property of the label control to 1 - Opaque. If you want the label control's background to match the background of the form, set its BackColor property to 0 - Transparent.

There are a handful of properties for text boxes that you will find useful when you're using text boxes in your dialog boxes. If you need to limit the number of characters the user can enter, set the MaxLength property of the text box accordingly. If the MaxLength property is 0 (the default), the capacity of the text box is roughly 32 KB.

The PasswordChar property of a text box is useful if you are using a text box to prompt the user for a password or for any other text that you don't want echoed to the text box. The character you specify for PasswordChar replaces any text typed in the text box. Instead of the password appearing as the user types, for example, you can have asterisks (*) appear for each character instead.

Command Buttons

Command buttons are an important part of most dialog boxes. Most dialog boxes at least have an OK button, and most also have a Cancel button. In many cases, you should consider setting the Default property for the OK button to True. If the Default property of a button is True, the button is "clicked" when the user presses the Enter key. If you don't want the OK button to be clicked when the user presses Enter, set the Default property of the button to False.

If your dialog box includes a Cancel button, consider setting the Cancel property of the button to True. If the Cancel property is true, the Cancel button is clicked when the user presses the Esc key. This provides a second method for the user to cancel the dialog box.

Frames

Frames offer a great way to group together controls by their logical function. In the EDITOR.MAK project, for example, the three radio buttons that control the text box's pointer are grouped in a frame. Only you can decide which of the controls on a dialog box should be grouped together, but you should examine the dialog boxes in similar programs for ideas on how to arrange your own. Figure 8.5 shows a dialog box with lots of frames.

In addition to providing a means to group controls, frames also provide a logical working structure for radio buttons. All of the radio buttons within a frame act together; when one is selected, all others are deselected.

TIP In addition to grouping controls together within a frame, you also can create an *array* of controls. All controls in the array have the same control name, but each is referenced by a different index number. Control arrays are explained later in this section.

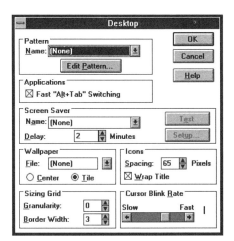

Figure 8.5
The Desktop dialog box contains lots of frames.

Although frames can't be selected by the user at run time, you can assign an access key to a frame's caption. To assign an access key, simply add the & character at the appropriate place in the frame's caption at design time. When the user presses the access key at run time, the first control within the frame receives focus.

Option Buttons

You had some practice with option (radio) buttons in exercises earlier in this chapter. In many situations, you can simply place option buttons within a frame (along with other controls, if you prefer), and reference each option button by its unique name. You'll learn later in this chapter, however, that you can create an array of option buttons and reference them by their index number instead of by a unique name. This method has advantages when you're working with many option buttons, as you'll later learn.

Option buttons have only two possible values—True or False. For that reason, you can incorporate an option button easily into a conditional test. In the EDITOR.MAK project, for example, you used an If...Then structure to test the value of each radio button to determine which pointer to use:

```
If dlgSettings!optPointerArrow Then frmEditor.Text1.MousePointer = 1
```

If the value of the option button is True (the button is selected), the condition evaluates as True. If the button is not selected, the condition evaluates as False. Therefore, you don't have to test for a specific value. Simply structure the code in the conditional structure such that a set of statements executes when the button is selected (the condition is True), and a different set of statements executes when the button is not selected (the condition is False). In the case of the pointer option buttons in EDITOR.MAK, the statement was executed only when the button was selected and the condition proved True.

Check Boxes

Check boxes haven't been covered much in previous chapters, but many dialog boxes include check boxes. Like an option button, a check box has only two possible values: True and False. If the check box contains a check, the Value property of the check box is True. If the check box is clear (unchecked), the Value property is False. This means that you can create conditional structures such as If...Then for check boxes much as you can for option buttons. Here's an example:

```
If chkSomeOption Then
     'Execute these statements if the check box is checked
Else
     'Execute these statements if the check box is unchecked
End If
```

The primary difference between option buttons and check boxes is that check boxes are not exclusive; two or more check boxes within a group of controls can be checked.

Using Control Arrays

A control array is a group of controls of the same type that have the same control name. A control array can contain from 1 to 254 control elements. Each control in the array has its own properties; only the control name is shared by all controls in the array.

But hold it a minute! What the frudally-flap is an array? An array in programming is a lot like a list. Each item in the list is referenced by an *index number*. The first item in the list is item 0, the second item is item 1, and so on. Assume you have an array in your program named *puppyDogsSmell* and want to read the value of the third item in the list and place it in a text box. Here's a statement that would do just that:

```
Text1.Text = puppyDogsSmell(2)
```

The index number follows the array name and is enclosed in parentheses. But if we were looking for the third smelly dog in this example, why use the array index 2? Recall that the first item in the array is item 0, so the third item is indexed by the value 2 instead of 3.

 NOTE Confused about arrays? You'll learn more about them in Chapter 13.

These lists (arrays) are used in list boxes, combo boxes, data structures, and... you guessed it: control arrays. What's so great about control arrays? Control arrays have two primary advantages. First, control arrays can simplify your program code to some degree. In the EDITOR.MAK project, for example, you could configure the pointer option buttons as a control array and use a single line of code to set the mouse pointer based on the option button selection. In this example, there are only three option buttons, requiring only three lines of code to set the mouse pointer. If there were 10 option buttons, however, you could replace 10 lines of code (or even 10 procedures) with a single statement, simplifying the program. Would you like an example? Of course you would.

Assume that you have 10 option buttons arranged inside a frame, but they aren't part of a control array. The value of the variable *whichOne* stores an integer from 1 to 10. Further assume that the program needs to set one of the option buttons to True (select it) based on the value of *whichOne*. Here's how you would do it *without* a control array (we can omit reference to the Value property since it is the default property for the option button):

```
Select Case whichOne
    Case 0
        Option1 = True
    Case 1
        Option2 = True
    Case 2
        Option3 = True
etc., ad nauseum...
```

To accommodate all 10 option buttons, you would actually need 22 statements. If you use a control array instead, you only need one statement.

Assume that you create a control array of option buttons and name the control array *smellyDogs*. Here's the line of code that would select the appropriate option button based on the value of your *whichOne* variable:

```
smellyDogs(whichOne) = True
```

That's it! You've replaced 22 statements with one statement just by using a control array instead of individual controls.

Another advantage to control arrays is that they make it possible for you to create controls at run time. You can't create a new, unique control at run time because the control would have no procedures associated with it. All controls in a control array share the same event procedures, however. You can simply add a new control index to the array, then set the properties for the new control instance as needed. Why add controls at run time? Take the example of an expanding dialog box. You might want to display only part of the dialog box for normal operation, but let the user choose a **M**ore button (or something like that) to see additional options. These additional options could be created by adding new elements to the control array.

Each control in the array is referenced by its *index number*. Control arrays work a lot like data arrays (which are explained in Chapter 13). You reference a control in the array simply by referring to its index number. Assume that you wanted to write a Calculator program. You could use a control array for the numeric command buttons (0 through 9) on the calculator's keypad. When the user clicked one of the numeric buttons, the number associated with the numeric key would be placed in the calculator's display. If each button were an individual control, you would need ten procedures to place a number in the display; one procedure for each numeric button on the calculator. If you create the buttons as a control array, however, you only need one procedure. Here's a simple procedure that will place a number in a label control based on the button that was clicked:

```
Sub cmdNumber_Click (Index As Integer)
    Label1.Caption = Label1.Caption & cmdNumber(Index)
End Sub
```

The name of the control array is `cmdNumber`. The reference `cmdNumber(Index)` returns the value of the index for the button that was clicked. How does a control in an array receive an index number? You assign the number when you create the array. In the calculator example, you would assign the index value 0 to button 0, 1 to button 1, and so on.

To understand how control arrays work, you have to remember that all controls in an array share the same event procedures. When the user clicks on any one of the numeric buttons in the calculator, the cmdNumber_Click event procedure is executed, and the index of the selected control is passed to the procedure as an integer variable named Index.

Putting a Control Array to Work

I'm not going to cover control arrays in a lot of detail. Instead, I'll give you a simple example to help you understand how control arrays work. The EDITOR.MAK project enabled you to select one of three pointers for the text editor window. The CTRLARAY.MAK project is identical to the EDITOR.MAK project with two exceptions: ARRAY.MAK uses an array of option buttons for selecting the pointer type, and CTRLARAY.MAK offers more than three pointer options.

Setting Up the Control Array

1. Open the project CTRLARAY.MAK from the *Understanding Visual Basic Disk*.

2. Display the dlgSettings form (DLGARRAY.FRM).

3. Select the frame control.

4. From the Toolbox, choose the option button control, then draw an option button inside the frame (see fig. 8.6).

Figure 8.6

An option button added inside the frame.

continues

5. Open the Properties window for the option button, which is now named Option1.

6. Change the Caption property of the option button to &Default.

7. Change the name of the option button to optPointer.

8. Set the Index property of optPointer to 0. By assigning an index property, you automatically define the control as part of an array. The name of the control array is optPointer. This option button is the first control in the array. Note that the Name property for this option button has changed to optPointer(0).

9. In the dlgSettings form, select the option button, then press Ctrl+C to copy the control to the Clipboard.

10. Select the frame control.

11. Press Ctrl+V to paste another option button into the form, then drag the new option button into location below the first one (see fig. 8.7).

Figure 8.7

A second option button added to the control array.

12. Change the Caption property of this new option button to &Arrow. Notice that the name of the control has automatically been assigned as optPointer(1) because it is the second control in the array.

13. Save the project.

You now have two option buttons in a control array named optPointer. The two controls have the same name but different index numbers. Also, they have different Caption properties. Although all other properties are the same for the two controls, the properties could be different for each one if necessary.

Next, complete the Settings dialog box by adding some more option buttons to the control array.

Completing the Control Array

1. Continue working with CTRLARAY.MAK.

2. In the dlgSettings form, select an option button inside the frame and press Ctrl+C to copy the control to the Clipboard.

3. Select the frame control.

4. Press Ctrl+V to paste an option button in the frame.

5. Change the Caption property according to the values in table 8.1.

6. Repeat steps 2 through 4 to add all of the option buttons listed in table 8.1 to the form.

7. Save the project.

Table 8.1
Option Buttons in the Control Array

Array index	Caption	Control name
0	&Default	optPointer(0)
1	&Arrow	optPointer(1)
2	&Cross	optPointer(2)
3	&I-Beam	optPointer(3)
4	Ico&n	optPointer(4)

Next, examine the code for the `mnuOptSettings_Click()` event procedure. This code has been included in the project for you, and is located in the frmEditor module:

```
Sub mnuOptSettings_Click ()
      'Set all of the option buttons to False
      For x = 0 To 4
            dlgSettings!optPointer(x) = False
      Next x
      'Set the optPointer option button to match the correct pointer
      'style setting in the text box
      dlgSettings!optPointer(frmEditor!Text1.MousePointer) = True
      'Show the dialog box modally
      dlgSettings.Show 1
      'Set the mouse pointer according to the selection in the
      'dialog box
      frmEditor!Text1.MousePointer = pointerStyle
End Sub
```

The first statement sets the option button to match the current pointer style in the text box. The Index value of the `optPointer()` control is based on the MousePointer property of the Text1 control. If the MousePointer is currently set to 2, for example, the statement evaluates as follows:

```
dlgSettings!optPointer(2) = True
```

The last statement, which is executed only after the modal Settings dialog box is closed, sets the MousePointer property of Text1 according to the selection in the dialog box. At this point, the program is not functional, however. The *pointerStyle* global variable, which is defined in the declarations section of the CTRLARAY.BAS file, needs to be set according to the user's selection in the dialog box.

There are five option buttons in the dialog box, so you must need either five procedures or five If...Then structures that test the value of each option button. Wrong! You only need one statement. Set it up now.

Adding a Procedure for the Control Array

1. Continue working with CTRLARAY.MAK and display the Settings dialog box form (`dlgSettings`).

2. Double-click on any one of the optPointer option buttons to display the Click event procedure for the optPointer control.

3. Modify the event procedure to read as follows:

```
Sub optPointer_Click (Index As Integer)
    pointerStyle = Index
End Sub
```

4. Save the project.

5. Run the program and test the Settings dialog box. Choose an option button, and choose OK and verify that the mouse pointer changes to the selected style when the pointer is over the text box.

6. End the program.

When the user clicks an option button, the Click event for the control array (optPointer_Click) is executed and the index value is passed to the procedure in the variable *Index*. The statement in the procedure sets the variable *pointerStyle* to the value of the control array index. The last line of the mnuOptSettings_Click() event procedure then sets the pointer style according to the value of *pointerStyle*. By using a control array instead of individual controls, the code for CTRLARAY.MAK is considerably simplified.

TIP At times you might want to use a control array to associate the index value of the array with some other value or property as you did in the previous examples. But what if you only need certain values? In the previous example, assume that you didn't want to make MousePointer 0 available, but did want to use values 1, 2, and 3. You can't skip optPointer(0) in the array, but you can make the control invisible. Any time you want to use a non-contiguous selection of controls in an array, just set the Visible property of the "extra" controls to False. The controls will be in the program, but they will be invisible and non-functional.

NOTE Visual Basic includes a sample project called CALC.MAK that uses control arrays. For more information regarding control arrays, examine the code in CALC.MAK.

9 CHAPTER

Even More Dialog Boxes!

If you've finished Chapter 8, you're probably sick of dialog boxes. I know I am. But there's a lot more to learn about dialog boxes, so you can't bail out yet. Besides, this chapter teaches you some *really* neat stuff like:

- Using combo boxes and list boxes
- Using scroll bars
- Using message and input boxes
- Using common dialog boxes

Okay, maybe this stuff isn't all that nifty, but it sure comes in handy. Common dialog boxes are a real time saver, for example. Before we get to those, wouldn't you just love some more information on combo boxes and list boxes? I knew you would.

More Controls for Your Dialog Boxes

Chapter 8 covered some of the most common controls found on dialog boxes, and you've seen examples of other controls in other chapters. This part of the chapter examines combo boxes and list boxes.

Combo Boxes and List Boxes

A list box presents a list of selections to the user. The list box remains a fixed size, but a scroll bar appears on the list when there are too many items to display in the list. The user can select an item from the list by clicking on it.

A combo box is a combination of a text box and a list box, which is why they have the highly inventive name *combo box*. You can select a choice from a combo box's list, or you can enter your own text in the combo box. Do you remember that wonderful FileMan program you worked with in Chapters 6 and 7? FileMan contains a combo box (see fig. 9.1).

Figure 9.1

A combo box in FileMan.

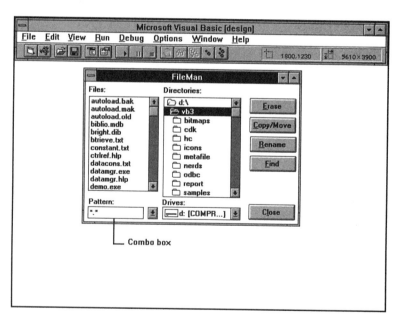

You can select a predefined file pattern from the list or enter your own file pattern in the edit box portion of the FileMan combo box. Combo boxes are useful when you want to provide a predefined list of options in a dialog box, but also want the user to be able to enter options not defined in the list. The file pattern in FileMan is a perfect example.

Types of Combo Boxes

There are three types of combo boxes: simple combo box, drop-down combo box, and drop-down list box. Figure 9.2 shows each of these three.

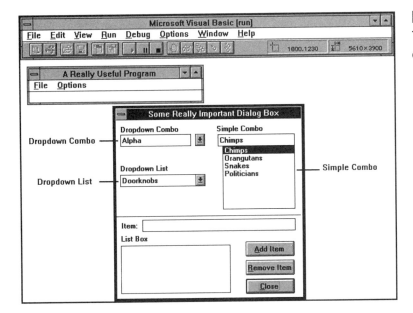

Figure 9.2

Three types of combo boxes.

The three types of combo boxes behave differently, although you add items to and remove items from the combo boxes in the same way. The following list explains the differences among the three types of combo boxes.

☐ **Simple combo box.** A simple combo box displays its list all of the time (all of the items are visible). You can select an item from the list or enter your own option in the edit box portion of the combo box. A scroll bar appears beside the list if there are too many items to display in the list box area.

☐ **Drop-down combo box.** A drop-down combo box displays its list only when you click on the drop-down arrow beside the edit box. You can select an item from the list or enter your option in the edit box.

☐ **Drop-down list box.** A drop-down list box displays its list only when you click on the drop-down arrow. You can only select items from the list; you can't enter your own option in this type of combo box.

Which type should you use in your dialog boxes? It really all depends on what type of information your dialog box is displaying, how much room you have in the dialog box for the combo box, and whether you want the user to be able to enter his or her own options. To conserve space, use either a drop-down combo box or a drop-down list box. Use the drop-down combo box if you want the user to be able to enter an option not defined in the list. Use a drop-down list box if you want to limit choices to only those that appear in the list. If space is not a problem, and you want all (or many) of the items displayed in the list all of the time, use a simple combo box.

To create a specific type of combo box, choose the combo box tool from the Toolbox and draw a combo box on the form. Then set the Style property of the combo box according to the type of combo box you need. The selections include 0-Dropdown Combo, 1-Simple Combo, and 2-Dropdown List.

Setting Up a Combo Box or List Box

Setting up a combo box or list box is really easy. You can use the AddItem method to add new items to the list, and use the RemoveItem method to remove an item from the list. Take a look at the code from the Load event procedure of the main form in FileMan:

```
Sub Form_Load ()
    Combo1.AddItem "*.*"
    Combo1.AddItem "*.exe;*.com"
    Combo1.AddItem "*.bat;*.pif;*.sys"
    Combo1.AddItem "*.doc"
    Combo1.AddItem "*.txt"
    Combo1.AddItem "*.ini"
    Combo1.AddItem "*.dll"
End Sub
```

The name of the control is Combo1. Each successive statement adds a new item to the list. Although this example adds the items to the combo box in the Load procedure for the form, you can add items to the list in any appropriate procedure.

TIP In the previous example, the items are added to the list in the same order in which the statements appear in the procedure. In this example, it's not really necessary or desireable to sort the items in the list. If you have a list of items you want sorted alphanumerically, set the Sorted property of the combo box to True.

Accessing Items in a Combo Box or List Box

Now that you have a combo box or list box full of items, how can you access those items in your program? The Text property of the control stores the value of the current selection. You can reference this property at run time. Assume, for example, that your dialog box includes a combo box from which the user can select a file name or enter his or her own file name. When the user clicks the OK button (cmdOK), the program calls a procedure called fileOpen and passes it the file name currently displayed in the combo box. Here's some code to do that:

```
Sub cmdOK_Click()
        theFile = Combo1.Text
        fileOpen(theFile)
End Sub
```

In most cases, you will have an OK or other button on the dialog box that closes the dialog box. You can include code in the Click event procedure for this button to process the contents of the list box or combo box, or you can reference the Text property later in another procedure (assuming you haven't unloaded the form).

Accessing Specific Items

The items in a combo box are like an array, and as such, you can access items in the list by an index number. To access a specific item in the list, use the List property of the control. In the following example, the third item in the list is stored in the variable *mySelection*:

```
mySelection = Combo1.List(2)
```

Why does the index number 2 return the third item in the list? The list index starts at 0, so 2 represents the third item in the list.

In addition to accessing a specific item in a list box or combo box, you can determine the location in the list of the selected item by using the ListIndex property. The following statement stores the index number of the current selection to a variable named *theIndexNum*:

```
theIndexNum = Combo1.ListIndex
```

The following statement sets the current item by setting the ListIndex property of the combo box:

```
Combo1.ListIndex = 3
```

If the value of the ListIndex property is 0, the first item in the list is selected, and if the value of the ListIndex property is 1, the next item is selected, and so on. If the ListIndex property is -1, no item is selected or the user has entered a choice in the text box portion of the control.

TIP When you set the ListIndex property of a combo box, a Click event is generated for the control. If a procedure changes the ListIndex property of the combo box, the Click event procedure of the combo box, if any, will execute. This means that you can cause the same code to be executed by either clicking on the combo box or by setting the ListIndex property.

To count the number of items in the list, use the ListCount property. The following statement stores the total number of items in a list box in a variable named *numOfListItems*:

```
numOfListItems = List1.ListCount
```

Removing Items and Clearing the List

You can use the RemoveItem method to remove items from a combo box or list box. Just specify the index number of the item you want to remove:

```
List1.RemoveItem index
```

Replace the *index* value with the actual index number or with a variable containing the index number of the item to be removed:

```
List1.RemoveItem theItem
List1.RemoveItem 4
```

To clear a list box or combo box completely, use the Clear method. This removes all items from the list:

```
List1.Clear
```

Putting It All Together

Now that you've had a quick primer on list boxes and combo boxes, put some of that knowledge to work. The following exercises use the project COMBO.MAK, which is included on your *Understanding Visual Basic Disk*, to help you learn to work with combo boxes and list boxes. As with many of the other sample programs on the sample disk, COMBO.MAK is absolutely useless (surprise!) except for its intrinsic learning value. Hey, the disk is free. If this were a Mexican restaurant, you'd get salsa with your disk.

Adding Items to a List

1. Open the project COMBO.MAK from the *Understanding Visual Basic Disk* and view COMBO.FRM. Figure 9.3 shows the main form and the dialog box containing the combo boxes and list box.

Figure 9.3

The frmMain and dlgComboList in the COMBO.MAK project.

continues

2. Select the form dlgComboList (COMBO.FRM) in the Project window, then choose the View Code button to open the Code window and display the Form1_Load() event procedure.

3. Examine the code in the Form_Load() procedure for the dlgComboList form.

Notice that each line in the procedure uses the AddItem method to add items to the three combo boxes. If you need to fill one or more combo boxes or list boxes as soon as your program starts, place the appropriate AddItem statement in the Load procedure of the startup form. If you don't need to fill the combo boxes or list boxes until you are ready to display the dialog box for the first time, place the AddItem statements in the Load procedure of the dialog box's form.

Next, try out the program to see if it does anything.

Taking COMBO.MAK for a Spin

1. Continue working with COMBO.MAK and run the program.

2. Choose **O**ptions, **C**ombo/List. Notice that the combo boxes don't automatically display item 0 in the list.

3. Choose an item from the Dropdown Combo.

4. Choose an item from the Dropdown List.

5. Choose an item from the Simple Combo.

6. Don't bother checking the control buttons—only the **C**lose button works. Choose the **C**lose button now to end the program.

Why don't the combo boxes automatically display item 0 when the program starts? They just don't—maybe it's a Zen sort of thing.... In any case, you have to initialize the combo boxes. Add some code to do that, and test the combo boxes again.

Initializing the Combo Boxes

1. Continue working with COMBO.MAK.

2. Open the Code window and display the Form1_Load() procedure for dlgComboList.

3. In the blank spaces between groups of AddItem statements, add a statement for each control that sets the combo box selection to the first item in the list. The statements you need to add are as follows (new statements are shown in bold):

   ```
   Combo1.AddItem "Delta"
   Combo1.ListIndex = 0


   Combo2.AddItem "Politicians"
   Combo2.ListIndex = 0


   Combo3.AddItem "Buttonholes"
   Combo3.ListIndex = 0
   ```

4. Run the program again. Notice that each of the combo boxes now automatically displays the first item in the list.

5. Choose **C**lose to close the dialog box, and **F**ile, E**x**it to end the program.

6. Save the project.

If you need to display an item other than 0, just set the ListIndex property of the combo box or list box to the required index number instead of setting it to zero. For example, if you wanted to display the "Politicians" item in Combo2, just specify its index number:

```
Combo2.ListIndex = 3
```

Adding Items to List1

I hope you're tired of playing with the combo boxes, because now it's time to fiddle with the list box. List1 in COMBO.MAK has no items in it yet. You could add statements to the Load procedure for the dialog box to fill List1 with items, but let's add some code to do it at run time based on the user's input. The text box in the bottom half of the dialog box (Text1) will be used to retrieve new items from the user. The **A**dd Item button will add the new item to the list.

First, add two statements to the Click event procedure for the **A**dd Item button. The first statement will add the contents of Text1 to the list if Text1 is not empty. The second statement will clear the text box.

Adding Items to List1

1. Continue working with COMBO.MAK.

2. Display the form dlgComboList, double-click on the **A**dd Item button to open the Code window and display the cmdAddItem_Click() event procedure.

3. Modify the procedure to read as follows:

   ```
   Sub cmdAddItem_Click ()
       If Text1.Text <> "" Then List1.AddItem Text1.Text
       Text1.Text = ""
       Text1.SetFocus
   End Sub
   ```

4. Run the program and choose **O**ptions, **C**ombo/List.

5. Type some text in the text box and choose the **A**dd Item button. The item should appear in List1.

6. Repeat step 5 as many times as you like to add new items to the list box.

7. Close the dialog box and end the program.

The first statement in the procedure evaluates the contents of Text1, and if there is something in the text box, the AddItem method adds the item to the list. Next, the second statement clears the text box to make it ready for another new entry. The third statement sets focus back to Text1 so the user can immediately begin typing a new item after adding the previous item.

TIP You can set the Sorted property of a list box to True to make the entries always appear in alphanumeric order. If you are dynamically adding and deleting items from the list, however, setting the Sorted property to True can complicate matters somewhat because the ListIndex property no longer matches the actual order of items in the list. Chapter 14 ("Creating Your Own Files") provides an example of how you can overcome that problem by using the ItemData property as a secondary index.

Removing Items from List1

Next, add some code to the **R**emove Item button that will remove the selected item from the list. This will enable the user to select an item from the list, then remove it.

Removing Items from List1

1. Continue working with COMBO.MAK.

2. Open the Code window for form dlgComboList and display the cmdRemoveItem_Click() procedure.

3. Modify the procedure to read as follows:

```
Sub cmdRemoveItem_Click ()
    If List1.ListIndex < 0 Then Exit Sub
    List1.RemoveItem List1.ListIndex
End Sub
```

4. Save the project and run the program.

5. Choose **O**ptions, **C**ombo/List to display the dialog box.

6. Type some text in the Item text box, and choose the **A**dd Item button.

7. Repeat step 6 to add a few more items to the list box.

8. Click on any one of the items in the list, and choose the **R**emove Item button. The item should disappear from the list.

9. End the program.

The first statement in the cmdRemoveItem_Click() procedure evaluates the ListIndex property of List1. If the ListIndex property is less than zero, there are no items in the list, so the program exits the procedure. Otherwise, the procedure removes the selected item with the RemoveItem method, specifying the ListIndex value to indicate which item to remove.

Using Message and Input Boxes

Unless you cheated and skipped a few chapters, you've already worked with message boxes and input boxes. Message boxes and input boxes offer a quick and easy means for you to display information in a dialog box and retrieve input from the user. First, let's take a look at message boxes.

Displaying Messages with Message Boxes

You're probably used to message boxes. Every time something goes wrong in a program you're using, you no doubt are blessed with the presence of a little dialog box telling you that the world just came to an end and would you please choose OK? Well, it's not OK! Why don't programmers put a **N**ot OK button on the dialog box?

You can't put a **N**ot OK button on a message box, but at least message boxes give you a quick and easy means of displaying an informational dialog box without creating a form for the dialog box.

The MsgBox statement and MsgBox( ) function enable you to display a message in a simple dialog box. The dialog box can contain various pre-defined buttons and icons. You specify the message, caption, buttons, and icon to be used for the dialog box. Figure 9.4 shows a typical dialog box issued by the MsgBox statement.

Figure 9.4

A typical dialog box issued by the MsgBox statement.

If you simply want to display a message box and only need to display an OK button on the message box, or you don't care which button the user selects in the message box, use the MsgBox statement. Here's the syntax for the statement:

```
MsgBox message, type, title
```

The *message* parameter specifies the text to be displayed in the message box. The *type* parameter, which is an integer, specifies which icon (if any) to display in the message box, which buttons to include in the message box, and whether the dialog box is application modal or system modal. The *title* parameter specifies the text that will appear in the message box's title bar. Here's a real example of a statement that displays the message box shown in figure 9.5:

```
MsgBox "The world just came to an end!", 16, "An Important Message"
```

Figure 9.5

End-of-the-world message box.

If you omit the *type* and *title* parameters, the message box contains only the message text and an OK button. The message box caption is taken from the application name.

I know you're asking yourself, "Self, how do I figure out which integer to use for the *type* parameter to display a particular combination of icon, buttons, and message box type?" The answer is, you add a few numbers together. Check out table 9.1.

Table 9.1
Message Box Type Values

Value	Result
0	Display OK button only
1	Display OK and Cancel buttons
2	Display Abort, Retry, and Ignore buttons
3	Display Yes, No, and Cancel buttons
4	Display Yes and No buttons
5	Display Retry and Cancel buttons
16	Stop sign icon
32	Question mark icon
48	Exclamation mark icon
64	Information icon
0	First button is default
256	Second button is default

continues

Table 9.1
Continued

Value	Result
512	Third button is default
0	Application modal
4096	System modal

Just add the numbers for the results you want. Assume you want Yes, No, and Cancel buttons, a question mark icon, the No button (second button) to be the default, and an application modal message box. Here are the values to use:

3	Yes, No, and Cancel
32	Question mark icon
256	Second button is default
291	Total value for *type* parameter

Here's a statement that displays the type of message box described previously and shown in figure 9.6:

```
MsgBox "Shall I erase your hard disk?", 291, "Just Checking..."
```

Figure 9.6

An obnoxious message box of type 291.

Although the previous statement will display the message box, you really shouldn't use the MsgBox statement for this particular message box. Why? The message box contains three buttons, and you want your program to take an action based on the button the user clicks. Instead of using the MsgBox statement, use the MsgBox function:

```
retval = MsgBox("Shall I erase your hard disk?", 291, "Just Check-
ing..."
Select Case retval
     Case 2
          'The user chose the Cancel button
          Exit Sub
     Case 6
          'The user chose the Yes button
          'Erase the hard disk
     Case 7
          'The user chose the No button
          'Don't erase the hard disk
End Select
```

Where do those numbers come from? Check out table 9.2.

Table 9.2
Return Values for the MsgBox() Function

Value	Meaning
1	OK button selected
2	Cancel button selected
3	Abort button selected
4	Retry button selected
5	Ignore button selected
6	Yes button selected
7	No button selected

In your procedure that issues the MsgBox() function, add a conditional test like the one in the previous example to test the return value of the function. Use the return value to determine what action to take in the program.

What's the bottom line with MsgBox? Use the MsgBox statement when the message box contains only one button (OK). Use the MsgBox() function when the message box contains more than one button and you need to base your program's action on the button that the user selected. Also, remember that you don't have to create a form for simple message boxes (dialog boxes). Just use the MsgBox statement or function to display the message box. Program execution pauses until the user closes the message box by choosing a button or pressing Enter. At that point, execution resumes with the statement following the one which issued the MsgBox statement or function.

Getting Input with Input Boxes

Input boxes are a little bit like message boxes except that they serve a different purpose. Input boxes are used to retrieve information from the user. For example, assume that you want your program to prompt the user to enter his or her name. A good way to do that is with an input box generated with the InputBox or InputBox$ functions. Figure 9.7 shows this type of input box.

Figure 9.7

An input box to prompt for a user's name.

The InputBox function returns a variant data type, and the InputBox$ function returns a string. The syntax of both functions is identical:

```
InputBox(prompt, title, default, xpos, ypos)
InputBox$(prompt, title, default, xpos, ypos)
```

The *prompt* parameter specifies the prompt message that appears in the input box. The *title* parameter specifies the caption that appears in the input box's title bar. The *default* parameter specifies the default value for the edit box portion of the input box. If you specify a default value, it appears in the edit box as soon as the input box appears on the display. The user can then modify the default answer and choose OK or press Enter.

The *xpos* and *ypos* parameters specify the location of the input box on the display. The values are measured in *twips*. I'm not going to tell you what a twip is, but it's not like a twit. If you want to open your input box at a specific location, open the VB Help file and search for the word InputBox to locate the Help topic for the InputBox function. It will tell you about *xpos, ypos,* and *twips*.

Let's return to the example of prompting for a user's name. In this example, we're looking for a string, so we'll use the InputBox$ function:

```
userName = InputBox$("Please enter your name.", "Name Box", "Bozo")
```

In this statement, the text "Please enter your name in the edit box below." appears in the input box as a prompt. The text "The Name Box" appears in the title bar of the input box. The text "Bozo" appears as the default text in the input box. In this example, the user's name is stored in the variable *userName*.

Using Common Dialog Boxes

The MsgBox and InputBox statements and functions are great if you need a simple message box or input box, but in many situations your program requires a more complex dialog box. You don't have to create every dialog box your program might need, however, because Visual Basic provides access to four common dialog boxes that you can use in your programs. These common dialog boxes are for opening and saving files, selecting fonts, selecting colors, and printing. You can add these dialog boxes to your program with the common dialog control. A little later in the chapter you'll learn how to use the common dialog control. First, you need to understand *why* you should use it.

Advantages of Common Dialogs

There are some advantages to using the common dialog control instead of creating custom dialog boxes for your programs. Here are four of those advantages:

☐ **Consistency.** By using common dialog boxes, you ensure that your program will share a consistent interface with many other Windows programs. Your program will use exactly the same File Open dialog box, for example, that is used by Notepad and Write. Using common dialog boxes makes it easier for your program's users to become familiar and productive with your program.

☐ **Reduced development time.** Why reinvent the wheel? If Windows already has a standard File Open dialog box that you can configure for your program, why create your own and waste a lot of time in the process?

☐ **Access to system functions.** Using a common dialog box can add functions to your program without the necessity of you adding any program code. If you use the common file dialog in your program, for example, and the user is running your program on a workstation that is networked, the Network button will automatically appear in the dialog box. This gives the user the ability to connect to new network drives and access files.

☐ **Professionalism.** When you use common dialog boxes, your programs look more polished and professional. If you want your program to make a good impression, common dialog boxes can help.

Perhaps more than any other feature of Visual Basic, the common dialog control can have the most positive impact on your programs. The reduced development time it allows is more than worth the effort to learn to use the control.

Before you read any more about common dialogs, open the project COMMDLG.MAK from the *Understanding Visual Basic Disk* and add a common dialog control to its form.

Adding a Common Dialog Control

1. Open the project COMMDLG.MAK.

2. From the Toolbox, choose the common dialog control, and draw the control anywhere on the form. Figure 9.8 shows the control added to the form.

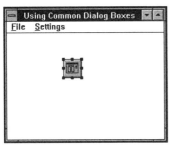

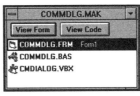

Figure 9.8

A common dialog added to the form.

3. Save the project.

You'll use COMMDLG.MAK in upcoming exercises.

Using Flags for Common Dialogs

When you use a dialog box that you have created as a form, it's easy to set controls on the dialog box—you just set the properties of the controls by referencing the form name, the control name, and the property. With common dialogs, however, you can do that only to a certain degree.

The common dialog control includes a number of properties that you can use to set the characteristics of controls in the dialog box. The Filter property, for example, specifies the file types that appear in the file dialog's Type drop-down list. Other common dialog properties can be read to determine which action the user took in the dialog box. The FileName property, for example, stores the name of the file the user entered in the Open or Save As file dialogs.

To set many of the properties of the controls on a common dialog before you display it, however, you must set some *flags*. These flags are variables that direct the common dialog control to set the properties of the controls when it displays the dialog.

There is a set number of predefined flags for each of the common dialogs. Each flag is a hexidecimal value that you apply to the Flags property of the common dialog control. The file CONSTANT.TXT that comes with Visual Basic defines all of the flags as global constants. Table 9.3 shows a selection of those flags to give you an example of what they look like.

I'm going to pass on a discussion of hexidecimal numbers because you will rarely use them except when setting flags or setting colors. If you're not familiar with hexidecimal numbers, check out Chapter 6 in the Visual Basic Programer's Guide. Otherwise, just use the values I've given in table 9.3.

Table 9.3
A Selection of Common Dialog Flags

Constant	Value	Description
OFN_ALLOWMULTISELECT	&H200&	Allows the user to select multiple files in the File Name list box of the common file dialog.
OFN_HIDEREADONLY	&H4&	Hides the Read Only check box from the common file dialog.
PD_DISABLEPRINTTOFILE	&H80000&	Disables the Print to File checkbox in the Print dialog.
PD_NOPAGENUMS	&H8&	Disables the Pages option button and the associated edit control in the Print dialog.
PD_PRINTSETUP	&H40&	Causes the system to display the Print Setup dialog box instead of the Print dialog.
CF_TTONLY	&H40000&	Specifies that the Font dialog will allow the selection of only TrueType fonts.
CF_EFFECTS	&H200&	Specifies that the Font dialog should enable strikethrough, underline, and color effects.

Table 9.3 shows just a few of the many flags. If you are writing a program that uses the common dialog control, open CONSTANT.TXT and select the statements that define the common dialog constants. Copy the statements to the Clipboard, and paste them into the declarations section of a module in your program's project.

TIP

For a complete description of the flags for each common dialog, open the Visual Basic Help file and search for the Flags property. The Help file contains a topic page covering the flags for each dialog.

Setting Flags for Common Dialogs

After you have defined the global constants for the common dialog flags, you can set them by applying them to the Flags property of the common dialog control. Assume that you want to display a common file dialog. You want to enable multiple selection, hide the Read Only check box, and specify that the user must enter the name of an existing file (if the user enters the name of a file that doesn't exist, an error message will be generated). After you have defined the necessary global constants, you would use a statement similar to the following:

```
CMDialog1.Flags = OFN_ALLOWMULTISELECT Or OFN_FILEMUSTEXIST Or
OFN_HIDEREADONLY
```

CMDialog1 is the name of the common dialog control. The Or operator is used to combine the flag constants and apply them to the Flags property. After setting any other properties for the dialog box (such as the Type filter), you display the dialog box by setting its Action property. Table 9.4 shows the valid values for the Action property.

Table 9.4
Values for the Action Property

Value	Description
0	No action
1	Open
2	Save As
3	Color
4	Font

continues

Table 9.4
Continued

Value	Description
5	Printer
6	Invokes WINHELP.EXE

In this example, we want to display the File Open dialog, so use a value of 1 for the Action property. The following statement would display the Open dialog:

```
CMDialog1.Action = 1
```

Now, let's put all this together and also set a couple of other properties before displaying the dialog box. Here's a sample procedure that sets the Filter property, InitDir property, OFN_FILEMUSTEXIST flag, and OFN_PATHMUSTEXIST flag, then displays the Open dialog:

```
mnuFileOpen_Click()
     CMDialog1.Flags = OFN_FILEMUSTEXIST Or OFN_PATHMUSTEXIST
     CMDialog1.Filter = "All files¦*.*¦TXT files¦*.txt¦DOC
     ➥files¦*.doc"
     CMDialog1.InitDir = App.Dir
     CMDialog1.Action = 1
     'Statements after this point would process the results
     'of the Open dialog
End Sub
```

In addition to specifying flags and properties before the dialog is displayed, you also must evaluate the flags and properties after the user closes the dialog to determine what action to take.

Reading Flags for Common Dialogs

Reading properties of the common dialog control after the user has closed the dialog is easy—just evaluate the property. For example, the file name the user selects in the Open dialog is stored in the FileName property. If the user cancels the dialog, the FileName property string is empty. The following statements display the Open dialog box, then take some actions based on the file name the user entered:

```
Sub mnuFileOpen_Click()
    '...other statements that set the flags and properties before
    'displaying the dialog
    CMDialog1.Action = 1   'Display the Open dialog
    If CMDialog.FileName = "" Then
        'The user cancels the dialog
    Else
        'Call a procedure called OpenFile to open the file
        OpenFile (FileName)
    End If
End Sub
```

That's great, but what if the user put a check in the Read Only check box? You need to open the file in read-only mode. Your OpenFile procedure would handle that task, but you still need to tell the OpenFile procedure that it should open the file in read-only mode. First, you have to evaluate the status of the OFN_READONLY flag. If this flag is on, the user checked the Read Only check box. You then take the appropriate action based on the value of the OFN_READONLY flag.

In the following example, a variable called IsReadOnly is set to 1 if the Read Only check box was checked, and is set to 0 if the Read Only check box was unchecked. The procedure then passes the file name and the IsReadOnly variable to the OpenFile procedure. Based on the value of IsReadOnly, the OpenFile procedure opens the file in the correct mode.

```
Sub mnuFileOpen_Click()
    CMDialog1.Flags = OFN_FILEMUSTEXIST Or OFN_PATHMUSTEXIST
    CMDialog1.Filter = "All files¦*.*¦TXT files¦*.txt¦DOC
    ➥files¦*.doc"
    CMDialog1.InitDir = App.Dir
    CMDialog1.Action = 1   'Display the Open dialog
    If CMDialog.FileName = "" Then
        'The user cancels the dialog
    Else
        If CMDialog.Flags And OFN_READONLY Then
            IsReadOnly = 1
        Else
            IsReadOnly = 0
        End If
```

```
                        'Call a procedure called OpenFile to open the file
                        OpenFile FileName, IsReadOnly
              End If
        End Sub
```

Notice that the And operator is used to test the value of the flag. If the flag is set, the condition evaluates as True. If the flag is not set, the condition evaluates as False. Based on the condition, the program can set variables or take other action accordingly.

 TIP   For more information about setting and reading common dialog flags, consult the Knowledge Base Help file that is included with Visual Basic.

File Dialogs

Many Windows programs use standard dialog boxes for opening and saving files. One of the dialogs provided by the common dialog control is the common file dialog. You've already seen some examples of the Open dialog box earlier in this chapter. Try adding a common Open dialog box to the COMMDLG.MAK project. This example prints some text to the form based on the selection in the dialog box. Printing is explained in more detail in Chapter 11, "Printing Stuff."

Adding Open Dialog to COMMDLG.MAK

1. Open the project COMMDLG.MAK.

2. Display the form, and choose **F**ile, **O**pen from the form's menu to display the mnuFileOpen_Click() event procedure.

3. Modify the procedure to read as follows (you can omit the comments):

```
        Sub mnuFileOpen_Click ()
            'Clear any previous text from the form
            Cls
            'Set a flag
            CMDialog1.Flags = OFN_FILEMUSTEXIST
            'Set the Filter property of the Type drop-down list
            CMDialog1.Filter = "All files|*.*|TXT files|*.txt|EXE
```

```
➥files¦*.exe"
'Clear the FileName property
CMDialog1.FileName = ""
'Display the dialog box
CMDialog1.Action = 1
If CMDialog1.Filename = "" Then   'User pressed Cancel
      Form1.Print "You canceled the dialog."
      Exit Sub
End If
'If the user checked the Read Only check box, set
'fileReadOnly accordingly
If CMDialog1.Flags And OFN_READONLY Then
      fileReadOnly = 1
Else
      fileReadOnly = 0
End If
'Print the name of the selected file on the form
Form1.Print "You selected " & CMDialog1.Filename
'Print a message indicating the status of the Read Only
'check box
If fileReadOnly Then
      Form1.Print "Read Only was checked."
Else
      Form1.Print "Read Only was not checked."
End If
End Sub
```

4. Run the program and choose File, Open.

5. In the Open dialog box, choose a file, and choose OK. The program prints the name of the file on the form and prints a message indicating that Read Only was not checked.

6. Choose File, Open and select a file. Place a check in the Read Only check box, and choose OK. The program prints the name of the file on the form, and prints a message indicating the Read Only check box was checked.

7. End the program.

8. Save the project.

Although this example doesn't actually open a file, it does illustrate how easy it is to use the common file dialog. Instead of printing a message to the form, your program would use the FileName property and any flags to actually open the file. Working with files is explained in Chapter 14, "Creating Your Own Files."

Print Dialogs

The common Print dialogs are just as easy to use as the common File dialogs. You simply set different flags and properties before displaying the dialog box. After the user closes the dialog box, you test for appropriate flags and take whatever action is required according to those flag settings and the dialog's properties.

There are two Print dialogs: the Print Setup dialog and the Print dialog. The Print Setup dialog enables the user to specify settings for the printer and to set the default printer. The Print dialog enables the user to specify other Print options and print the document. Figure 9.9 shows the Print Setup dialog, and figure 9.10 shows the Print dialog. Note that the user can access the Print Setup dialog box by choosing the **S**etup button in the Print dialog box.

Figure 9.9

The Print Setup dialog.

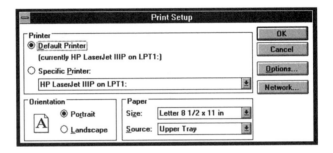

Figure 9.10

The Print dialog.

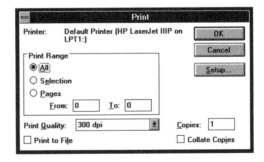

As with the File dialogs, the example in this section only shows you how to set flags, display the Print dialog, and read its flags and properties after it is closed. The code in your program would instead issue statements as necessary to print the document or set other printer options.

First, let's get the P**r**int Setup menu item working.

Adding a Print Setup Feature

1. Continue working with COMMDLG.MAK and display the form.

2. From the form's menu, choose File, and Print Setup to display the Code window for the mnuFilePrintSetup_Click() event procedure.

3. Modify the procedure to read as follows:

```
Sub mnuFilePrintSetup_Click ()
     'Set flag to make CMDialog1 display Print Setup dialog
     CMDialog1.Flags = PD_PRINTSETUP
     CMDialog1.Action = 5
End Sub
```

4. Save the project.

5. Run the program and choose File, Print Setup. The Print Setup dialog box displays.

6. Set some printer options or select a different printer, and choose OK. The printer options or default printer are set automatically by Windows.

7. Choose File, Print Setup again and set your printer options back to their original settings.

8. End the program.

You can see that setting the printer options is easy. All it takes is two lines of code, and Windows handles the rest of the chore.

Using the Print dialog is a bit more complex, but not difficult. You simply have to set more flags and properties, and evaluate those flags and properties to determine how to print the document.

Add some code to the COMMDLG.MAK project to enable the Print item in the File menu.

Enabling the Print Command

1. Continue working with COMMDLG.MAK.

2. Open the Code window and choose mnuFilePrint from the Object drop-down list. This displays the Click event procedure for mnuFilePrint.

continues

3. Modify the mnuFilePrint_Click() event procedure to read as follows:

```
Sub mnuFilePrint_Click ()
    Cls
    'Disable the Print to File check box
    CMDialog1.Flags = PD_DISABLEPRINTTOFILE
    'Set minimum page
    CMDialog1.Min = 1
    'Set maximum page
    CMDialog1.Max = 100
    'Display the dialog
    CMDialog1.Action = 5
    If CMDialog1.Flags And PD_SELECTION Then
        Form1.Print "You chose the Selection option."
        'You would put some code here to set the program
        'up to print just the current selection
    Else
        If CMDialog1.Flags And PD_PAGENUMS Then
            Form1.Print "You chose the Pages option."
            Form1.Print "Printing from page " &
            ➥CMDialog1.FromPage & " to page " &
            ➥CMDialog1.ToPage
            'You would put some code here to set up the
            'program to print the specified pages
        Else
            Form1.Print "You chose to print all pages."
            'You would put some code here to set up the
            'program to print all of the document
        End If
    End If
    If CMDialog1.Copies = 1 Then
        Form1.Print "You want 1 copy."
        'Put some code here to print only one copy
    Else
        Form1.Print "You want " & CMDialog1.Copies & " copies"
        'Put some code here to print the requested number
        'of copies
    End If
End Sub
```

4. Save the project.

5. Run the program and choose <u>F</u>ile, <u>P</u>rint. The Print dialog box appears.

6. Choose some settings in the Print dialog box, and choose OK. The program prints on the form a message about your selections.

7. Repeat step 6 to try different settings.

8. End the program.

The procedure in the previous exercise isn't very useful, but at least it gives you an idea of how you can set control properties in the Print dialog box by setting flags and properties of the common dialog control. Actually printing the document is more complex. Chapter 11 ("Printing Stuff") explains printing. For additional information on setting other Print dialog box properties, search the VB Help file on the keywords Common Dialog, then choose the Common Dialog Control topic. This topic provides four popup lists of the properties that apply to the four common dialog boxes. For information on the various flags that you can use to control the dialog boxes, choose the Flags item from the appropriate Properties pop-up list.

Using the Font Dialog

The common dialog control provides access to the Font dialog box (see fig. 9.11). As with other common dialogs, you simply set the necessary flags and properties, and display the dialog. Write some code to change the font characteristics of Form1 when the user chooses font settings in the Font dialog box.

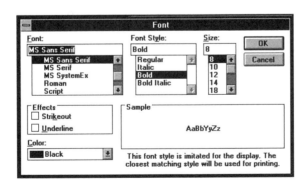

Figure 9.11

The Font dialog box.

Using the Font Dialog Box

1. Continue working with COMMDLG.MAK.

2. From Form1's menu, choose $\underline{S}$ettings, and $\underline{F}$ont to display the mnuSettingsFont_Click() event procedure.

3. Modify the procedure to read as follows:

```
Sub mnuSettingsFont_Click ()
    'Set the dialog properties to match the form's
    'current settings
    CMDialog1.FontName = Form1.FontName
    CMDialog1.FontBold = Form1.FontBold
    CMDialog1.FontItalic = Form1.FontItalic
    CMDialog1.FontSize = Form1.FontSize
    CMDialog1.FontStrikeThru = Form1.FontStrikethru
    CMDialog1.FontUnderLine = Form1.FontUnderline

    'Set some flags
    CMDialog1.Flags = CF_FORCEFONTEXIST Or CF_EFFECTS Or CF_BOTH

    'Display the dialog
    CMDialog1.Action = 4

    'Set Form1's text properties to match selection
    'in dialog box
    Form1.FontName = CMDialog1.FontName
    Form1.FontBold = CMDialog1.FontBold
    Form1.FontItalic = CMDialog1.FontItalic
    Form1.FontSize = CMDialog1.FontSize
    Form1.FontStrikethru = CMDialog1.FontStrikeThru
    Form1.FontUnderline = CMDialog1.FontUnderLine

    'Print some stuff
    Cls
    Form1.Print "This is some text."
    Form1.Print "This is yet another line of text."
    Form1.Print "Are we having fun yet?"
End Sub
```

4. Save the project.

5. Run the program and choose $\underline{S}$ettings, $\underline{F}$ont.

6. Select the font characteristics of your choice from the Font dialog, and choose OK. The text in the Form will take on the characteristics you specified in the Font dialog box.

7. End the program.

You must set a flag to tell the dialog box which types of fonts to display. In this example, the flag CF_BOTH was used to cause the dialog to display printer and screen fonts. Other flags enable you to display only screen fonts, only printer fonts, only TrueType fonts, and so on. If you don't set one of the flags, the dialog generates an error informing you that no fonts are installed.

Using the Color Dialog

The common Color dialog (see fig. 9.12) is even easier to use than the other common dialogs because the Color dialog only returns one property—a color value. You can use this color value to set the color of text, the background of a form, and so on. The color value returned by the Color dialog is stored in the Color property of the common dialog control.

You also can change the color of text by applying the Color property of the common dialog box control to the text or to the form's ForeColor property.

Figure 9.12

The Color
dialog box.

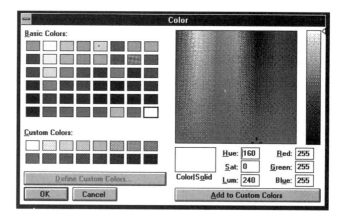

In the following exercise, add the option to specify the color of the form background. First, set the Color property of CMDialog1 to match the current BackColor property of the form. Next, use the CC_RGBINIT flag to set the initial color value for the dialog box. Then, display the Color dialog box. Finally, set the BackColor property of the form to match the color selected in the Color dialog.

Using the Color Dialog

1. Continue working with COMMDLG.MAK.

2. Display the form and choose **S**ettings, **C**olor to open the Code window and display the mnuSettingsColor_Click() event procedure.

3. Modify the procedure to read as follows:

```
Sub mnuSettingsColor_Click ()
    CMDialog1.Flags = CC_RGBINIT
    CMDialog1.Color = Form1.BackColor
    CMDialog1.Action = 3
    Form1.BackColor = CMDialog1.Color
End Sub
```

4. Save the project.

5. Run the program and choose **S**ettings, **C**olor to display the Color dialog box.

6. Choose a color from the dialog box, and choose OK. The background color of the form changes to match the selected color.

7. Choose **S**ettings, and **C**olor. Notice that the currently selected color in the dialog box matches the color of the form.

8. Choose the Cancel button. Note that the form color does not change (because the Color property of the CMDialog1 control did not change).

9. End the program.

There are four flags that you can use with the Color dialog. In most cases, you won't need to use any of the flags except the CC_RGBINIT flag. You can, however, use the CC_FULLOPEN flag to automatically open the Color dialog expanded to include the custom color definition controls. Or if you want to limit selection to standard colors, use the CC_PREVENTFULLOPEN flag. This disables the Define Custom Colors button. The fourth flag, CC_SHOWHELP, causes a Help button to be displayed in the dialog box.

10
CHAPTER

Working with Pictures

One picture is worth a thousand words, unless you have a picture of a well-known political figure in a compromising situation. In that case, the picture is worth a federal appointment and a large sum of money. I promise not to include any such pictures in this chapter. Instead, let's talk about picture and image controls—two topics not quite as juicy, but certainly more useful in Visual Basic.

This chapter provides an overview of using graphics in your programs. It hits the following all-too-interesting, though tame and non-scurrilous, topics:

- Adding graphics to forms
- Using image and picture controls
- Using image controls in place of command buttons
- Creating a toolbar
- Optimizing memory when using graphics

The time has come to talk of ships and shoes and...

Pictures, Images, and Ceiling Wax

Yes, I know it's *sealing wax*. Take your medication, OK? Anyway, I'm not going to discuss sealing wax—I'm going to tell you all about pictures and images.

Windows is a graphical environment, so it's a sure bet that you at one time or another will want to include graphics in your programs. Windows supports bit maps, icons, and metafiles directly. With additional software, you can work with other types of graphics files. Bit maps and icons are static images essentially made up of small dots; when you resize them, you lose image quality. No, that isn't a technical description, but it's close enough for geeks like me.

Metafiles, however, are images made up of lines, circles, and so on. When you resize a metafile, these graphic elements are redrawn, sustaining the same image quality as the original.

Visual Basic provides two types of controls that you can use to place graphics in your program—picture box controls and image controls. In addition, you can assign graphics files to forms (as a background), picture controls, image controls, and OLE (Object Linking and Embedding) controls. This chapter covers the first three of these items. Sorry, but *Understanding Visual Basic* doesn't cover OLE. What did you expect for this price?

NOTE

Okay, the lack of OLE coverage is a little more complicated than a few bucks here and there. Most of the programs you'll write probably will not need OLE support. Those are the types of programs we're targeting with this book. As you get more experience, you might want to add OLE support to your programs. Understanding and using OLE takes up more pages than we can spare in an introductory book. To get a good understanding of OLE, check out *Ultimate Windows 3.1, Maximizing Windows 3.1,* or *Inside Windows 3.11* (due soon), all available from New Riders Publishing.

Assigning an Image to a Form

Forms have a Picture property. You can assign a picture (bit map, icon, or metafile) to a form by setting the Picture property to the name of the image file. The image then appears on the background of the form behind any other controls that you add to the form. Figure 10.1 shows a form with its Picture property set to display the WINLOGO.BMP file.

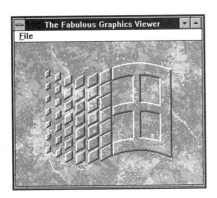

Figure 10.1

A form with its Picture property set to display an image.

If you assign a bit map (BMP) or icon (ICO) file to the Picture property of a form, either at run time or design time, the image will not automatically resize itself to fill the form. Metafiles, however, will resize automatically to fill the form if the form is resized.

The project GRAPHICS.MAK on your *Understanding Visual Basic Disk* lets you apply an image to the Picture property of a control. The project consists of a form called frmViewer, which contains a common dialog control and a simple menu structure. The code that assigns the Picture property of the form has already been added to the project.

In the next exercise, experiment with GRAPHICS.MAK and examine the code that displays the picture.

Assigning an Image to a Form

1. Open the project GRAPHICS.MAK and run the program.

2. Choose **F**ile, **O**pen.

continues

3. From the common file dialog box, locate and select a BMP file. Your Visual Basic directory contains subdirectories full of BMP files. The Windows directory also contains a number of BMP files. When you choose OK or double-click on the file name, notice that the bit map appears on the form. Resize the form. The image doesn't change size.

4. Repeat step 3, but this time choose an icon file. Your Visual Basic directory contains subdirectories with icon files in them. The icon displays on the form in place of the previous bit map. Resize the form. The image doesn't change size.

5. Repeat step 3, but this time choose a metafile. Your Visual Basic directory contains subdirectories with metafiles in them. The metafile replaces the icon from the previous step. Resize the form. The image resizes accordingly. Figure 10.2 shows a metafile loaded into the program.

Figure 10.2

A metafile
loaded into
the form.

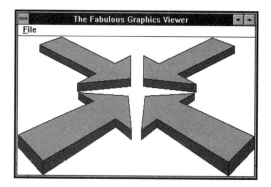

6. End the program.

7. Display the Code window and select the `mnuFileOpen_Click()` event procedure from the Object drop-down list.

Most of the mnuFileOpen_Click() event procedure consists of statements that set flags for the common dialog box, display the dialog box, and store the file name in the variable *fileToOpen*. The statement that actually loads the picture into the form is the following:

```
frmViewer.Picture = LoadPicture(fileToOpen)
```

The statement uses the LoadPicture function (a standard VB function) to assign the image to the Picture property of the form. Any time you need to load an image and assign it to a form, image, or picture control at run time, use the LoadPicture function.

You also can assign an image to a form or control at design time by simply setting its Picture property in the Properties window. In the following exercise, assign a picture to the frmViewer form.

Assigning an Image at Design Time

1. Continue working with GRAPHICS.MAK and display the form frmViewer.

2. Click on the blank area of the form to select it, and press F4 to open the Properties window.

3. Locate the Picture property in the window and double-click on it or select the button labeled with an ellipses (...). A file dialog box opens that you can use to locate a BMP, ICO, or WMF file.

4. Locate a WMF file in your Visual Basic subdirectories, then select it and choose OK. The file appears on the background of the form (see fig. 10.3).

5. Run the program. Notice that the picture appears on the background automatically.

6. End the program.

7. Open the Properties window for frmViewer again, and click once on the Picture property.

8. Highlight (Metafile) in the Settings box, and press Del to set the Picture property to (none).

Figure 10.3

An image added to a form at design time.

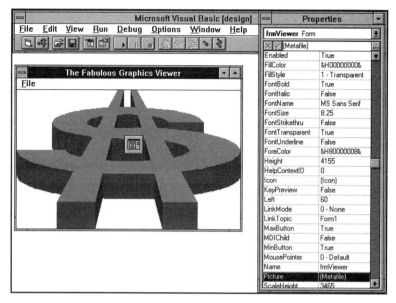

Now you know how to assign an image to a form at design time and at run time. Big deal! Most of the time, you'll use a picture control or an image control to contain an image rather than apply it to the form itself. If you want your form to have a background image, however, you now know how to apply the image to the form.

TIP   If you assign an image to a form or control at design time, the image becomes part of the EXE file when the program is compiled. Therefore, you don't have to distribute the image with the program, but the size of the EXE file is larger and takes more memory than if you load the picture at run time. If you load the picture at run time, however, you must distribute the file with the application.

Using a Picture Box Control

A picture box control (picture control) offers a better means to display an image than simply applying the image to the form because the picture control provides greater control over the image. The picture control has a number of properties that you can modify at design time and at run time to control the appearance and behavior of the image inside the control.

TIP Image controls use less memory than picture box controls. If you're planning on adding a picture control to your form, first read the section of this chapter that explains image controls to determine if an image control will work instead of a picture control.

Picture box controls can contain other controls, such as image controls. For that reason, picture box controls are great for creating a toolbar on your application's form. You'll learn how to do that later. For now, experiment with displaying graphics files in a picture box.

NOTE In addition to displaying an image in a picture box, you also can use the Print method to print text to a picture box.

Displaying a Graphics File

The BMPVIEW.MAK project in Chapter 0 used a picture control to display an image. Add a picture control to the frmViewer form in the GRAPHICS.MAK project.

Adding a Picture Control

1. Continue with GRAPHICS.MAK and display the frmViewer window.

2. From the Toolbox, choose the picture box control (it's the one with the cactus on it).

3. Draw the picture control at any size inside the form. It's okay to cover up the common dialog control with the picture control.

4. From frmViewer's menu, choose File, Open to open the Code window and display the code for the mnuFileOpen_Click() event procedure.

continues

5. Locate the following statement:

    ```
    frmViewer.Picture = LoadPicture(fileToOpen)
    ```

    Change the statement to read as follows:

    ```
    Picture1.Picture = LoadPicture(fileToOpen)
    ```

6. Run the program, choose <u>F</u>ile, then <u>O</u>pen, and select a BMP, ICO, or WMF file. Choose OK to load the file. The image appears in the picture box.

7. Resize the form so its bottom or right border crosses over the picture box. The picture box doesn't resize to fit the window and the image is occluded by the form's border (see fig. 10.4).

8. End the program.

Figure 10.4

Picture box occluded by the form's border.

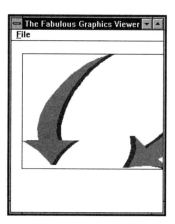

Great! Now you have a working picture control. But wouldn't it be nice if the picture control would automatically resize to fit the form when the form is resized? It's a two-step process to make the picture box act like that. First, align the picture control with the top of the form. Second, add a statement to the Resize event of the frmViewer form to resize the picture control when the form is resized.

Sizing a Picture Box to a Form

1. Continue working with GRAPHICS.MAK and display frmViewer.

2. Select the Picture1 control, and open the Properties window.

3. Set the Align property of the picture control to 1-Align Top.

4. Open the Code window and display the Form_Load() procedure.

5. Modify the Form_Load() procedure to read as follows:

```
Sub Form_Load ()
    Picture1.Height = frmViewer.ScaleHeight
End Sub
```

6. From the Proc drop-down list, choose the Resize event and the same statement to the procedure as in step 5:

```
Sub Form_Resize ()
    Picture1.Height = frmViewer.ScaleHeight
End Sub
```

7. Run the program and load a graphics file.

8. Resize the form and notice that the picture control resizes automatically to match the form's size (see fig. 10.5). If the loaded image is a metafile, it also resizes to match the new window size.

9. End the program.

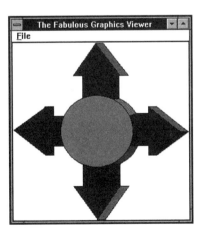

Figure 10.5

Picture box resized to match the form's size.

By aligning the picture control to the top of the form, you cause the picture box to automatically resize to match the width of the form. That doesn't take care of the height, however, so you have to add some code to make the control resize to match the height of the form. The ScaleHeight property lets you do that. The Load and Resize event procedures for the form set the Height property of the picture box to match the ScaleHeight property of the form. The ScaleHeight property is the current height of the form, and changes when the form is resized.

Removing a Picture at Run Time

Now it's time to add some code to the File, Close menu item. When the user chooses this item, the image displayed in the picture control should disappear. To remove a picture from a picture control at run time, use the LoadPicture function without an argument.

Removing a Picture at Run Time

1. Continue working with the GRAPHICS.MAK project.

2. Open the Code window, then choose the mnuFileClose procedure from the Object drop-down list.

3. Modify the mnuFileClose_Click() event procedure to read as follows:

```
Sub mnuFileClose_Click ()
    'Clear the picture from the control
    Picture1.Picture = LoadPicture()
    'Disable the Close menu item
    mnuFileClose.Enabled = False
End Sub
```

4. Choose mnuFileOpen from the Object drop-down list to display the mnuFileOpen_Click() event procedure.

5. Right after the statement that loads the picture, add a statement to enable the Close menu item as follows (add only the statement in bold):

```
Picture1.Picture = LoadPicture(fileToOpen)
mnuFileClose.Enabled = True
```

6. Run the program and open a file.

7. Choose **F**ile, **C**lose. The image should disappear from the picture box.

8. End the program.

Now you've had some experience loading and unloading pictures from a picture box. You've also had some experience in enabling and disabling menu items. If you want to add an image to a dialog box, you can place a picture box or image control on the form and assign an image to its Picture property at design time. Figure 10.6 shows a dialog box that contains a picture box.

Figure 10.6

A picture box control in a dialog box.

TIP   If you are using a picture box to fill a form with an image, you might want to set the BorderStyle of the picture box to 0-None. This eliminates the border line around the picture box.

Using Image Controls

Picture and image controls both can display icons, bit maps, and metafiles. To use an image control instead of a picture box, just draw the image control on the form and size it in the same way you would size the picture box. You can assign an image to the image control at design time by setting its Picture property. Or, you can use the LoadPicture function to load an image into an image control at run time, just as you would with a picture box:

```
Image1.Picture = LoadPicture(someImageName)
```

The image control doesn't have an Align property, so if you want align the image to the top of the form and resize the image to fit the form, you have to use a couple of extra statements to do so. Here's a sample Load procedure that uses the Top and Left properties of the image control to locate the top-left corner of the control at the top-left corner of its container, which is the form:

```
Sub Form_Load ()
    Image1.Visible = False
    Image1.Left = 0
    Image1.Top = 0
    Image1.Height = frmViewer.ScaleHeight
    Image1.Width = frmViewer.ScaleWidth
    Image1.Visible = True
End Sub
```

TIP Unless you were dozing off, you probably noticed in this example that the image control is made invisible while the resizing takes place. Why? The image control actually redraws more than once. By making the control invisible while the resizing takes place, you prevent the user from seeing these extra redraws.

The primary advantage of a picture control over an image control is that the picture box can contain other controls. An image control can't contain other controls, but it uses less memory than a picture control. So, unless you are creating a toolbar, you should use an image control in place of a picture control whenever possible.

Using the Stretch Property

The Stretch property of an image control specifies whether the image stretches to fit the image box. If Stretch is set to True, the image stretches to fit the image box. If Stretch is set to False, the image does not stretch. The Stretch property really only has an effect on bit maps and icons; metafiles always stretch to fit the image control.

In the following exercise, check out the Stretch property in the IMAGE.MAK project.

Using the Stretch Property

1. Open the IMAGE.MAK project included on the *Understanding Visual Basic Disk*.

2. Open the Code window and display the mnuOptStretch_Click() event procedure. Here's the code from that procedure with some comments added to explain it:

```
Sub mnuOptStretch_Click ()
      'Reverse the state of the menu check
      mnuOptStretch.Checked = Not mnuOptStretch.Checked
      'If the menu is checked, set the Stretch property to True
      If mnuOptStretch.Checked Then
    Image1.Stretch = True
      'Otherwise, set it to False
      Else
          Image1.Stretch = False
      End If
      'Call the ResizeImage procedure, which updates the
      'image control
      'if the Resize menu item is checked
      ResizeImage
End Sub
```

3. Run the program and choose File, Open.

4. Choose a bit map and notice that the bit map doesn't resize to fit the image control.

5. Choose Options, Stretch. The bit map stretches to fit the image control.

6. Choose Options, Stretch to set the Stretch property to False. The bit map snaps back to its original size.

7. End the program.

The Stretch property has the same effect on icons that it has on bit maps. In most cases, you won't want the bit map or icon to stretch to fit the window. If you're writing a bit map or icon editing program, however, the Stretch property provides a quick and easy way to resize the working image when the user resizes the window.

Although you didn't use it, the **R**esize option in the **O**ptions menu controls whether the image control resizes to fit the form. Experiment on your own to see how the **R**esize option works.

Saving an Image

Graphics files are complex, so it must take a lot of effort to save a bit map, metafile, or icon, right? Nope! It just takes one statement—SavePicture().

The frmViewer form in the IMAGE.MAK project includes a Save **A**s item in the **F**ile menu. At this point, the menu item isn't functional, although I have added code to the program to enable and disable the Save **A**s menu at the appropriate times. All you need to do to make the Save **A**s item work is add some common dialog stuff to its procedure and include a SavePicture() statement to save the image based on the user's file name selection.

Saving an Image to a File

1. Continue working with IMAGE.MAK.

2. Open the Code window and display the mnuFileSaveAs_Click() event procedure. Modify the procedure to read as follows:

```
Sub mnuFileSaveAs_Click ()
    'Do some common file dialog stuff
    CMDialog1.DialogTitle = "Save As"
    CMDialog1.Flags = OFN_FILEMUSTEXIST Or OFN_PATHMUSTEXIST
    CMDialog1.Filter = "All pictures¦*.bmp;*.wmf;*.ico"
    CMDialog1.Action = 2
    'Store name of file to save
    fileToSave = CMDialog1.Filename
    If fileToSave = "" Then Exit Sub
    'Just in case we can't save the file, set up error handler
    On Error GoTo notSave
    'Save the picture in Image1 to the file name specified
    'by fileToSave
    SavePicture Image1.Picture, fileToSave
    Exit Sub

notSave:
    MsgBox "Could not save file.", 48, "File Error"
    Resume Next
End Sub
```

3. Save the project.

4. Run the program, load a graphics file, and choose File, Save As.

5. Specify a new file name and choose OK.

6. Choose File, Open and search for the new file you just created. When you locate the file, open it.

7. End the program.

That's all there is to it! You can save any ICO, BMP, or WMF file quickly and easily with the SavePicture statement. If you actually want to edit the image, you'll have to add a lot more code to the program. If you're interested in how you can edit an image file such as an icon, open the sample project ICONWRKS.MAK that comes with Visual Basic. ICONWRKS.MAK is a full-featured (a Madison Avenue term for "does a lot of nifty stuff") icon editor that lets you create your own icons and modify existing icons.

Creating a Toolbar

In addition to using image controls to display images on a form or in a dialog box, you can use a combination of a picture box and image controls to create a toolbar for an application. Figure 10.7 shows a toolbar on a system file editor.

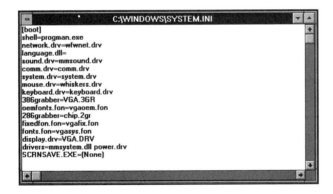

Figure 10.7

A toolbar on a system file editor.

It's really fairly simple to create a toolbar. All you have to do is follow these steps:

1. Add a picture box control to the form and align it with the top of the form. This creates a container for your toolbar buttons. If you want

the toolbar to appear at the bottom of the window instead of the top, set the Align property of the picture control to 2-Align Bottom.

2. Draw one image control in the picture box for each of your toolbar buttons. These image controls are what the user will click on to access the function represented by a toolbar button.

3. Size the picture box to match the size of the image control buttons you will be putting on the picture box (your toolbar buttons).

4. Add extra image controls to the toolbar to contain images of the "up" state and "down" state of each button. These image controls will be invisible, and will be used to store the images that will make the toolbar buttons look like they're being pushed down when the user clicks on them.

5. Add code for the Click, MouseUp, MouseDown, and MouseMove events for each toolbar button. These procedures will control the appearance of the button when the user clicks it, and also will invoke the code that performs the function associated with the toolbar button (such as opening a file).

Creating a toolbar is further simplified by the fact that Visual Basic comes with lots of bit maps that you can use as toolbar buttons. Even if you need a button with an image not included with Visual Basic, you can use Paintbrush or some other graphics editor to edit one of the buttons to suit your needs.

I know you're just dying to add a toolbar to IMAGE.MAK, so get busy.

Drawing the Toolbar

1. Continue working with IMAGE.MAK and display the form frmViewer.

2. From the Toolbox, choose the picture control tool and draw a picture control anywhere on the form and at any size.

3. With Picture1 selected, open the Properties window and set the Align property of Picture1 to 1-Align Top. The picture control will snap to the top of the form as shown in figure 10.8.

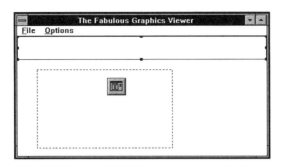

Figure 10.8

A picture control aligned to the top of the form.

Next, you need to add some image controls inside the picture box. These image controls will contain the images of the toolbar buttons.

Drawing the Buttons

1. Draw an image control (Image2) inside the picture control.

2. Open the Properties window for Image2. Change the Name property to **btnFileOpen**. Change the Width property to **330**. Change the Height property to **360**.

3. Position the image control at the upper left corner of the picture box as shown in figure 10.9.

TIP If you want to save some time, you can copy the first image control to the Clipboard and then paste it into the picture box control to create the remaining toolbar buttons. This will take the place of steps 4 through 6.

4. Draw another image control inside the picture control. Change its Name property to **btnFileSave**. Change its Width, Height, and BorderStyle properties to match the image control created in step 2.

5. Position the btnFileSave image control next to the btnFileOpen image control.

6. Draw four more image controls inside the picture control and name them **btnFileOpenUp**, **btnFileOpenDown**, **btnFileSaveUp**, and **btnFileSaveDown**. Set their Width and Height properties to match the other two image controls. Set the Visible property of these four image controls to False.

7. Position the four image controls as shown in figure 10.10.

8. Drag the bottom of the picture control up to the bottom of the image controls as shown in figure 10.10.

Figure 10.9

Image control placed in the upper left corner of the picture control.

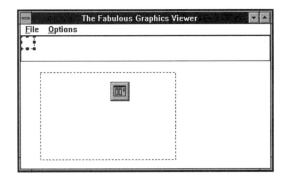

Figure 10.10

Completed and resized toolbar.

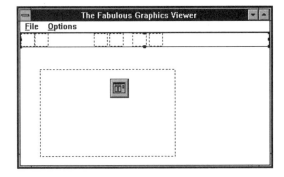

You now have all of the image controls you'll need for this toolbar. All you have to do now is assign some bit map images to the buttons and add some code to make them work.

Assigning Images to the Buttons

1. Continue working with IMAGE.MAK and select the btnFileOpen image control.

2. Open the properties window for btnFileOpen and double-click on the Picture property to open the Load Picture dialog box.

3. Locate the file OPEN-UP.BMP in the .\BITMAPS\TOOLBAR3 directory (in your Visual Basic directory). Select the file and choose OK. The image appears on the button.

4. Repeat steps 2 and 3 for the btnFileSave image control. Assign the bit map file SAVE-UP.BMP to the Picture property of btnFileSave.

5. Assign the file OPEN-UP.BMP to the Picture property of the btnFileOpenUp control.

6. Assign the file OPEN-MDS.BMP to the Picture property of the btnFileOpenDown control.

7. Assign the file SAVE-UP.BMP to the Picture property of btnFileSaveUp.

8. Assign the file SAVE-MDS.BMP to the Picture property of btnFileSaveDown. Your toolbar should now look like the one in figure 10.11.

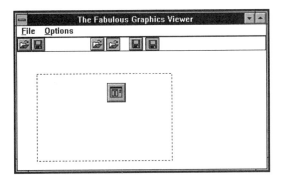

Figure 10.11

Images assigned to the toolbar image controls.

The hard part of creating the toolbar is over. All you have to do now is add some code to make the toolbar buttons work. The image controls support a Click event, so you could simply add some code to the Click event of the btnFileOpen and btnFileSave controls to issue a Click event for the mnuFileOpen and mnuFileSave controls. When the user clicks the btnFileOpen image control, for example, a Click event is generated for mnuFileOpen, which is the same as clicking File, Open. There's no time like the present to write that code.

Making the Toolbar Buttons Work

1. Continue working with IMAGE.MAK and double-click on the btnFileOpen control to display the Code window for the btnFileOpen_Click() event procedure.

2. Modify the procedure to read as follows:

```
Sub btnFileOpen_Click ()
     mnuFileOpen_Click
End Sub
```

3. Select the btnFileSave control from the Object drop-down list to display the Code window for the btnFileSave_Click() event procedure.

4. Modify the procedure to read as follows:

```
Sub btnFileSave_Click ()
     mnuFileSaveAs_Click
End Sub
```

5. Run the program.

6. Click on the mnuFileOpen button in the toolbar. The Open dialog box should appear. Choose a BMP, ICO, or WMF file, and choose OK. The file should appear in the image control below the button bar.

7. End the program.

Unfortunately, the image controls don't behave like buttons *visually*. If you want the button to look like it's being pushed down, you have to add some code to do that. Also, you might have noticed that the image control that contains the picture is partially hidden by the toolbar. Instead of positioning the image control at the top of the form (where the toolbar is located), we need to move the Image1 control down to the bottom of the toolbar.

First, let's reposition the Image1 control.

Repositioning the Image1 Control

1. Continue working with IMAGE.MAK.

2. Open the Code window and display the Form_Load() event procedure.

3. Modify the Form_Load() event procedure to read as follows (the new line is shown in bold):

```
Sub Form_Load ()
    mnuOptResize.Checked = False
    mnuOptStretch.Checked = False
    Image1.Top = Picture1.Height
End Sub
```

4. From the Object drop-down list, choose general. From the Proc drop-down list, choose the ResizeImage procedure.

5. Modify the ResizeImage procedure to read as follows (the changed lines are shown in bold):

```
Sub ResizeImage ()
    Image1.Visible = False
    Image1.Left = 0
    Image1.Top = Picture1.Height
    Image1.Height = frmViewer.ScaleHeight - Picture1.Height
    Image1.Width = frmViewer.ScaleWidth
    Image1.Visible = True
End Sub
```

6. Save the project. We'll test it shortly.

When the form loads, the Form_Load procedure will now position the Image1 control at the bottom of the toolbar. The toolbar (Picture1) is 360 twips in height, so setting Image1.Height equal to Picture1's Height property moves the Image1 control down 360 twips from location 0, which is the top of the form. When the image is resized, the ResizeImage procedure positions the Image1 control at the bottom of the toolbar and sets the height of the Image1 control to the height of the form minus the height of the toolbar.

We're almost home now. The toolbar works perfectly. All you need to do is make it *look* like it's working perfectly. It's really easy; here's what you need to do:

MouseDown. Add code to the MouseDown event for each button to change the image in the button to display the "down" state of the button when the mouse is pressed down over the button. The "down" state images are stored in btnFileOpenDown and btnFileSaveDown.

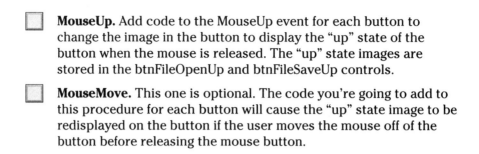 **MouseUp.** Add code to the MouseUp event for each button to change the image in the button to display the "up" state of the button when the mouse is released. The "up" state images are stored in the btnFileOpenUp and btnFileSaveUp controls.

MouseMove. This one is optional. The code you're going to add to this procedure for each button will cause the "up" state image to be redisplayed on the button if the user moves the mouse off of the button before releasing the mouse button.

Making the Buttons Look "Pushed"

1. Continue working with IMAGE.MAK.

2. Double-click on the btnFileOpen image control to display the Code window for the btnFileOpen_Click() event procedure.

3. From the Proc drop-down list, choose the MouseDown procedure and modify the btnFileOpen_MouseDown() event procedure to read as follows:

```
Sub btnFileOpen_MouseDown (Button As Integer, Shift As Integer, x
➥As Single, y As Single)
    btnFileOpen.Picture = btnFileOpenDown.Picture
End Sub
```

4. From the Proc drop-down list, choose the MouseUp procedure and modify the btnFileOpen_MouseUp() event procedure to read as follows:

```
Sub btnFileOpen_MouseUp (Button As Integer, Shift As Integer, x
➥As Single, y As Single)
    btnFileOpen.Picture = btnFileOpenUp.Picture
End Sub
```

5. From the Proc drop-down list, choose the MouseMove procedure and modify the btnFileOpen_MouseMove() event procedure to read as follows:

```
Sub btnFileOpen_MouseMove (Button As Integer, Shift As Integer, x
➥As Single, y As Single)
    'If the button is pressed, display the up bitmap if the
    'mouse is dragged outside the button's area. Otherwise
    'display the down bitmap
    Select Case Button
```

```
Case 1
    If x <= 0 Or x > btnFileOpen.Width Or y < 0 Or y >
    ➡btnFileOpen.Height Then
        *btnFileOpen.Picture = btnFileOpenUp.Picture
    Else
        btnFileOpen.Picture = btnFileOpenDown.Picture
    End If
End Select
End Sub
```

6. Repeat steps 3, 4, and 5 for the btnFileSave control, substituting btnFileSave wherever btnFileOpen appears in the procedure.

7. Save the project.

8. Run the program and test the appearance of the buttons as you click on them. If you move the pointer away from the toolbar button with the mouse button held down, the toolbar button should return to its "up" state.

9. End the program.

That's it for image controls. There is more to learn about picture controls and image controls, but now you have enough knowledge to begin working with them. If you want more information about these two types of controls, check out the chapter on graphics in your Visual Basic *Programmer's Guide* and browse through the Help file for the image and picture controls.

Printing Stuff

Do you want to add the capability to print stuff from your Visual Basic programs? As long as you don't want to combine text and graphics or write your own word processor, printing isn't very difficult. When you begin writing programs that create complex documents, printing becomes a much more complicated process. Can you guess what I'm leading up to? We're not going to cover those complex document types! I hope you're not distraught, destroyed, or even mildly disappointed. At least you'll learn enough about printing to print text to the printer. When you do reach the point in your programming career that you need to work with these complex document types, take a look at the TIMECARD.MAK sample project that comes with Visual Basic.

Here's a list of the topics in this chapter that will make you a Printer Programmer First Class (okay, maybe Second Class):

- [ ] Working with fonts
- [ ] Printing text using the Printer object
- [ ] Formatting text
- [ ] Setting left and top printer margins
- [ ] Using tabs

Before you start printing stuff, you need a quick refresher course in using fonts.

Working with Fonts

You've used fonts to a limited degree in previous chapters. If you intend to print text from your program, you probably want to be able to print the text using its current font settings. Printing with the current font settings isn't difficult, but you should review some information on fonts before you start working with them in your program.

About Fonts

There are two general categories of fonts:

- **Screen fonts.** Screen fonts are designed to display on the computer's screen.

- **Printer fonts.** Printer fonts are designed to be used to reproduce text on a printer.

In addition, fonts can be *scalable* or *non-scalable*. A scalable font can be scaled to nearly any size without losing resolution. Scalable fonts are defined by routines that draw the character at the selected font size. Non-scalable fonts consist of bit maps of specific sizes. You can't scale a non-scalable font; instead, the font file must include font descriptions for each of the font sizes you want to use. There are scalable and non-scalable printer fonts and screen fonts.

You can distribute custom fonts with your program, but it's best to rely on the standard fonts provided with Windows. If you want the user to be able to specify the font used in a text editor, for example, let the user choose the font from the common Font dialog box. This ensures that the selected font will be on the user's system, because only fonts that are installed on the system will show up in the dialog box. If you attempt to use a font that isn't installed on the user's system, either Windows will attempt to approximate the font with another, or your program will generate an error. Both can lead to unpredictable results.

When you print text to the printer, keep in mind that the results you get on the printed page might not match the font used in the program. The type of printer and type of font can affect the printed output. By relying on the user's existing fonts, however, you leave control of printed output quality up to the user.

Setting Font Characteristics

Most controls have a selection of font properties. These properties include FontName, FontBold, FontItalic, FontSize, and others. To apply a specific font characteristic to a control, you simply set the appropriate font property. To determine which font properties a control supports, just look in the Properties window—all of the font properties are prefixed by the word Font.

The PRINT.MAK project on the *Understanding Visual Basic Disk* is a simple text editor (see fig. 11.1). PRINT.MAK uses a multi-line text box as the text control. The project already contains a majority of its code. The common dialog control has already been coded for you to provide Open, Save As, and Font dialog boxes in the PRINT.MAK project. By using the Font dialog box (see fig. 11.2), you can apply a font to the text in the text box.

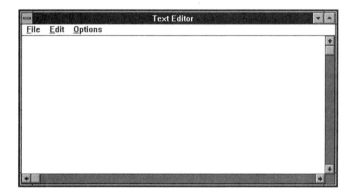

Figure 11.1

The text editor in PRINT.MAK.

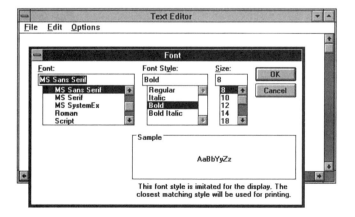

Figure 11.2

The Font dialog box.

The Font dialog box is displayed by the mnuOptFont_Click() event procedure, as shown in the following code:

```
Sub mnuOptFont_Click ()
    'Set dialog to generate error 32755 if user chooses Cancel
    CMDialog1.CancelError = True
    On Error GoTo FontErr
    'Set the current font in the dialog box to match the font
    'being used by Text1
    CMDialog1.FontName = Text1.FontName
    'Set Bold option in dialog to match Text1
    CMDialog1.FontBold = Text1.FontBold
    'Set Italic option in dialog to match Text
    CMDialog1.FontItalic = Text1.FontItalic
    'Set Strikethru option in dialog to match Text
    CMDialog1.FontStrikethru = Text1.FontStrikethru
    'Set Underline option in Text1 to match Text1
    CMDialog1.FontUnderline = Text1.FontUnderline
    'Set font size to match Text1
    CMDialog1.FontSize = Text1.FontSize
    'Set a couple of dialog flags
    CMDialog1.Flags = CF_FORCEFONTEXIST Or CF_PRINTERFONTS
    'Display the Font dialog box
    CMDialog1.Action = 4
    'Set the font properties of Text1 to match the settings the
    'user selected in the Font dialog box.
    Text1.FontName = CMDialog1.FontName
    Text1.FontBold = CMDialog1.FontBold
    Text1.FontItalic = CMDialog1.FontItalic
    Text1.FontStrikethru = CMDialog1.FontStrikethru
    Text1.FontUnderline = CMDialog1.FontUnderline
    Text1.FontSize = CMDialog1.FontSize
    Exit Sub

FontErr:
    Resume Next
End Sub
```

When you take out all of the comments, you can see that there really are very few statements required to set all of the font characteristics of the text box.

 NOTE Because some of the font characteristics are dependent on the font being used (specified by the FontName property), you should always set the FontName property first, then set other font properties to avoid errors and unpredictable results.

If necessary, you can limit the types of fonts that are displayed in the Font dialog box. In this example, the CF_PRINTERFONTS flag directs the Font dialog box to display only fonts supported by the printer (which includes TrueType fonts). A look at the COMMDLG.BAS file included with PRINT.MAK will show you the other constants for the Font dialog flags. Table 11.1 shows the flags that define the types of fonts to be displayed in the Font dialog box.

Table 11.1
Font Dialog Box Display Flag Settings

Flag	Description
CF_SCREENFONTS	List only screen fonts supported by the system.
CF_PRINTERFONTS	List only printer fonts supported by the current printer.
CF_BOTH	List printer and screen fonts.
CF_ANSIONLY	Limits user's selection to only those fonts that contain the Windows character set. Prevents users from selecting fonts that contain only symbols.
CF_NOVECTORFONTS	Prevents selection of vector fonts (such as TrueType and screen fonts).
CF_FIXEDPITCHONLY	Lists only fixed-pitch fonts.

continues

Table 11.1
Continued

Flag	Description
CF_WYSIWYG	Limits selection to fonts that are available to both the printer and the display. If you use this flag, you must also use the CF_BOTH and CF_SCALEABLEONLY flags.
CF_SCALABLEONLY	Limits selection to only those fonts that are scalable.
CF_TTONLY	Limits selection to only TrueType fonts.

Set the flags according to the types of fonts you want displayed in the Font dialog box, and also set flags if necessary to limit the user's selection of fonts in the dialog box.

TIP

In the next section of the chapter, you learn about the Printer object. You can set various font properties of the Printer object to control the font characteristics that are used when you print text to the printer. If you attempt to assign a font property to a printer that isn't supported by the printer, an error occurs. For that reason, you should enable the user to select only fonts supported by the printer, or add code to your program to select an alternate font if the selected font is not supported. If you don't do either, the printer will approximate the font with the closest matching font that it supports. In many cases, this match won't be very close.

About the Printer Object

The Printer object enables you to print text and graphics to the default printer. The Printer object, like other objects in VB, has a number of properties associated with it. In particular, the Printer object supports the same font properties as other objects like forms, picture boxes, and text boxes.

To print using the Printer object, use the Print method. The Print method prints text or graphics on an object. The COMMDLG.MAK project in Chapter 9 used the Print method to print information describing your dialog box selections to a form. You'll use the Print method in this chapter to print information to the Printer object (which sends it to the printer).

The syntax of the statement you'll use to print information to the Printer object is as follows:

```
Printer.Print expressionList
```

The *expressionList* parameter specifies the information that is sent to the printer. To print the contents of Text1 to the printer, for example, use the following statement:

```
Printer.Print Text1.Text
```

What about fonts? If you want to print using a specific font name or characteristic such as bold, you need to set the font properties of the Printer object accordingly. Here's a fragment of a procedure from PRINT.MAK that sets the font properties of the Printer object:

```
On Error Resume Next
Printer.FontName = Text1.FontName
Printer.FontBold = Text1.FontBold
Printer.FontItalic = Text1.FontItalic
Printer.FontStrikethru = Text1.FontStrikethru
Printer.FontUnderline = Text1.FontUnderline
Printer.FontSize = Text1.FontSize
```

The On Error Resume Next statement is important in this procedure. If the current printer doesn't support the font assigned to Text1, attempting to set the Printer.FontName property to the Text1.FontName property will generate an error. By adding the error statement, you ensure that the program continues to function.

If the FontName property defined by Text1 *is* supported by the Printer object, no error occurs, and the printer uses the font to print the next time the Print method is used. If the FontName property isn't supported, the printer uses a font that matches as closely as possible the one associated with the FontName property. In many cases, the substituted font will have only a few characteristics in common with the font used by the text box. For this reason, you might want to limit user font selection to fonts supported by the printer (by using the CF_PRINTER flag) or add code to your program to warn the user that the font is not supported by the printer.

Controlling the Printer Object

Just sending information to the Printer object with the Print method isn't quite enough to print a document. You also have to worry about positioning the document on the Printer object, ending a page when it's finished, and ending the document.

If you don't specify otherwise, issuing the Print method with the Printer object prints the information at the current location on the Printer object. If you print a line of text, for example, and then print another line of text, the second line follows the first line. If you want to print information at a specific location, you can set two of the Printer object's properties to control the location where the data is printed: CurrentX and CurrentY.

The CurrentX and CurrentY properties specify the X and Y coordinate locations of the current print location on the Printer object based from the upper left corner at 0,0. The coordinates are expressed in twips (1/20 of a printer's point) or in the current scale defined by the ScaleMode property.

When you want to begin a new page by issuing the statement `Printer.NewPage`, the CurrentX and CurrentY properties both are set to zero, placing the printing location at the upper left corner of the page.

When should you use the NewPage method? Whenever you want to start a new page, use the NewPage method. You also should use the NewPage method when you are finished printing the document. In addition, you must use the EndDoc method when you want to finish printing the document. Therefore, the last two statements that should execute when you are printing are the following:

```
Printer.NewPage
Printer.EndDoc
```

NOTE There is a lot more to controlling the Printer object than what is described in this section, but using additional control options is only necessary when you need to closely control the position and arrangement of data on the printed page. It's also necessary when you want to print specific pages of the document. Neither of these topics is covered in this chapter because they generally relate to more complex programs.

Printing Text

Now it's time to print some text. Oh, joy! (I knew you'd be beside yourself with emotion.) We'll cover two options: printing the entire document and printing the selection. The only difference in these two options is a single statement that determines what is sent to the Printer object.

First, you need to set your upper and left page margins.

Setting the Left and Top Margins

The upper left corner of the print area on the Printer object is defined by the Printer object's ScaleTop and ScaleLeft properties. Setting the ScaleTop property sets the location of the print area in relation to the upper edge of the Printer object (in this case, the upper edge of the page). Setting the ScaleLeft property sets the location of the left edge of the printing area in relation to the left edge of the Printer object.

To set a top margin, set the ScaleTop property of the Printer object. If you want the margin to move to the right, specify a negative value. To shift the printing area to the left, use a positive value. To move the printing area down on the page, specify a negative value for the ScaleTop property.

The PRINT.MAK project enables you to set the left and top margins for printing the contents of a text box using the Page Setup dialog box. The dialog box provides controls for setting the document's margins and also provides label controls that display the Printer.Height, Printer.Width, Printer.ScaleLeft, and Printer.ScaleTop properties.

Although the scroll bars for the bottom and right margins are synchronized with the scroll bars for the left and top margins, setting the right and bottom margins has no effect. I included the controls for the right and bottom margins only to show you how to synchronize them with the controls for the left and top margins. The methods for controlling the right and bottom margin are beyond the scope of this chapter (yes, that means it's a lot of hard work).

NOTE There are a couple of general methods you can use to print using a right and bottom margin. You can print one character at a time, checking the CurrentX property of the Printer object after each character has been printed to determine if the right margin has been reached. If it has been reached, start a new line. This method will work for fixed-width fonts as well as proportional fonts.

To use a specific bottom margin, print the document one line at a time, checking the value of the CurrentY property after each line. If the CurrentY property has reached or exceeded the bottom margin, start a new page.

Fortunately, setting the top and left margins is easy. PRINT.MAK does it this way: when the user clicks one of the margin scroll bars, the value in the associated label changes accordingly. The Click event procedure for the scroll bar then calls the UpdateSettings procedure, which is located in PRINT.BAS. Here's the UpdateSettings procedure:

```
Sub UpdateSettings ()
    On Error Resume Next
    'Convert the value in the label from a string to a Single,
    'then multiply the value by 1440 to convert from inches to
    'twips
    '(there are about 1440 twips in a logical inch).
    'Then, the Printer.ScaleLeft
    'property is set to the negative of this value
    'to make the left margin move
    'to the right
    Printer.ScaleLeft = -(CSng(frmPageSetup!lblMarginLeft) * 1440)
    'Perform a similar calculation for the top margin
    Printer.ScaleTop = -(CSng(frmPageSetup!lblMarginTop) * 1440)
    'Display the information in the Page Setup dialog box
    'for reference.
```

```
frmPageSetup!lblPageHeight = Printer.Height
frmPageSetup!lblPageWidth = Printer.Width
frmPageSetup!lblScaleTop = Printer.ScaleTop
frmPageSetup!lblScaleLeft = Printer.ScaleLeft
End Sub
```

TIP In the previous example, you might consider defining 1440 as a constant rather than using its literal value.

Try running PRINT.MAK and set the top and left margins. Figure 11.3 shows the Page Setup dialog box you'll use to set the margins.

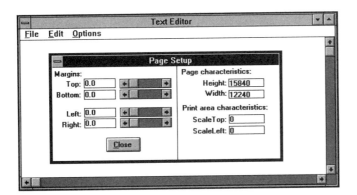

Figure 11.3

The Page Setup dialog box.

Setting Top and Left Margins

1. Open the project PRINT.MAK.

2. Run the project.

3. In the text editor program window, choose File, Page Setup.

4. In the Page Setup dialog box (see fig. 11.3), set the top margin to 1" by clicking on the scrollbar to the right of the Top label. The value of ScaleTop changes accordingly.

5. Set the left margin to 1.5" by clicking on the scrollbar to the right of the Left label. The value of ScaleLeft changes accordingly.

continues

6. Choose <u>C</u>lose to close the dialog box.

7. Choose <u>F</u>ile, <u>O</u>pen, and open a text file of your choice.

8. Choose <u>F</u>ile, <u>P</u>rint, and OK to print the entire document using the top and left margins you have just set.

9. End the program.

Although the UpdateSettings procedure uses the default ScaleMode property of the Printer object (twips), you could set the ScaleMode property to inches to eliminate the need to convert from inches to twips. Here's the same procedure modified to use inches as the ScaleMode for the Printer object:

```
Sub UpdateSettings ()
    On Error Resume Next
    'Set ScaleMode to 5, which is inches
    Printer.ScaleMode = 5
    Printer.ScaleLeft = -CSng(frmPageSetup!lblMarginLeft)
    Printer.ScaleTop = -CSng(frmPageSetup!lblMarginTop)
    'Display the information in the Page Setup dialog box
    'for reference.
    frmPageSetup!lblPageHeight = Printer.Height
    'Etc...
End Sub
```

Both functions have the same effect on the printed page. All you have to do to set the left or top margins, therefore, is set the ScaleTop and ScaleLeft properties of the Printer object. If you want to set the values within the program and don't want to give the user the option of setting the margin, you could use a procedure similar to the following, which sets the top margin to 1" and the left margin to 1.5":

```
Sub SetMargins ()
    Printer.ScaleMode = 5
    Printer.ScaleTop = -1
    Printer.ScaleLeft = -1.5
End Sub
```

Next, let's take a look at printing the entire document.

Printing the Entire Document

In the PRINT.MAK text editor, the editor consists of a multi-line text box. Multi-line text boxes are limited to about 32 KB, but that's enough for a simple text editor.

To print the entire contents of the text box, all you have to do is issue the following statements:

```
Printer.Print Text1.Text
Printer.NewPage
Printer.EndDoc
```

The first of these statements prints the entire contents of the text box to the Printer object, which you can think of as a *virtual printer* (a printer that doesn't really exist except in the computer's memory). The second statement ends the current page and advances to the next page. The EndDoc method in the third statement then ends the document and releases it to the printer.

Although this statement would work to print the entire contents of the Text1 control, PRINT.MAK uses a slightly different approach. This is because PRINT.MAK also enables you to print a selection of text.

Printing a Selection

The mnuFilePrint procedure, which executes when you choose the **P**rint item in the **F**ile menu, displays the common Print dialog box. After the dialog box is displayed and the user chooses OK, the following statements are executed:

```
If CMDialog1.Flags And PD_SELECTION Then
     'Store the currently selected text in the variable
     'stuffToPrint
     stuffToPrint = Text1.SelText
Else
     'Store the entire contents of Text1 in the variable
     stuffToPrint = Text1.Text
End If
```

The If statement tests the condition of the PD_SELECTION flag. If the user chooses the Selection option button in the dialog box, the condition returns True and the following statement is executed:

```
stuffToPrint = Text1.SelText
```

The SelText property of the Text1 control identifies the text that is highlighted in the text box. If no text is highlighted, the SelText property is empty.

If the user does not choose the Selection option, the condition evaluates as False and the following statement is executed:

```
stuffToPrint = Text1.Text
```

This statement copies the entire contents of the text box to the variable *stuffToPrint*, even if part of the text is highlighted.

By using this If statement and storing the text to be printed in the *stuffToPrint* variable, the procedure can use these three statements to print the text, regardless of whether the All or Selection options were chosen:

```
'Set print location to upper left corner
Printer.CurrentX = 0
Printer.CurrentY = 0
'Print the stuff
Printer.Print stuffToPrint
'Start a new page to flush the last page
Printer.NewPage
'End the document to send it to the printer
Printer.EndDoc
```

Experiment on your own using the PRINT.MAK project to print a text file (or any ASCII file, such as an INI file). Try printing using both the All and Selection options.

Combining Items on a Line

You learned earlier in this chapter that you can set the next print coordinate by using the CurrentX and CurrentY properties of the Printer object. In the previous section, the sample code placed the printer coordinate at the upper left corner of the Printer object by setting CurrentX and CurrentY to zero.

You also can control printing in another way. By default, each Print method begins printing on a new line. For example, issuing these two statements causes the two lines to be printed one after the other on separate lines:

```
Printer.Print "I really need a nap."
Printer.Print "But I have to finish this chapter first."
```

Placing a semicolon or comma at the end of a Print statement, however, starts the next line at the next print position, not on the next line. Here's an example:

```
Printer.Print "I can't keep my eyes open much longer.";
Printer.Print "Snore... "
```

These two lines result in the following output:

```
I can't keep my eyes open much longer.Snore...
```

Notice that there isn't any space between the two lines. If you want to add space between lines, insert the spaces as part of the Print statement.

Using Tabs

If you need to print tables or print columns of data, you can use Visual Basic's preset tabs or you can set your own tabs. Each print zone is 14 columns wide, and the column width is based on the width of an average character of the font and font size you are currently using.

To print items using these preset tabs, include a comma between the items to be printed on a line. To skip a print zone, add an extra comma in the statement at the appropriate place. The following code is an example that prints three columns of data using preset tabs. Figure 11.4 shows how the output to the form would look based on this example.

```
Form1.FontName = "Arial"
Form1.FontSize = 10
Form1.Print "First name", "Last name", "Sex"
Form1.Print
Form1.Print "Fred", "Jones", "No"
Form1.Print "Nancy", "Knuckle", "No"
Form1.Print "Amy", "Knicker", "Yes"
```

Figure 11.4

Output using
preset tabs.

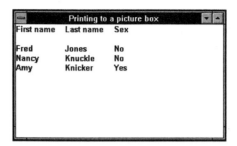

How do you know that the text you're printing will fit in a print zone? You don't. Before printing, test the length of the longest string that is going in each print zone, then base the print location on whether this longest string will fit. If it won't fit, you need to either add an extra tab to move to the next print zone, or use custom tabs.

To print with custom tab settings, use the Tab function within the Print statement. The Tab function has the following syntax:

```
Tab(column)
```

The *column* parameter specifies the column number to which the line will tab. The following statements print text in columns in a picture box at columns 3 and 20:

```
Picture1.FontName = "MS Sans Serif"
Picture1.FontSize = 10
Picture1.Print Tab(3); "Name:"; Tab(20); "Occupation"
Picture1.Print Tab(3); "Ferdinand"; Tab(20); "Baker"
Picture1.Print Tab(3); "Harley"; Tab(20); "Whiner"
Picture1.Print Tab(3); "Anne"; Tab(20); "Candlestick dipper"
Picture1.Print Tab(3); "Tiffany"; Tab(20); "Independently wealthy"
```

Figure 11.5 shows the resulting output of this sample code.

Formatting Your Output

Visual Basic provides two functions—Function() and Function$()—to enable you to quickly and easily format numbers, dates, and times. The Format() function converts numeric values to Variant types, and the Format$() function converts numeric values to strings.

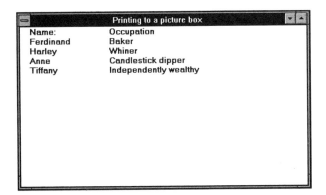

Figure 11.5

Printing to a picture box using custom tabs.

In addition to formatting numbers with these two functions, you can format date and time variables. Rather than repeat all of the possible options (there are a lot), I'll give you some quick examples. Table 11.2 lists some format statements and the resulting output.

Table 11.2
Sample Format$() Function Output

Format$ statement	Resulting output
Format$(1234.567, "00000.00")	01234.56
Format$(1234.567, "#####.##")	1234.56
Format$(1234.567, "##,###.##")	1,234.56
Format$(1234.567, "Currency")	$1,234.56
Format$(Now, "ddd, mmmm dd, yyyy")	Tue, March 22, 1994
Format$(Now, "dddd, mmm dd, yyyy")	Tuesday, Mar 22, 1994
Format$(Now, "Short Date")	3/22/94
Format$(Now, "Long Date")	Tuesday, March 22, 1994

Figure 11.6 shows examples of data that has been formatted and printed to a picture box.

There are many other options in addition to those shown in table 11.2, but these will give you an idea of how the Format$() function works. For a list of all of the predefined formats and a description of how to create your own formats, search the Visual Basic Help file on the keyword Format$.

Figure 11.6

Numbers and dates formatted and printed to a picture box.

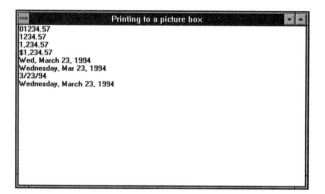

Getting Serious

If you start learning too much about the more complex aspects of Visual Basic, you might morph into an expert yourself. Tread carefully in this part of the book—you'll learn some pretty nerdy details in it that will come close to making you a fully-functional programmer.

Here's what you can expect in this part of the book:

12: Handling Errors. This chapter introduces the concept of *error trapping and handling.* In it you learn how to anticipate potential errors that might occur when someone is using your program, and you learn to write *error handlers* that will trap the error and take corrective action. No program is complete without error handling.

13: Using Lots of Data. Chapter 13 introduces some topics that you'll find particularly useful as you begin writing programs that work with larger amounts of data. You learn about data types and arrays, and begin writing an address book program.

14: Creating Your Own Files. Many programs are useless if they can't open and save files. Chapter 14 teaches you to use three different methods to open files. You'll create a simple text editor that works with text files, and you'll use two different methods to add file-handling capability to the address book program you started in Chapter 13.

15: Da Bugs! Programmers affectionately refer to bugs as *undocumented features,* but a bug is a flaw in your program (a fly in your ointment?). Chapter 15 teaches you the basics of testing and debugging a program.

Handling Errors

I'll be honest and even a bit humble: I don't make mistakes. Other people simply misinterpret my meaning. I'm sure you're the same way. Programs are not so perfect; errors happen in them all the time. This chapter explains error handling and will give you a good understanding of how you can error-proof your programs. I know you're expecting a list of the topics in this chapter, so not to disappoint you, here it is:

- Understanding how and why errors happen
- Writing local error handlers
- Writing general error handlers
- Causing your own problems (testing)
- Making the IRS believe that the errors on your return are just misinterpreted—but valid—deductions

The first four topics will take some time. The last topic can be summed up in two words: fat chance (no way, good luck, get real, dream on, yeah sure— just pick the two words you prefer).

You Can't Make It Foolproof

I read somewhere recently that you can't make anything foolproof because fools are so ingenious. How true. Your task as a programmer is to anticipate the things the user will do with your program and enable him only do those things that won't wreak havoc on his system, change the balance of world power, affect trade balances, ruffle the feathers of the spotted owl, or alter the nature of reality as we know it.

In addition to preventing the user from doing stupid things with your program (like erasing the hard disk), you also have to anticipate errors that might happen in your program because of things beyond the user's control: a font isn't available, the printer is off-line, a network drive suddenly becomes unavailable, there is no disk in drive A, and so on. All of these things fall under the general umbrella of *errors*.

What Are Errors?

If your program did nothing but make some internal calculations and gnash on its own internally defined data, it's unlikely that any errors would occur in the program when it runs. But your programs probably need to at least interact with the Windows environment. This brings up the possibility of errors.

What are errors? Anytime something doesn't go as you planned it, it's an error. If you expected the user to enter a number and she entered a letter, and your program then tries to perform some math calculations on that input, an error will likely occur. If the user tries to connect to a disk that isn't available, an error occurs. If you try to assign a FontName property to the Printer object that the printer doesn't support, an error occurs.

Let's chew on a specific example brought up by the FileMan project from Chapter 6. Figure 12.1 shows the FileMan form to refresh your memory.

If you double-click on a file name in the file list box, FileMan attempts to execute the file you have double-clicked upon. You could write the function as a simple procedure containing one line:

```
Sub File1_DblClick ()
    retval = Shell(File1.FileName, 1)
End Sub
```

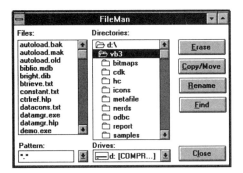

Figure 12.1
The FileMan form.

If the file specified by the FileName property of File1 is an executable file recognized by Windows (EXE, COM, BAT, or PIF), Windows executes the program without generating an error. If you double-click on the name of any other type of file, an error occurs because Windows doesn't know how to run the program. The attractive but relatively unhelpful dialog box shown in figure 12.2 appears on the display informing you that the program has experienced an "illegal function call" error. Your program then *terminates*, which is a polite way of saying that your program blows up.

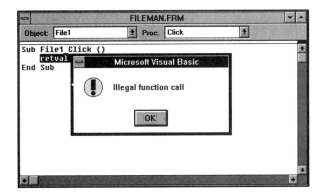

Figure 12.2
A typical error dialog box.

There are all sorts of errors that can occur in a program, either through unexpected user actions, problems with availability of system resources, or other unexpected snags. Your task as a programmer is to anticipate all possible errors and *handle them*.

NOTE If you don't trap and handle an error, your program will go belly up and die a horrible death.

Error Handling

There's one important rule about errors that you need to understand, and it is: You have to plan for the possibility that an error will occur in all but the simplest procedures.

If you had to anticipate every possible error that could occur while your program is running, you'd never be able to complete a program. Fortunately, you can handle many errors in a general way. In a lot of situations, it doesn't matter *what* error occurred; it only matters that an error did occur. In other situations, you probably will need to handle *specific* errors. If the program tries to access a disk in the floppy drive and it can't read the file, for example, your program needs to respond to the resulting error by displaying a dialog box that prompts the user to verify that the disk is inserted in the drive.

The term *handling an error* means that your program needs to be ready to respond to an error when it occurs. When the error does occur, your program needs to *trap* the error. Trapping an error simply means that the program anticipates the error and prevents it from terminating the program. The program can then examine the type of error and take some action that is appropriate for the error. In some cases, this means simply going on with the next statement and ignoring the error. In other cases, the program needs to display an error message. In still other cases, the program needs to be able to reattempt the action that generated the error.

Adding code to your program to trap and deal with errors isn't particularly difficult, but it is a very necessary step of developing the program. Here is a list of three things you have to do to error-proof a procedure:

☐ **Set an error trap.** No, those steel-toothed snap traps won't work for this one. Instead, you need to add statements in appropriate places in the procedure that tell the program how to behave when an error occurs.

☐ **Write an error handler.** This is a chunk of code that goes in the procedure. When errors occur that can't be ignored, program execution passes to this error handler. The error handler then determines what action to take based on the type of error that occurred.

☐ **Exit the error handler.** After the error handler has determined what action to take, the error handler needs to initiate some action to correct the error. To do this, the error handler has to include some code to exit the handler and initiate the corrective action.

First, let's take a look at trapping errors.

Using the On Error Statement

A number of different ways exist to trap and handle an error. You can cause the program to ignore the error and continue execution, redirect execution to a block of code called an *error handler*, or turn off error handling altogether. The On Error statement makes all of these options available. Here are three On Error statements that perform different error-trapping functions:

```
On Error Resume Next
On Error GoTo lineLable
On Error GoTo 0
```

The first of these—On Error Resume Next—causes the program to continue execution with the statement immediately following the statement that caused the error to occur. Here's an example of a procedure that uses this technique.

```
Sub WetWilly ( )
    On Error Resume Next
    Printer.FontName = Text1.FontName
    Printer.FontSize = Text1.FontSize
End Sub
```

If the Printer object doesn't support the font specified by the statement Printer.FontName = Text1.FontName, an error occurs. Because the On Error statement directs the program to execute the next statement if an error occurs, the program executes the next statement to set the FontSize property of the Printer object to match the FontSize property of the text box.

By using the On Error Resume Next statement, we've prevented the program from crashing if the font isn't supported by the Printer object. In this particular case, however, we should at least warn the user that the font isn't supported and that the font that appears on the printed page might not look the same as the one used in the program. To do that, we need to write an error handler.

Using On Error GoTo

An error handler is a block of code that you place in a procedure to handle errors that occur within the procedure. To make program execution jump to the error handler when an error occurs, use the On Error GoTo statement and specify a label that names the error handler. Here's a small example:

```
Sub Drive1_Change ()
      On Error GoTo SomeError
      Dir1.Path = Drive1.Drive
      Exit Sub

SomeError:
      MsgBox "Something screwed up...", 0, "File Error"
      Exit Sub
End Sub
```

In this example, if an error occurs (such as the drive is not available), execution jumps to the SomeError label. The code within this error handler displays a mostly harmless dialog box, then the Exit Sub statement causes execution to exit the procedure. In a moment, you'll create a much more useful error handler. First, however, you need to understand how long an error trap can live.

The Life of an Error Trap

An error trap is active until you set a different trap or until the Exit Sub, Exit Function, End Sub, or End Function statements are executed. If you issue the statement On Error Resume Next, for example, program execution will continue with the next statement any time an error occurs until you set a different trap or issue one of the four statements described previously. Here's a code example that might make the concept clearer to you:

```
Sub SlideDownBannister ()
      On Error Resume Next
      'If an error occurs here, the next statement executes.
      'Ditto for this line...
      '...and for this line
      On Error GoTo OuttaHere
      'Now if an error occurs, execution contiues at the
      'OuttaHere label...
      'and same goes for this line...
      Exit Sub
```

```
OuttaHere:
    'This code would handle the error
    '...and this code
    '...etc.
    Exit Sub
End Sub
```

After execution jumps to the OuttaHere label, the statements within its block of code execute. When the Exit Sub function finally executes, the trap On Error GoTo OuttaHere is no longer in effect. The next procedure will have to have its own set of error traps.

NOTE You can't use the same label for an error trap in two different procedures. The label names must be unique. Also, the error handler must be before the End Sub or End Function statement. Therefore, you need to include an Exit Sub statement *before* the error handler label. This ensures that the error handler code is not executed if no errors occur during the procedure.

Getting Out of the Error Handler

When an error occurs and execution jumps to the error handler, whatever code you have written in the error handler will execute to try to determine which error occurred and take corrective action. At some point, execution will have to exit from the error handler to enable the program to continue, or in the case of a terminal error, to stop.

Here are the statements you can use to exit an error handler:

Resume. This statement causes execution to resume with the statement that caused the error. Use this statement in an error handler after your code has attempted to correct the problem and you want the program to again try the process that caused the error to occur. If you detected that there was no disk in the floppy drive, for example, use a message box to direct the user to insert a disk, then issue the Resume (0) statement.

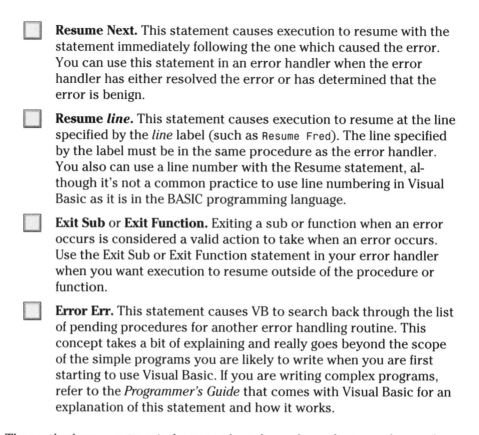

Resume Next. This statement causes execution to resume with the statement immediately following the one which caused the error. You can use this statement in an error handler when the error handler has either resolved the error or has determined that the error is benign.

Resume *line*. This statement causes execution to resume at the line specified by the *line* label (such as Resume Fred). The line specified by the label must be in the same procedure as the error handler. You also can use a line number with the Resume statement, although it's not a common practice to use line numbering in Visual Basic as it is in the BASIC programming language.

Exit Sub or **Exit Function.** Exiting a sub or function when an error occurs is considered a valid action to take when an error occurs. Use the Exit Sub or Exit Function statement in your error handler when you want execution to resume outside of the procedure or function.

Error Err. This statement causes VB to search back through the list of pending procedures for another error handling routine. This concept takes a bit of explaining and really goes beyond the scope of the simple programs you are likely to write when you are first starting to use Visual Basic. If you are writing complex programs, refer to the *Programmer's Guide* that comes with Visual Basic for an explanation of this statement and how it works.

The method you use to exit the procedure depends on the type of error, how your program handles the error, and other factors. You'll see some specific examples as you read through the rest of the chapter.

A Real Life Example

Now, let's create a decent error handler. Do you remember the FileMan program from Chapter 6? Here's the code that executes if the user selects a different drive using the Drive1 drive list box:

```
Sub Drive1_Change ()
    On Error Resume Next
    Dir1.Path = Drive1.Drive
End Sub
```

Although this trap prevents the program from crashing if the user selects a drive that isn't available (such as an empty floppy drive), we're really not giving the user any indication that something is wrong. Therefore, let's spruce up the error capability of this procedure a bit.

Adding Error Handling to FileMan

1. Open the FILEMAN.MAK project, and display the frmFileMan form.

2. Double-click on the Drive1 control to open the Code window and display the Drive1_Change() procedure.

3. Modify the procedure to read as follows:

```
Sub Drive1_Change ()

        'If the drive isn't available, jump to the
        'DriveChangeError label
        On Error GoTo DriveChangeError
        'Set the directory path to match the newly selected drive
        Dir1.Path = Drive1.Drive
        Exit Sub
DriveChangeError:
        MsgBox "Sorry, but something screwed up.", 0, "File Error"
        Exit Sub
End Sub
```

4. Save the project, and run the program.

5. With no disk in drive A, select drive A from FileMan's drive list box. An error should occur and you should see the message box shown in figure 12.3.

6. Close the dialog box and end the program.

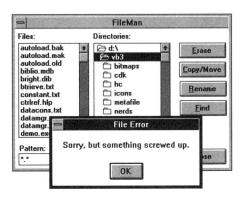

Figure 12.3

Message box generated by the error handler.

If an error occurs in this procedure, execution passes to the DriveChangeError label. The message box appears, and when you close the message box, the Exit Sub statement executes.

The Exit Sub statement is required because Visual Basic expects that the error handler will terminate in a specific way. You can't just let the program execute a bunch of statements until it hits the end of the procedure (the End Sub statement). That will generate an error. One of the accepted methods is to use an Exit Sub or Exit Function statement. Another is to use some form of the Resume statement.

Although this error handling method is a little better than our previous one, it still is a bit lame. Instead of blindly spitting out a message box, we need to determine what error occurred and take appropriate action. To do that, we need the Err and Error$ functions.

Using the Err and Error$ Functions

Each potential error has a unique number that identifies it. The Err function returns the value of the error number of the last error. By testing the value of Err after an error occurs, your program can determine which error occurred and base its action on that information.

The Error$ function performs a similar function, except that Error$ returns a unique error message string associated with the error. You can use the value of Error$ in a message box to inform your user of the specific error that occurred.

It's a good idea to combine the error number and error message in the message box you display to inform the user that an error has occurred. You also can add your own text to the message box to instruct the user what to do to alleviate the error. Here's an example of a chunk of code that will do just that:

```
myErrorHandler:
    NL = Chr$(10) & Chr$(13)
    Msg = Str$(Err) & ": " & Error$ & NL & NL
    Msg = Msg & "An error occurred in your program. Please send "
```

```
        Msg = Msg & "$1000 in cash to the address listed in your "
        Msg = Msg & "user's manual, and the programmers will get "
        Msg = Msg & "back to you as soon as possible."
        MsgBox Msg
        Exit Sub
    End Sub
```

Figure 12.4 shows a dialog box that might result from such an obnoxious bit of code.

Figure 12.4

An obnoxious error message generated with Err and Error$.

Even this error handler isn't quite enough. We really should check the value of Err to determine what error occurred and take appropriate action. Using the drive change procedure in the previous example, we probably should test for the following errors:

- **68.** Device unavailable. This error will occur if there is no disk in a floppy drive. The procedure should offer the user the options of retrying or canceling.

- **76.** Path not found. This error will occur if a network drive suddenly becomes unavailable (it is no longer being shared, for example). The procedure should offer the user the option of retrying or canceling.

- Anything else. If any other error occurs, add some code to offer the user the option of continuing or ending the program.

Okay! Now we're cooking. Let's modify the error procedure to test for these errors.

Writing the Final Error Handler

1. Continue working with the FILEMAN.MAK project.

2. Open the Code window for the frmFileMan object and display the Drive1_Change( ) event procedure.

3. Modify the procedure to read as follows:

```
Sub Drive1_Change ()
      'If an error occurs, jump to the error handler
      On Error GoTo DriveChangeError
      'Set the directory path to match the newly selected drive
      Dir1.Path = Drive1.Drive
      'If no errors, exit the sub
      Exit Sub


DriveChangeError:
      'Store the error number and string to a variable for
      'later use
      ErrTitle = Err & ": " & Error$
      'Choose action based on the value of Err
      Select Case Err
          Case 68
              Msg = "This drive is currently unavailable. If
              ➥this is a floppy"
              Msg = Msg & " drive, make sure the disk is
              ➥inserted and the"
              Msg = Msg & " drive door is closed."
              retval = MsgBox(Msg, 5, ErrTitle)
          Case 76
              Msg = "An error occured accessing the drive. If
              ➥this is a network"
              Msg = Msg & " drive, the drive may have become
              ➥unavailable."
              retval = MsgBox(Msg, 5, ErrTitle)
          Case Else
              Msg = "An unexpected error occurred. Choose Yes to
              ➥continue program,"
              Msg = Msg & " or choose No to end program."
              retval = MsgBox(Msg, 4, ErrTitle)
              If retval = 6 Then
                    Drive1.Drive = Dir1.Path
```

```
                        Exit Sub
              Else
                        End
              End If
      End Select
      'If the Case Else condition didn't execute, the error was
      'either 68 or 76. So, test the value of retval to determine
      'if the user selected the Retry or Cancel button in the
      'message box that was displayed
      Select Case retval
            Case 4   'User chose Retry, so try the Dir1.
            'Path = Drive1.Drive again.
                  Resume
            Case 2   'User cancelled, so restore the original drive
            'to match Dir1
                  Drive1.Drive = Dir1.Path
                  Exit Sub
      End Select
End Sub
```

4. Save the project, and run the program.

5. With no disk in drive A, attempt to select drive A. An error 68 should occur and you should see the message box shown in figure 12.5. Insert a disk in drive A and choose **R**etry.

6. End the program.

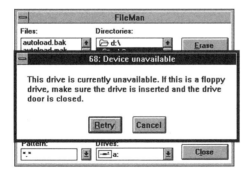

Figure 12.5

Error message generated by the error handler.

TIP

If you want to test the error 76, here's one way to do it: If your system is on a network, share a floppy disk at a remote node, then connect to the remote floppy from your system. After connecting to the remote floppy, remove the floppy disk from the remote drive. Then run FileMan and attempt to access the remote floppy drive. An error 76 should occur.

In this example, the error handler is about ten times as long as the actual core procedure. But by adding the error handler, your program will handle drive errors more gracefully and will seem more professional and polished.

Wait, I Didn't Expect That...

You should always allow for the possibility that an error will occur that you didn't anticipate. If the error is relatively benign and won't adversely affect the program, you can simply display an error message containing the error, then resume execution. The only problem is that if you didn't anticipate the error, you have no way of knowing if it will be benign or evil incarnate.

One option is to display a message box containing the error number and error that occurred, and give the user the option of continuing or ending the program. The previous example used this technique by adding a Case Else structure to the error handler. If the error was neither 68 nor 76, the statements following the Case Else statement displayed a message box giving the user the option of ending the program or continuing execution.

Another option is to create a centralized error procedure to handle all unanticipated errors. The next section explains how to do that.

Using Common Error Handlers

Although an error handler has to be located in the procedure in which the error occurs, there is nothing to prevent the error handler from calling another procedure. This means that you can create one or two common error handling procedures to handle the majority of errors that occur in your program. Why would you want to do that? As you begin writing more complex programs, you'll soon realize that you are duplicating a lot of the same code in each error handler you add to your procedures. Instead of duplicating that code, you can create a centralized procedure to handle the errors instead.

Consider the error handler that you just added to FileMan. The two errors handled by the error handler could possibly happen in other procedures. Why not create a single procedure to handle all file, path, and drive related errors? By doing that, you avoid duplicating a lot of code in your program.

Here's how we'll set it up: each procedure in which a drive, path, or file error might occur will contain its own error handler. This error handler will contain a call to a function called, for lack of a more inventive name, DiskErrorHandler(). The DiskErrorHandler() function will contain the code necessary to handle all anticipated file, directory, and disk problems.

First, move your existing error handling code to a new function called DiskErrorHandler.

Creating the DiskErrorHandler Procedure

1. Continue working with FILEMAN.MAK.

2. Open the Code window for frmFileMan and choose the Drive1_Change() event procedure.

3. Select all of the statements below the DriveChangeError label (except for the End Sub statement), and press Ctrl+X to cut the statements to the Clipboard.

4. Choose <u>V</u>iew, <u>N</u>ew Procedure to display the New Procedure dialog box.

5. Choose the <u>S</u>ub radio button, and enter DiskErrorHandler in the same edit box. This will create a new procedure called DiskErrorHandler.

6. In the new DiskErrorHandler function, press Ctrl+V to paste the statements from the Clipboard to the procedure.

7. Modify the DiskErrorHandler function to read as follows:

```
Function DiskErrorHandler ()
        'Store the error number and string to a variable for
        'later use
        ErrTitle = Err & ": " & Error$
        'Choose action based on the value of Err
        Select Case Err
            Case 68
                Msg = "This drive is currently unavailable. If
                ➥this is a floppy"
```

```
                    Msg = Msg & " drive, make sure the disk is
                    ➡inserted and the"
                    Msg = Msg & " drive door is closed."
                    retval = MsgBox(Msg, 5, ErrTitle)
                Case 76
                    Msg = "An error occured accessing the drive. If
                    ➡this is a network"
                    Msg = Msg & " drive, the drive may have become
                    ➡unavailable."
                    retval = MsgBox(Msg, 5, ErrTitle)
                Case Else
                    Msg = "An unexpected error occurred. Choose Yes to
                    ➡continue program,"
                    Msg = Msg & " or choose No to end program."
                    retval = MsgBox(Msg, 4, ErrTitle)
            End Select
            'Return the value of the message box action
            DiskErrorHandler = retval
        End Function
```

8. Select Drive1_Change from the Proc drop-down list and modify the Drive1_Change() event procedure to read as follows:

```
    Sub Drive1_Change ( )
            'If an error occurs, jump to the error handler
            On Error GoTo DriveChangeError
            'Set the directory path to match the newly selected drive
            Dir1.Path = Drive1.Drive
            'If no errors, exit the sub
            Exit Sub

    DriveChangeError:
            errorAction = DiskErrorHandler()
            Select Case errorAction
                Case 2, 6
                    'User pressed Cancel
                    Drive1.Drive = Dir1.Path
                    Exit Sub
                Case 4
                    Resume
                Case Else
                    MsgBox "An unrecoverable error occurred.
                    ➡Terminating program."
```

```
                    End
            End Select
        End Sub
```

9. Save the project, and then run the program and test your error handling capability by attempting to access an empty floppy drive. The program should display a message box with **R**etry and **C**ancel buttons. Test the **R**etry button, and test the **C**ancel button.

10. End the program.

As you add other procedures to your FileMan program, you can expand the error checking capability in the DiskErrorHandler function by adding additional Case statements for specific errors.

Causing Your Own Problems (Testing)

No, this section isn't about making snide comments to your spouse about how he/she dresses. It's about generating specific errors so you can test your error handler. As you are testing your program, you should test each of the possible errors your error handler is designed to handle. Assume you've written some code in an error handler to trap and react to an error 71, Disk not ready. An easy way to determine if your error handler will handle this particular error properly is to generate the error yourself within the program.

You can generate specific errors by using the Error statement, followed by the number of the error. Here's an example that generates the error 71:

```
    Error 71
```

This statement will cause an error 71 to be generated when the statement is executed. Assuming that a previous statement has set the error trap to direct program execution to the error handler, the error handler will respond to this error as if it had been generated by the system, rather than by the program.

Give the Error statement a try. Make a small change to the DiskErrorHandler procedure in FileMan to trap error 71. Then, add an Error statement in the Drive1_Change event procedure to cause the error to occur.

Causing Your Own Errors

1. Continue working with FILEMAN.MAK.

2. Open the Code window for the Drive1_Change event procedure and insert, as the first line of the procedure, the following statement:

    ```
    Sub Drive1_Change ()
        Error 71
        '...existing statements...
    ```

3. Choose General from the Object drop-down list, and choose the DiskErrorHandler procedure from the Proc drop-down list.

4. Modify the DiskErrorHandler procedure to handle error 71 as shown below (the change is shown in bold):

    ```
    Select Case Err
        Case 68, 71
    ```

5. Save the project.

6. Run the program and select a different drive from Drive1 control. An error 71 will be generated.

7. Choose **R**etry. The error will occur again because the statement Error 71 will be repeated.

8. Choose **C**ancel.

9. End the program.

It's a good idea when you're writing a program to test the error handler by generating all of the errors that it is designed to handle. Also generate a few errors that it isn't designed to handle to test the error handler's capability to deal with unanticipated errors. For a list of trappable errors, display the Contents page of the Help file and click on the Trappable Errors item.

13

CHAPTER

Using Lots of Data

It's fine to start out writing programs that make obnoxious noises or print lovely but useless graphics on the display, and some of the simple programs you write will probably be very useful. Sooner or later, however, you'll want to graduate to writing more complex and useful programs. Generally, that means writing programs that can manipulate and store data. You learned how to work with small amounts of data in earlier chapters. This chapter teaches you to work with big chunks of data. It covers the following topics:

- Using arrays
- Moving data to and from the Clipboard
- Using a custom data structure

A lot of this material will help you in Chapter 14 when you start learning how to create your own files, so wipe that silly grin off of your face and pay attention!

Using Arrays

The variables you have worked with in previous chapters have served to store a single piece of data, whether it was a number, a string, a date, or some other type of data. *Arrays* also enable your program to store data, but arrays enable you to store multiple elements of data under the same name. Instead of storing one person's name in a variable called *lastName*, you can store the names of a bunch of people in a variable array called *lastName*. Each item in an array is of the same data type. If you declare an array as an integer array, for example, all of the elements in the array must be integers.

In many ways, arrays are just data lists. As with list boxes, you access elements in the list by their index numbers. The first element in an array has the index number zero. The second element in the array is element 1, and so on. Arrays make it possible to simplify the design of a program because it is much easier to track large amounts of data in an array rather than handle each data element individually. You've seen brief examples of arrays— including control arrays—in earlier chapters.

Creating Static (Fixed) Arrays

You create an array in much the same way you create variables. Unlike variables, however, you must declare an array before you can use it. Arrays can be global, module-level, or local. To create a global array that is available in all procedures and functions, use the Global statement in the Declarations section of a code module, as I've done in the first of the following three examples:

```
Global LastNames(9) As String      'In the Declarations section of
'a module
Dim LastNames(9) As String 'In the Declarations section of a form
'or code module
Static LastNames(9) As String      'In a procedure or function
```

These examples each create a static array of ten elements with index numbers 0 through 9. Each element in the array is a string. The first statement creates a global array, the second statement creates a module-level array, and the third statement creates a local array. If you don't declare the data type of the array, it's created as an array of Variant elements.

In addition to creating a static array—one that contains a set number of elements—you also can create a dynamic array. A dynamic array can change size if you need to add more elements to the array or reduce the size of the array to eliminate unused elements and conserve memory. You'll learn later in the chapter how to create and use dynamic arrays.

Storing Data in an Array

It's easy to store data in an array; all you have to do is reference the index number of the location in the array where you want the element to be added. Here's an example that stores some string data as the third element in an array:

```
someArray(2) = "Fungus"
```

 It's always a good idea to initialize ANY variable, but arrays take on a special need. You should always know exactly what's inside your containers at any moment. When you create an array, there's the off chance that it'll have some left over memory garbage inside. Programmers should automatically initialize arrays right after creating them.

That was easy enough. What if you want to store the same information in each element in the array? This is called *initializing* the array, and you can do it by using a For...Next structure:

```
For x = 0 to 9
    LastName(x) = "None"
Next x
```

Retrieving Data from an Array

How can you access a specific element in the list? Just reference its index number. The following statement prints the third element in the array to the Printer object:

```
Printer.Print LastNames(2)
```

What if you want to print all of the names to the Printer object? Just set up a For...Next loop that uses the value of the For...Next counter as the index number:

```
For x = 0 to 9
    Printer.Print LastNames(x)
Next x
```

Arrays—a Practical Example

Now it's time to put to use some of that great array of knowlege you've just picked up (cheap pun intended). Let's start writing a program to keep track of the names, addresses, and phone numbers of your favorite friends and enemies. True to my agreeable and solicitous nature, I've designed the program for you. Figure 13.1 shows the interface for the address book program. It isn't pretty, but it's functional.

Figure 13.1

The interface for the address book program.

For now we'll just worry about keeping track of the last name and first name of each person in the address book, and use two arrays to store the names.

First, start by declaring the two arrays to hold the first name and last name of each person.

Declaring an Array

1. Open the project PEOPLE1.MAK that is included on the *Understanding Visual Basic Disk.*

2. Open the Code window for PEOPLE1.FRM and choose General from the Object drop-down list.

3. In the Declarations section of the form, add the following statements:

    ```
    Dim LastName(3) As String
    Dim FirstName(3) As String
    Dim indexCounter As Integer
    ```

    The first two statements create two arrays of four elements each to contain the last name and first name strings. The last statement defines an integer array you'll use to keep track of the array index.

4. From the Object drop-down list, choose cmdAdd to display the cmdAdd_Click event procedure.

5. Modify the cmdAdd_Click event procedure to read as follows:

    ```
    Sub cmdAdd_Click ()
        If txtLastName = "" Then
            MsgBox "Please enter a last name."
            Exit Sub
        Else
            LastName(0) = txtLastName
            FirstName(0) = txtFirstName
        End If
    End Sub
    ```

6. Save the project, and run the program.

7. Enter a last name in the Last Name text box, a first name in the First Name text box, and choose **A**dd.

8. Choose **V**iew, **A**rray. This displays a new form and prints the contents of the array to the form.

9. Choose the **C**lose! menu to close the output form.

10. Choose the **C**lose button to end the program.

You have succeeded in storing one element in an array. Oooh, ahhh, what a triumph! But now you have a problem. How do you place other items in the array? With the current procedure, you can't. Instead of using the actual index value to store the data in the array, use a variable. The integer variable *indexCounter* is defined in the Declarations section of the form, making it a module-level variable. You can use *indexCounter* to incrementally add items to the arrays.

Using a Variable for the Index

1. Continue working with PEOPLE1.MAK.

2. Open the Code window and display the code for the cmdAdd_Click event procedure. Modify the procedure to read as follows:

```
Sub cmdAdd_Click ()
        If txtLastName = "" Then
                MsgBox "Please enter a last name."
                Exit Sub
        Else
                'Store the last name in the LastName array
                LastName(indexCounter) = txtLastName
                'Store the first name in the FirstName array
                FirstName(indexCounter) = txtFirstName
                'Display the current index number in a label on the
                'form
                lblCurrentIndex = indexCounter
                'Increment the indexCounter variable by 1
                indexCounter = indexCounter + 1
                'Set focus to the txtLastName edit box to make it ready
                'for next entry
                txtLastName.SetFocus
        End If
End Sub
```

3. Run the program.

4. Enter a last name and first name in the appropriate boxes, and choose **A**dd.

5. Repeat step 4 three more times, placing a total of four names in the array.

6. Choose **V**iew, **A**rray to view the contents of the array (see fig. 13.2), and choose **C**lose! to close the output window.

7. End the program.

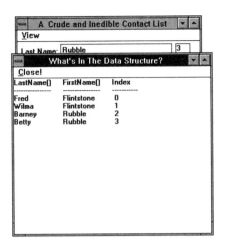

Figure 13.2
Four names
added to the
array.

 The cmdAdd_Click event procedure should really clear the contents of the text boxes to make them ready for the next entry, but we'll add that bit of code later.

The cmdAdd_Click event procedure is now much better. You can add up to four names to the array, filling it completely. But what happens if you try to put in a fifth name? The array is only designed to hold four elements, so you'll be rewarded with the error dialog box shown in figure 13.3 if you try to add another name.

Figure 13.3
The "Subscript
out of range"
error dialog
box.

The error message "Subscript out of range" means that you tried to access an array element that doesn't exist. In this case, you tried to access LastName(4), a non-existent fifth element in the array.

This PEOPLE1.MAK program is really bogus! Who needs an address book that only allows four entries? Maybe you don't have that many friends, but you probably have at least that many enemies. We need to modify the array so it will hold as many names as we want. To do that, we need to use a dynamic array.

TIP In addition to creating one-dimensional arrays such as the one in the PEOPLE1.MAK project, you also can create multidimensional arrays. No, multidimensional arrays don't live in parallel universes. *Understanding Visual Basic* doesn't cover multidimensional arrays. For an explanation of multidimensional arrays, refer to the *Programmer's Guide* that comes with Visual Basic.

Using Dynamic Arrays

The arrays we've been playing with so far are known as *static* arrays. Static arrays are great when you know exactly how many elements there will be in the array, but what if you need to change the size of the array as the program is running? Maybe you want the user to be able to add as many names as she wants to the array. If that's the case, you can create a *dynamic array* that can change size while the program is running.

Why not just create a big array that is large enough to contain as many names as the user could possibly want, and just ignore any extra unused elements? The first problem with this approach is that it uses more memory than is necessary. If you make a habit of this approach, you're likely to cause your users' systems to run low on memory. The other problem is that unless you create an array of an unrealistically large size, you still have no guarantee that the array will be as large as the user needs it to be. She might have a lot more friends and enemies than you can imagine. The answer still is to use a dynamic array.

There are two ways to create a dynamic array. The first method is to declare the array without specifying its size. Here are a couple of statements we can use in this program to create the two name arrays as dynamic arrays:

```
Dim LastName() As String
Dim FirstName() As String
```

Notice that the size isn't specified. When the program runs, the arrays are declared but they aren't sized. You'll have to size them later when you start putting data into the arrays. How do you resize an array? I thought you'd never ask. You use the ReDim statement.

Redimensioning an Array

The ReDim statement redimensions an array. Here's the syntax of the ReDim statement for redimensioning a one-dimensional array (I'll explain *one-dimensional* later):

```
ReDim [Preserve] arrayName(size) [As type]
```

If you simply want to redimension the array LastName as an array of twenty elements, for example, you can use this statement:

```
ReDim LastName(19)
```

If there is any data in the array, however, you're going to lose it when the array is redimensioned. If you want to retain the existing data in the array and simply resize it, use the Preserve keyword:

```
ReDim Preserve LastName(19)
```

Now you're ready to do some real damage. Modify the cmdAdd_Click event procedure to redimension the arrays each time a new item is added.

TIP   You add the As type parameter to the ReDim statement if you're declaring the array using an explicit type of variable. To redimension an array of integers, for example, you can tack on the As Array parameter to the end of the statement.

Redimensioning an Array

1. Continue working with PEOPLE1.MAK.

2. Open the Code window and display the cmdAdd_Click event procedure. Modify the procedure to read as follows (new lines and modified lines are shown in bold):

```
Sub cmdAdd_Click ()
      If txtLastName = "" Then
            MsgBox "Please enter a last name."
            Exit Sub
      Else
            ReDim Preserve LastName(indexCounter)
            ReDim Preserve FirstName(indexCounter)
            LastName(indexCounter) = txtLastName
            Firstname(indexCounter) = txtFirstName
            vsbArrayIndex = indexCounter
            lblCurrentIndex = vsbArrayIndex
            indexCounter = indexCounter + 1
            txtLastName.SetFocus
      End If
End Sub
```

3. Choose general from the Object drop-down list. In the declarations section, remove the 3 from the first two Dim statements to make them read as follows:

```
Dim LastName() As String
Dim Firstname() As String
Dim indexCounter As Integer
```

4. Save the project.

5. Run the program and enter at least 5 names to the array.

6. Choose View, and Array to view the contents of the array (see fig. 13.4).

7. Close the output window and end the program.

Figure 13.4
Multiple names added to the array.

The first time the cmdAdd_Click procedure is executed, indexCounter has not been set so it defaults to 0. The first time the ReDim statements execute, they create a single-element array. For example, the first ReDim statement evaluates as follows:

```
ReDim Preserve LastName(0)
```

Subsequent executions of the procedure redimension the array to contain one element more than its current size. By redimensioning the arrays in this way, you make it posssible to expand the array to contain as many elements as the user requires.

You might also have noticed in the last exercise that you added some code to make the scroll bar semi-functional. As you add new names the scroll bar increments by one. You will add a procedure in the next exercise to enable the user to select an element from the array by clicking on the scroll bar. To do that, you need to understand the UBound and LBound functions.

Using the UBound and LBound Functions

The *UBound* and *LBound* functions return the upper and lower bounds of an array. These functions are particularly useful with dynamic arrays because the functions enable you to determine the size of the array at any given time. The LBound function returns the lowest index value for the array, and the UBound function returns the upper index value for the array.

The mnuViewArray_Click event procedure, which executes when you choose <u>V</u>iew, <u>A</u>rray from the program's menu, uses the LBound and UBound functions in a For...Next structure to output the contents of the array to the output form. Here is that procedure:

```
Sub mnuViewArray_Click ()
    frmArrayOutput.Show
    frmArrayOutput.Cls
    frmArrayOutput.Print "LastName()", "FirstName()", "Index"
    frmArrayOutput.Print "----------", "----------", "----------"
    'Start at the lower bound and end at the upper bound
    For x = LBound(LastName) To UBound(LastName)
        frmArrayOutput.Print Firstname(x), LastName(x), x
    Next x
End Sub
```

The LBound function sets the start value of the For...Next counter and the UBound function sets the ending value for the For...Next counter.

In the next exercise you'll add some code to the program to enable the user to select a name from the array by clicking on the scroll bar. A potential problem, however, is that the scroll bar's Max property could exceed the size of the array. If the user tries to select past the end of the array, a "Subscript out of range" error will occur. Therefore, we need to set the Max property of the scroll bar equal to the UBound (highest index) value of the array.

Fixing the Scroll Bar

1. Continue working with PEOPLE1.MAK.

2. Open the Code window for the cmdAdd_Click event procedure and insert a statement as follows (the new statement to be inserted is shown in bold):

   ```
   FirstName(indexCounter) = txtFirstName
   vsbArrayIndex.Max = UBound(FirstName)
   vsbArrayIndex = indexCounter
   ```

3. Open the Code window for the vsbArrayIndex_Change event procedure and modify the procedure to read as follows:

```
Sub vsbArrayIndex_Change ()
     txtLastName = LastName(vsbArrayIndex)
     txtFirstName = FirstName(vsbArrayIndex)
     lblCurrentIndex = vsbArrayIndex
End Sub
```

4. Save the project, and run the program.

5. Enter four names in the array. Notice that the scroll bar moves to its bottom-most position after each name is entered.

6. Click the scroll bar up and down to choose names from the array. The data shown in the txtFirstName and txtLastName text boxes will change accordingly (see fig. 13.5).

7. End the program.

Figure 13.5

The scroll bar can be used to select a name from the array.

In this example, the UBound function makes it possible to set the Max property of the scroll bar to match the upper bound of the array. This prevents the user from attempting to select an element of the array that doesn't exist, and it also provides a means for synchronizing the scroll bar with the array.

The UBound function will also prove useful in enabling you to make the array smaller. The next section explains how.

Making the Array Smaller

Making an array larger is easy, but what if your user wants to delete a name from the list? In that case, you need to make the array smaller, because it will contain one fewer element. To make an array smaller, use the ReDim statement, just as you do when making the array larger. The only difference is that making the array smaller will "cut off" the element(s) in the array that have an index number higher than the newly defined upper bound.

Therefore, you'll have to add some code to copy the last element of the array into the location where the "deleted" name resides, then reduce the size of the array by one element. You're still cutting off the last element, but it has been copied into the place of the name the user wants to delete. This changes the order of the names in the array, but it enables you to make the array smaller without losing the content of the last element.

How will the program "know" which element the user wants to erase? We're using the lblCurrentIndex label to display the current array element index value, so if the user clicks the **D**elete key, we'll just delete the currently displayed item. The procedure you're going to write performs the following steps:

1. Determine if the user is deleting the last item. If so, just redimension the array, reducing its size by 1. This will "cut off" the last element, effectively deleting it. Exit the procedure.

2. If the user is not deleting the last element, copy the last element in the array to the current element.

3. Redimension the array, reducing it by one element.

Add some code to the cmdDelete_Click event procedure to perform these steps.

Adding Delete Capability

1. Continue working with PEOPLE1.MAK.

2. Open the Code window and display the cmdDelete_Click event procedure. Modify the procedure to read as follows:

```
Sub cmdDelete_Click ()
        'If lblCurrentIndex is lower than upper bound, copy the last
        'element to the current element
        If lblCurrentIndex < UBound(LastName) Then
            FirstName(lblCurrentIndex) =
```

```
        FirstName(UBound(FirstName))
                LastName(lblCurrentIndex) = LastName(UBound(LastName))
            End If
            'Redimension the arrays
            ReDim Preserve LastName(UBound(LastName) - 1)
            ReDim Preserve FirstName(UBound(FirstName) - 1)
            'Reset the Max property of the scroll bar
            vsbArrayIndex.Max = UBound(LastName)
            'Refill the text boxes with the current name
            txtFirstName = FirstName(vsbArrayIndex)
            txtLastName = LastName(vsbArrayIndex)
          indexCounter = UBound(FirstName) + 1
        End Sub
```

3. Save the project and run the program.

4. Enter four or five names in the array.

5. Use the scroll bar to select the last name in the array; choose the **D**elete button. The last item will disappear from the display and will be replaced by the new last item (if 5 is the last item, 4 is displayed). The index counter label also will change.

6. Choose a name in the middle of the list (such as element 1 or 2), and choose **D**elete. The name will change to show the new element, but the index value will not change. The currently displayed name used to be the last element in the array.

7. End the program.

Although you now can delete an element from the array, the program really provides no means for sorting the names alphabetically. Later in this chapter you'll work with a completely different version of the People program, which will give you the ability to sort the names.

Controlling the Lower Bound of an Array

One final topic you should learn about arrays is how to control the lower bound. By default, the lower bound (lowest list element) of an array has the index number zero. If you prefer, you can use a lower bound of 1 instead of zero for an array by placing the following statement in the Declarations section of a module:

```
Option Base 1
```

This will cause arrays declared in the module to start at a lower bound of 1 instead of zero. This isn't the only way, however, to declare a variable with a lower bound of 1. You also can do it directly by using the To keyword:

```
Dim someHairyArray (1 to 25)
```

This statement creates an array named someHairyArray with a lower bound of 1. The first element in the array has an index property of 1, the second index is 2, and so on.

Declaring an array with a lower bound of 1 can sometimes make it easier to access elements in the array by eliminating the need to subtract 1 in your calculations to access the correct element. If nothing else, it's easier to remember that element 1 in the array has the index 1 instead of the index zero.

 NOTE You can't change the lower bound of an array when you redimension the array. You can only change the upper bound.

Working with the Clipboard

As you start writing programs that handle larger amounts of data, it's likely that you will want to add the ability to cut and paste data to and from the Clipboard. Like almost everything else in Visual Basic, using the Clipboard is easy. Before you start using it, however, you need to understand Clipboard *formats*. Table 13.1 lists the data formats supported by Visual Basic for the Clipboard object.

Table 13.1
Clipboard Formats Supported by Visual Basic

Constant	Value	Description
CF_LINK	&HBF00	DDE conversation information
CF_TEXT	1	Text
CF_BITMAP	2	Bitmap (BMP files)

Constant	Value	Description
CF_METAFILE	3	Metafile (WMF files)
CF_DIB	8	Device-independent bitmap
CF_PALETTE	9	Color palette

NOTE The constants shown in table 13.1 are defined in the file CONSTANT.TXT that is included with Visual Basic. You can paste these constants into the Declarations section of a module in your program and use the constant rather than the value.

Clipboard formats are predefined data formats for text, graphics, and DDE (Dynamic Data Exchange) data. If you are working with a program such as Notepad and copy text to the Clipboard, for example, it is copied to the Clipboard in CF_TEXT format (format 1). If you are working with a graphics program like Paintbrush, the data is copied in one or more of the four graphics formats.

The Clipboard object has no properties or events, but it supports six methods, which are listed next:

- **Clear.** This method clears the Clipboard object, removing all data currently on the Clipboard.
- **GetData.** This method retrieves a picture from the Clipboard. If the picture is present on the Clipboard in more than one format, you can specify which format to retrieve.
- **GetFormat.** This method returns an integer indicating if a requested data format is available on the Clipboard object.
- **GetText.** This method returns a text string from the Clipboard.
- **SetData.** This method places a picture on the Clipboard object.
- **SetText.** This method places text on the Clipboard object.

The procedure for placing data on the Clipboard is relatively simple. If you want to place text on the Clipboard object, use the SetText method. If you want to place graphics on the Clipboard object, use the SetData method. Here are two examples that copy data to the Clipboard:

```
Clipboard.SetText "I love fried earthworms in guacamole."
Clipboard.SetData Picture1.Picture
```

Are you ready to try some specific examples? Well, do it anyway.

Working with Text and the Clipboard

Do you remember the simple text editor you worked with in Chapter 11? Figure 13.6 shows its interface to help jog your sluggish memory. The Text Editor program (PRINT.MAK) includes an **E**dit menu, but none of the items in the **E**dit menu function. In this section of the chapter, you'll add some code to the project to enable the user to cut, copy, and paste text to and from the Clipboard.

Figure 13.6

The text editor interface from Chapter 11.

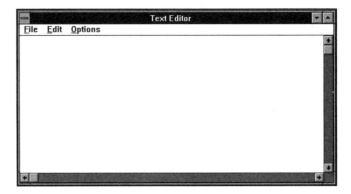

First, add the ability to select all of the text in the document. This will require only three statements.

Adding a Select All Feature

1. Open the project PRINT.MAK that you worked with in Chapter 11 (if you haven't worked through Chapter 11 yet, you can still use PRINT.MAK).

2. Open the Code window and display the mnuEditSelectAll_Click event procedure. Modify the procedure to read as follows:

```
Sub mnuEditSelectAll_Click ()
    Text1.SetFocus
    Text1.SelStart = 0
    Text1.SelLength = Len(Text1.Text)
End Sub
```

3. Save the project and run the program.

4. Choose File, Open, and select any text file.

5. Choose Edit, Select All. All of the text in the text box will be selected and highlighted.

6. End the program.

The first statement in the procedure sets focus to the Text1 control in case the user has just opened the file and has not yet clicked in the text box to locate the insertion point. The second statement sets the beginning of the text selection to 0, which places it at the beginning of the text box. The third statement selects all of the text in the text box by setting the end of the selection to the number of characters in the text box.

That was easy enough. Now, add a few statements to copy the current text selection to the Clipboard when the user chooses the Copy item in the Edit menu. Next, add a statement to the mnuEditPaste_Click event procedure to paste the contents of the Clipboard into the text box when the user chooses the Paste item from the Edit menu.

Enabling the Copy and Paste Items

1. Continue working with PRINT.MAK.

2. Open the Code window and display the mnuEditCopy_Click event procedure. Modify the procedure to read as follows:

```
Sub mnuEditCopy_Click ()
    Clipboard.Clear
    Clipboard.SetText Text1.SelText
End Sub
```

3. Display the mnuEditPaste_Click event procedure and modify the procedure to read as follows:

continues

```
Sub mnuEditPaste_Click ()
    Text1.SelText = Clipboard.GetText()
End Sub
```

4. Save the project and run the program.

5. Choose **F**ile, **O**pen and open a text file.

6. Select some of the text and choose **E**dit, **C**opy to copy the text to the Clipboard.

7. Choose **F**ile, **N**ew to clear the contents of the text box.

8. Choose **E**dit, **P**aste to paste the text from the Clipboard to the text box.

9. End the program.

Let's take a look at the mnuEditCopy_Click event procedure. Here is its code:

```
Sub mnuEditCopy_Click ()
    Clipboard.Clear
    Clipboard.SetText Text1.SelText
End Sub
```

The first statement clears the contents of the Clipboard. The second statement uses the SetText method to place the currently selected text (defined by Text1.SelText) on the Clipboard object. The SelText property of the text box returns the selected text. If no text is selected, SelText returns an empty string.

The mnuEditPaste_Click event might be a little confusing to you. Here is its code:

```
Sub mnuEditPaste_Click ()
    Text1.SelText = Clipboard.GetText()
End Sub
```

Why does this move the text from the Clipboard to the text box? It works like this because of the way the SelText property is designed to work. Setting SelText to a new value sets the SelLength property to zero and replaces the selected text (if any) with the new string. In this example, setting the SelText property of the text box replaces the current selection with the contents of the Clipboard. If no text is selected when you choose **P**aste, the text is simply inserted into the text box. If text is selected when you choose **P**aste, the text from the Clipboard replaces the selected text.

Your editing functions are almost complete. You only need to get the Cut menu item working. The procedure you create will be almost identical to the one that copies text to the Clipboard. The only difference is that the procedure will also set the SelText property to an empty string. This will replace the selected text with an empty string.

Programming the Cut Function

1. Continue working with PRINT.MAK.

2. Display the mnuEditCut_Click event procedure and modify the procedure to read as follows:

```
Sub mnuEditCut_Click ()
    Clipboard.Clear
    Clipboard.SetText Text1.SelText
    Text1.SelText = ""
End Sub
```

3. Save the project and run the program.

4. Open a text file or type some text in the text box.

5. Select some of the text and choose Edit, Cut. The text will be removed from the text box.

6. Choose Edit, Paste. The text will be inserted into the text box.

7. End the program.

TIP Although you can specify a format of 1 with the GetText method, there is no need to do so in a Visual Basic program when retrieving text from the Clipboard because Visual Basic will automatically use format 1 (CF_TEXT).

There is just one more small addition you should make to your program to polish it up. When you click on the Edit menu, the program should check the contents of the Clipboard. If there is text on the Clipboard, the Paste menu item should be enabled. If there is no text on the Clipboard, the Paste item should be disabled. Also, the <u>C</u>opy and Cu<u>t</u> menu items in the <u>E</u>dit menu should be enabled only if some text is selected. If you want to polish the program in this way, add the following code to the program:

```
Sub mnuEdit_Click ()
    mnuEditPaste.Enabled = Clipboard.GetFormat(1)
    If Text1.SelText <> "" Then
        mnuEditCopy.Enabled = True
        mnuEditCut.Enabled = True
    Else
        mnuEditCopy.Enabled = False
        mnuEditCut.Enabled = False
    End If
End Sub
```

The first statement needs a little explanation. Rather than use an If...Then structure to test for the presence of text on the Clipboard and enable or disable the mnuEditPaste menu item accordingly, the statement simply sets the Enabled property of the mnuEditPaste item to the result of the GetFormat method. If there is text on the Clipboard, the Clipboard.GetFormat(1) returns True, setting the Enabled property of the menu item to True. If there is no text on the Clipboard, Clipboard.GetFormat(1) returns False, setting the Enabled property of the menu item to False.

The If...Then structure in the procedure tests the SelText property of the text box to determine if any text is selected. It then sets the Enabled property of the <u>C</u>opy and Cu<u>t</u> menu items accordingly.

That's all there is to moving text to and from the Clipboard in a Visual Basic program. Working with graphics is just as easy.

Working with Graphics and the Clipboard

Unless you're writing a program that lets you cut out just a portion of an image and put it on the Clipboard, copying and pasting graphics is even easier than copying and pasting text. Working with just a portion of an image requires a completely different mechanism for loading the file and maintaining it in memory, and goes beyond the scope of this book. So, we'll concentrate on working with entire images.

To copy an image to the Clipboard, use the SetData method. To paste data from the Clipboard, use the GetData method. The important point to understand when performing either action is that the graphics data might be available on the Clipboard in more than one format, or you might be able to place the data on the Clipboard in more than one format. If you are pasting a bit map from the Clipboard, it might be available in BMP and DIB formats.

If your program displays metafiles or bit maps in a picture box, you can place on the Clipboard the bit map or metafile displayed in the picture box. If the picture box displays an icon, however, you can't place the icon on the Clipboard because the Clipboard doesn't support the icon format. How do you determine which type of data is in the picture box? Unfortunately, there's no way to determine the format of the image in the picture box, but you can simply paste the data in multiple formats, using a "shotgun" approach to placing the data on the Clipboard. Here's some sample code that does that:

```
'Clear the contents of the Clipboard
Clipboard.Clear
'If an error occurs, continue with the next statement
On Error Resume Next
'Place the data on the Clipboard using each of the four
'graphics formats
Clipboard.SetData frmViewer.Picture, 2
Clipboard.SetData frmViewer.Picture, 3
Clipboard.SetData frmViewer.Picture, 8
Clipboard.SetData frmViewer.Picture, 9
```

If there is a picture in the picture box, these statements will place the picture on the Clipboard in as many formats as possible. The project file CLIPBORD.MAK uses this method to place the contents of a picture box on the Clipboard. CLIPBORD.MAK also enables you to paste the data from the Clipboard to a picture box. Here's the code that performs that task:

```
frmViewer.Picture = Clipboard.GetData()
```

Notice that the program doesn't specify a particular format with the GetData method. If you don't specify a format with the GetData method, GetData automatically chooses an appropriate format. If you want to paste the data from the Clipboard to the picture box in a specific format, you can check the Clipboard to determine if it contains the format you want by using the GetFormat method. GetFormat returns True if the format is available on the

Clipboard or False if the format isn't available. Here's a bit of code that pastes a metafile image from the Clipboard to a picture box only if the CF_METAFILE format (format 3) is available:

```
If Clipboard.GetData(3) Then
    Picture1.Picture = Clipboard.GetData(3)
Else
    MsgBox "Sorry, Charlie! Metafile format isn't available."
End If
```

Examine CLIPBORD.MAK on your own if you want to experiment more with graphics and the Clipboard.

Creating a Data Structure

Arrays offer a good mechanism for handling large amounts of the same type of data (such as a list of strings, or a list of integers). Arrays are limited, however, because you can store only one type of data in an array, regardless of the size of the array. You can use multiple arrays to maintain different types of data or multiple variables as you did in the PEOPLE1.MAK project to store the last name and first name of each entry in your address book. Using multiple arrays can be cumbersome, however, and can require a lot of extra programming. In many cases, a *data structure* is a much more efficient way to store data.

A data structure, also called a user-defined type, enables you to store different types of data or multiple elements of the same type of data in a single variable name. In the PEOPLE1.MAK project, wouldn't it be great if we could create a variable named *person* to keep track of the last name, first name, phone, address, and other information for each person? With a user-defined data type, you can do just that.

Creating a User-Defined Data Type

You create a user-defined data with the Type statement in the Declarations section of a code module (data types are always global). The Type statement contains multiple declaration statements that define the data to be stored in the data type. Following is an example you could have used with the PEOPLE1.MAK project to store all of the data in an address book entry in a single variable. This code would be placed in the Declarations section of a code module:

```
Type Person
      LastName As String
      FirstName As String
      Address1 As String
      Address2 As String
      City As String
      State As String
      Zip As Long
      Phone As Long
End Type
```

TIP You can use any combination of standard variable types in a Type declaration. You can even include a fixed-size array in a data type (but not a dynamic array).

After you have declared the type, you also can create an array using the type. The following statement creates a dynamic array named People that uses the Person data type as its variable type:

```
Dim People As Person
```

I bet you're now wondering how in the world you access elements in the data type. Okay, I'll tell you.

Using the Data Type

After you've declared a data type, what good is it? It isn't any good at all until you put some data in it. You access the elements in a data type in much the same way you access the properties of an object. Using the previous data type example, you could store a name from a text box in the LastName variable in a data type named Person using the following statement:

```
Person.LastName = Text1.Text
```

If you've created an array of this special data structure, you can access it in much the same way you access the elements of an array. Using the People array from the previous example, here is the code you would use to access the third person in the list:

```
People(2).LastName = Text1.Text
```

Now we have a data type that we can use to store all of the information associated with an address book entry in a single variable named *Person*. And, we've created an array called *People* to store lots of *Person* elements.

The PEOPLE2.MAK project included on the *Understanding Visual Basic Disk* uses a data type just like the one in the previous example to store information in an address book. PEOPLE2.MAK declares a data type named Person in the Declarations section of PEOPLE.BAS and dimensions a dynamic array called People as follows:

```
Type Person
      LastName As String
      FirstName As String
      Address1 As String
      Address2 As String
      City As String
      State As String
      Zip As String
      Phone As String
End Type
Global People() As Person
```

Here's the procedure that stores a new entry in the array:

```
Sub cmdAdd_Click ()
      If txtLastName = "" Then
            MsgBox "Please enter a last name."
            Exit Sub
      Else
            ReDim Preserve People(indexCounter)
            People(indexCounter).LastName = txtLastName
            People(indexCounter).FirstName = txtFirstName
            People(indexCounter).Address1 = txtAddress1
            People(indexCounter).Address2 = txtAddress2
            People(indexCounter).City = txtCity
            People(indexCounter).State = txtState
            People(indexCounter).Zip = txtZip
            People(indexCounter).Phone = txtPhone
            vsbArrayIndex.Max = UBound(People)
            vsbArrayIndex = indexCounter
            lblCurrentIndex = vsbArrayIndex
```

```
                indexCounter = indexCounter + 1
                txtLastName.SetFocus
            End If
    End Sub
```

You can see that this procedure is very similar to the procedure in the PEOPLE1.MAK project. The only real difference is that instead of storing each item in a separate array, all of the data is stored in an array of Person data types called People. Instead of having to search through lots of different arrays to find all of the information for a single person, you can reference one data type element in a single array.

As you've probably been grumbling about for the last half of this chapter, this address book program is not very useful because it doesn't store the names permanently. What good is an address book if you have to fill it out every time you want to use it? The solution is to store the address book in a file. That's what you'll learn in Chapter 14.

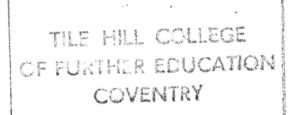

CHAPTER 14

Creating Your Own Files

A lot of utility programs don't need to store information in files. Other programs, however, are basically useless without the ability to store data in files. The address book program in Chapter 13, for example, needs the added capability to store the addresses in a file. Would you pay $29.95 for an address book you had to fill out each time you wanted to use it? I think not (unless, of course, you're still interested in that marsh... I mean, beachfront property I have for sale).

This chapter explains the types of file access you can use in a Visual Basic program. The chapter covers the following topics:

- Understanding files (just a little bit)
- Random access
- Sequential access
- Binary access
- Storing data in various types of files

About Files and File Access

A file is just a series of related bytes on a disk. When you add the ability to read and write files to a program, you're really just adding the ability for the program to open a file and either store or retrieve those bytes. The way your program stores or retrieves that information depends on the type of information being read from the file or stored in it. The three types of file access you can use in a Visual Basic program are *random* access, *sequential* access, and *binary* access.

Random Access

Use random access when you want to work with files that contain a series of records of identical length. Each record in the file might contain a single string or number, or it might contain a data type, but each record must be the same total number of bytes. Figure 14.1 shows an example of the first few bytes in a file. The data was stored using a user-defined data type called *Person*, which is declared as follows:

```
Type Person
    LastName As String * 10
    FirstName As String * 10
End Type
```

Figure 14.1

A file opened for random access.

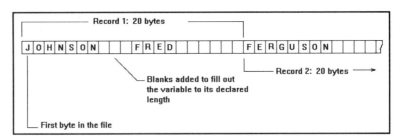

The important point to understand is that a file opened for random access must contain records that all have the same length.

Sequential Access

Sequential access is used mainly to read and write text files. Visual Basic expects each character in a file that is opened for sequential access to be either an alphanumeric text character like 4 or Z, or a formatting character like a tab. Sequential access makes it very easy to write procedures that read and write text files. You can open a text file, for example, and copy its entire contents into a text box with a single statement.

Binary Access

Binary access is the most flexible of all the three file-access methods. You can store information in a file in any format you want using binary access. You can store records of different lengths in the file, which can make the file size smaller than it might otherwise be if you used random access. Figure 14.2 shows the first part of a file containing data that was stored using binary access.

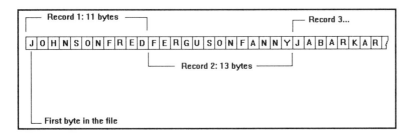

Figure 14.2

Records of different lengths in a file created using binary access.

If you take a moment to gander and gawk at figure 14.2, you'll probably realize that you're going to have a problem telling one record from another. Why? The problem is that because the records can be any length, you have no sure way of knowing where one record stops and another record begins. The only solution is to add some additional information to the file to separate one variable from the next, and to separate one record from the next. Figure 14.2 doesn't show this additional information. You'll learn how to add it to the file later in this chapter.

Choosing the Type of File To Use

If you're working with text files, sequential access probably is your best choice for reading and storing information in the files. You can write very simple procedures that read and write the contents of a text file. Sequential access does have a couple of disadvantages, however. If you're mainly storing long series of numbers, sequential access will waste storage space. Storing a four-digit number as a string requires four bytes, for example, but storing it as an integer requires only two bytes. Using random or binary access, you can store the number as an integer. Using sequential access, however, you can only store it as a string.

Sequential access also is generally a poor choice if you want to access the file at any point other than at the beginning of the file. Sequential access is great for starting at the beginning of the file and working straight through to the end, but is cumbersome when you want to start at a specific point in the file.

If you are working with types of data other than text, such as data types or numbers, random and binary access are much better alternatives. If you want to simplify the procedures you write for file access at the expense of disk space, use random access. If the records you are working with are not very large (in bytes), or they are all fairly close to the same size, the little bit of storage space wasted through random access will usually be unimportant.

If the data types contain strings or other variables that can vary by large amounts, however, you should use binary access to optimize disk space. You'll learn more about binary access later in the chapter.

Are you ready to start working with files? Pull that thumb out of your mouth and get with it!

Using Sequential Access

Sequential access is primarily used for reading and writing text files, so we'll use a text editor as the sample project for learning about sequential access. Do you remember the PRINT.MAK project from Chapter 11? This chapter uses a similar project named USEFILES.MAK to teach you about using sequential file access. Figure 14.3 shows the interface for USEFILES.MAK, which already contains the code necessary to open a text file and place the contents of the file in a text box. You'll learn in this section of the chapter how USEFILES.MAK does that, and you'll also add some code to the project to enable you to save the contents of a text box to a file.

First, you need to understand how to open a file for sequential access.

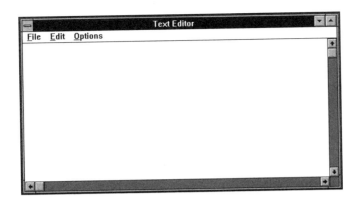

Figure 14.3
The interface for the USEFILES.MAK project's startup form.

Opening and Reading a File

Before you can read a file or write to it, you must *open* the file. The Open statement enables you to open a file for sequential, random, or binary access. I know you're salivating to find out what the syntax is for the Open statement, so here it is:

```
Open file For mode As #filenumber Len = bufferSize
```

Are you happy now? I thought not. You need some explanation of what the parameters in the statement are for. There are a lot of them, so I'll thoughtfully place them in a neat little list for you:

- *file.* This parameter specifies the file name. You can use a literal string or a variable that contains a valid file name.

- *mode.* This parameter specifies the file access method to be used. You can specify Input, Output, and Append when opening a file for sequential access.

- *filenumber.* This parameter specifies an integer between 1 and 255 that is used to identify the file while the file is open. Think of this parameter as a "handle" you use to identify the file in other I/O operations (such as later writing to the file).

bufferSize. This parameter specifies the number of characters to be buffered before the contents of the buffer are read from or written to the disk. The default buffer size is 512 KB. Using a larger buffer requires more memory but speeds file access. Using a smaller buffer requires less memory but slows file access.

Here's an explanation of the three *mode* keywords that you can use with the Open statement when you are opening a file for sequential access:

Input. This operation enables you to read from the file.

Output. This operation enables you to write to the file.

Append. This operation enables you to append data to the end of the file.

If you're opening the file to read it, use the Input keyword. You need an example, and here it is:

```
Open "DEAD.DUK" for Input As #1
```

This example opens a file called DEAD.DUK for input and assigns the integer 1 as the file handle. After you have opened the file, you can begin reading characters or lines of text from it.

You can use the *filenumber* handle with other statements that perform I/O actions on the file. When it's time to close the file, for example, you would use the following statement:

```
Close #1
```

Also, if you issue the open statement and the file doesn't exist, an error will occur.

Let's take a look at the USEFILES.MAK project to see how it opens a file. USEFILES.MAK contains a multi-line text box that you can use to edit a text file or create your own text file. Take a look at USEFILES.MAK's OpenFile procedure.

Opening an Existing File for Sequential Access

1. Open the project USEFILES.MAK included on the *Understanding Visual Basic Disk* (the same USEFILES.MAK project you worked with in Chapter 11).

2. Open the Project window and choose Form1; choose the View Code button to open the Code window.

3. In the Code window, choose mnuFileOpen from the Object drop-down list. The mnuFileOpen_Click procedure, which executes when the user chooses **O**pen from the **F**ile menu, appears in the Code window. Most of the code in the procedure is used to display the Open common file dialog box and retrieve a file name, which is stored in the variable *fileToOpen*. The following statement then passes the file name to another procedure, which actually opens the file:

   ```
   OpenFile (fileToOpen)
   ```

4. In the Project window, choose the file USEFILES.BAS, and choose the View Code button.

5. In the Code window, choose general from the Object drop-down list, and choose OpenFile from the Proc drop-down list. Search for the following statement:

   ```
   Open fileToOpen For Input As #1
   ```

Only three of the statements in the OpenFile procedure actually deal with opening, reading, and closing the file. The statement shown in step 5 of this exercise is the one that opens the file. The file, which is specified by the variable *fileToOpen*, is opened for input. The file handle is #1, and this handle will be used in later statements to read from the file and to close it.

Reading from a File with Sequential Access

Now that you have the file open, how do you read it and store its contents in the Text1 control? How does Input$ sound? The Input$ function returns a specified number of characters (bytes) read from a file. Here is the syntax of the Input$ statement:

```
Input$(bytes, #filenumber)
```

The *bytes* parameter specifies the number of bytes to be read from the file, and the *filenumber* parameter is the handle previously specified in the `Open` statement when the file was opened. Take a look at how the OpenFile procedure in the USEFILES.MAK project opens the file and inputs all of the file to the text box.

Reading a Text File Into a Text Box

1. Continue working with the USEFILES.MAK project.

2. Open the Code window for USEFILES.BAS, choose General from the Object drop-down list, and choose OpenFile from the Proc drop-down list to display the OpenFile procedure.

3. Search through the OpenFile procedure for the following statement:

```
Form1.Text1 = Input$(LOF(1), 1)
```

The statement uses the `LOF` function to determine the length of the file in bytes. Both instances of the number 1 in the statement are the file's handle. So, `LOF(1)` returns the length of file 1 in bytes. The `Input$` function then inputs that many bytes (the entire file) from the file and stores them in Text1.

Later in this chapter you'll learn how to read only portions of a file. Next, learn how to save the changes you've made in your letter to crazy-but-rich Aunt Gertrude.

Saving the Changes

In this example, we're using a text box as the editor. Therefore, changing the contents of the file really involves just loading the entire file into the text box, changing the contents of the text box, and saving the contents of the text box to the same file. Because we've already loaded the file, changing the text is easy—just click in the text box and start editing to your heart's content. Tell Aunt Gertrude how lovely she is. Tell her you would love to take care of her in her golden years and that you would exercise her power of attorney with the utmost discretion.

Saving the contents of the file is a little more difficult than buttering up your crazy aunt, however, but not very much so. All you have to do is use the `Print #` statement.

Using the Print # Statement

The `Print #` statement writes data to a sequential file (a file that you have opened for sequential access). The basic syntax of the statement is as follows:

```
Print # filenumber, expressionlist
```

The *filenumber* parameter is that familiar file handle of which you've grown so fond. The *expressionlist* parameter specifies the data that will be written to the file. To print a string to a file opened as # 4, for example, you can use the following statement:

```
Print # 4, "I am definitely not wearing my underwear."
```

In addition to printing a literal string to the file, you also can print the contents of a variable or data type to the file.

The USEFILES.MAK project doesn't have any code to save the contents of the text file, so it's up to you to add it. Start by adding a general SaveFile procedure. Then add a statement in the mnuFileSaveAs procedure to enable the user to save the contents of the text box to a file.

Saving a Sequential File

1. Continue working with USEFILES.MAK.

2. Choose USEFILES.BAS from the Project window, and choose the View Code button to display the Code window.

3. Choose **V**iew, **N**ew Procedure to open the New Procedure dialog box.

4. In the New Procedure dialog box, select the **S**ub option button, type **SaveFile** in the **N**ame edit box, and choose OK. This creates a new procedure called SaveFile.

5. Modify the SaveFile procedure to read as follows:

```
Sub SaveFile (fileToSave)
    On Error GoTo NoFileSave
    Open fileToSave For Output As #2
```

continues

```
        Print #2, Form1!Text1.Text
        Close #2
        Exit Sub

    NoFileSave:
        MsgBox "Can't save the file"
        Exit Sub
    End Sub
```

6. In the Project window, choose Form1, then choose the View Code button to open the Code window for Form1.

7. From the Object drop-down list, choose mnuFileSaveAs to open the Code window for the mnuFileSaveAs_Click procedure.

8. Add the following statement to the end of the procedure. An existing statement has been included next to help you place the new statement in the correct location, and the new statement is shown in bold:

```
        If fileToSave = "" Then Exit Sub
        SaveFile (fileToSave)
    End Sub
```

9. Save the project, and run the program.

10. Type some text in the text box, and choose File, Save As.

11. In the Save As dialog box, enter a new file name to be used to save the file, and choose OK. This saves the file.

12. Choose File, Open and search for the new file you just created. Cancel the dialog box after you have verified that the new file exists.

13. End the program.

The SaveFile procedure has three statements that open the file, output the text to the file, and close the file. Here are those three statements:

```
    Open fileToSave For Output As #2
    Print #2, Form1!Text1.Text
    Close #2
```

The Open statement actually creates the file. If you open a file using Output or Append modes, and the file doesn't exist, a new file is created and then opened. If the file already exists, it is opened. If you open a file using Input mode and the file doesn't exist, an error occurs instead.

The `Print #` statement is the one that actually places the text in the file. In this example, the statement prints all of the contents of the text box to the file.

After you open a file, always close it. Failing to do so could result in the loss of the file. Even if you are not through with the file, you can close it and open it again later when you need to access it again.

The mnuFileSaveAs_Click event procedure contains a few statements that you should examine a little more closely. Here is the first one:

```
CMDialog1.DefaultExt = "TXT"
```

This statement sets the DefaultExt property of the common dialog control to TXT. By setting this property, you force the file to assume the TXT extension if the user omits a file extension in the Save As dialog box. If the user includes a different file extension, the user's file extension is used instead of the default file extension.

The other statement in the mnuFileSaveAs_Click event procedure that you should examine is the following:

```
SaveFile (fileToSave)
```

This statement passes to the SaveFile function the file name that was returned by the Save As dialog box. The SaveFile function then uses this file name to store the file.

That's really all there is to reading and saving text files. If you want to read or write just a portion of a file, however, you have to use a somewhat different method.

Writing and Reading Strings

In addition to reading an entire text file in one operation, you also can read only a certain number of bytes or a certain number of lines. If you find that you need to read only a specific number of bytes, just specify the number of bytes in the `Input$` statement. The following is an example that reads 512 bytes from a file:

```
Open "LINGERIE.TXT" For Input As #3
Input$ (512, 3)
Close #3
```

If you want to read the file one line at a time, you can do so with the `Line Input #` statement. This statement reads from the file until it detects a newline character, which consists of the carriage return character (`Chr(13)`) and the linefeed character (`Chr(10)`). Note, however, that the `Line Input #` statement doesn't include the newline character in the string. If you want to retain the newline character, you need to concatenate one to the string after you read it. Here is a fragment of a procedure that reads a text file one line at a time and stores each line as an element in an array:

```
Dim lineFromFile As String
ReDim lineArray(0) As String
IsFirstLine = 1
Show
Open "PLATYPUS.TXT" For Input As #1
Do Until EOF(1)
    Line Input #1, lineFromFile
    If IsFirstLine Then
        lineArray(0) = lineFromFile
        IsFirstLine = 0
    Else
        ReDim Preserve lineArray(UBound(lineArray) + 1)
        lineArray(UBound(lineArray)) = lineFromFile
    End If
Loop
```

This little procedure uses the `EOF()` function in a Do...Loop structure to keep reading lines from the file until the end of file mark is encountered.

Using Random Access

Sequential access is great for text files, but isn't very good for reading and writing other types of files, such as files in which you are storing a record from a data type. Random access, however, is great for reading and writing files that contain multiple records. Do you recall the address book program from Chapter 13? You'll use random access in following exercises to add the capability of storing and reading address records in a file.

Setting Up

The project you'll use for the following exercises is PEOPLE3.MAK. Unlike the address book project you used in earlier chapters, PEOPLE3.MAK is nearly complete. All it needs is for you to add file capabilities to it.

Figure 14.4 shows the interface for the PEOPLE3.MAK address book. Unlike the previous address book projects, this one stores the last name and first name of each entry in a list box. You can select a name from the list box to view the address of the selected person. As with the previous address book projects, the addresses are stored in an array of data types.

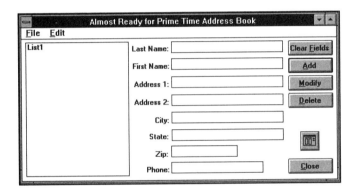

Figure 14.4

The interface for the address book program.

Most of the code in the PEOPLE3.MAK project builds on topics you've learned in previous chapters. Before you start adding file procedures to the project, however, you should have a basic understanding of how the data array and the list box are synchronized. Keeping track of an array with a list box is a useful technique, and you might need to use the same technique in one of your own programs. First, let's take a look at the data type you'll be using.

Defining a Record

The data type you'll be using in PEOPLE3.MAK is very similar to the one used in the PEOPLE2.MAK project. The only difference is that this data type uses fixed-length variables. The LastName variable, for example, is fixed at 20 characters. The FirstName variable is fixed at 15 characters. In the following exercise, have a look at the type declaration that defines the data type you'll be using to store each address.

Defining the Data Type and Array

1. Open the project PEOPLE3.MAK that is included on your *Understanding Visual Basic Disk*.

2. In the Project window, choose PEOPLE3.BAS, and choose the View Code button to display the Code window. You should see the Declarations section of the module.

3. Examine the Type declaration statement. Here's a copy of it:

```
Type Person
      LastName As String * 20
      FirstName As String * 15
      Address1 As String * 20
      Address2 As String * 20
      City As String * 15
      State As String * 15
      Zip As String * 10
      Phone As String * 12
      Deleted As Integer
   End Type
```

Notice that each of the string variables in the type are a fixed length, creating a fixed-length record. (The integer requires two bytes of storage space.)

4. Search for the following statement in the Declarations section of the module:

```
Global People() As Person
```

This statement creates a global dynamic array called *People*, which will contain *Person* record elements.

If you have completed Chapter 13, none of this should be new to you. As the user adds a new address, the address is stored in the array, just as it was in the PEOPLE2.MAK project. The only differences are that the strings are of a fixed length, and the data type contains an additional integer variable called *Deleted*, which will be used to keep track of whether a record has been deleted or not. When the user selects a name from the list box and then chooses the **D**elete button, the Deleted variable in the selected array element is set to 1 to indicate that the record has been deleted.

Why are all of the variables in the data type a fixed length? Random access requires that each record in the file be of the same length. By creating a data type using fixed-length variables, each record will require the same number of bytes as every other record in the file. In this example, each Person data record is 134 bytes long. To verify that, add up the numbers for each string (each character requires one byte of storage space), then add two bytes for the integer. You should get a result of 134 bytes.

Synchronizing the Array and List Box

The List1 list box in PEOPLE3.MAK has its Sorted property set to True so it will display the names in alphabetical order. As each new address is added to the array, the last name and first name also are added to the list box using the AddItem method. The first element in the array and the first item in the list box both have the index value 0. If the list box was not sorted, it would be an easy matter to synchronize the array and the list box—their index numbers would match.

Unfortunately, the index numbers don't match when you sort the list box. Also, deleting an address record from the array requires that you delete the associated name from the list box. Because we are simply setting the Deleted flag to true in the record and not actually removing the record from the array, this means that the array can and will have more elements in it than the list box. This further prevents you from synchronizing the list box and the array using their index numbers.

Fortunately, there is another way to synchronize them. Each element in the list box has an ItemData property. Each element in the list box can have a different value for ItemData. Even though the index number for each element in the list box won't match the index number of a corresponding address in the array, you can set the ItemData property of a list box element to match the index number of its corresponding address entry in the array.

When the user adds an address record, the program checks the upper bound of the People array and sets the variable *theIndex* to a value of one number higher than the upper bound of the array. If the upper bound is 6, for example, the program sets *theIndex* to 7. The program adds the new record to the array, then calls the AddRecord function and passes it the variable *theIndex*. Here is the AddRecord function, with comments:

```
Sub AddRecord (theIndex As Integer)
     'Add an item to List1 consisting of the
     'last name and first name
     frmPeople!List1.AddItem People(theIndex).LastName & ", "
     ➡& People(theIndex).FirstName
     'Set the ItemData property of the new list box element to
     'match the index number of the array
     frmPeople!List1.ItemData(frmPeople!List1.NewIndex) = theIndex
     'Clear the text box fields
     ClearFields
     'Set focus to the txtLastName edit box
     frmPeople!txtLastName.SetFocus
End Sub
```

This AddRecord procedure places the last name and first name of the new
address entry in the list box, then sets the ItemData of the new list box item
to match the index of the address entry in the array.

I know this could be confusing to you. Bear with me. You now know that
each element in the list box has an ItemData property that has been set to
match the index number of the associated address in the array. What good is
that? It enables the user to select a name from the list box and have the
associated address displayed in the edit boxes. Here is the procedure that
executes when the user selects an item from the list box:

```
Sub List1_Click ()
     'If ListIndex = -1, no item is selected, so don't do anything.
     'If ListIndex <> -1, then an item is selected.
     If List1.ListIndex <> -1 Then
          'Set the array index variable equal to the ItemData
          'property of the selected list box item
          theIndex = List1.ItemData(List1.ListIndex)
          'Copy the data from the array to the edit boxes
          txtLastName = People(theIndex).LastName
          txtFirstName = People(theIndex).FirstName
          txtAddress1 = People(theIndex).Address1
          txtAddress2 = People(theIndex).Address2
          txtCity = People(theIndex).City
          txtState = People(theIndex).State
          txtZip = People(theIndex).Zip
          txtPhone = People(theIndex).Phone
```

```
                cmdDelete.Enabled = True
                cmdModify.Enabled = True
            End If
    End Sub
```

This procedure reads the ItemData property of the selected list box item, then uses the value of that ItemData property to read information from the associated address entry in the array.

The important point for you to understand is that even though a name might not appear in the list box, its deleted record may still exist in the array. This point will become even more important when you start creating the procedures to read and write the array to a file.

I'm glad we got that out of the way. Now we can move on to some file stuff. The *Understanding Visual Basic Disk* includes a sample address file. In the following section you'll learn how to create a procedure to read the file and copy its contents into the array.

Opening and Reading the File

As with sequential access, you open a file for random access by using the Open statement. To open a file for random access, you have to include the For Random keywords and also specify the record length. Here is the statement you will use in PEOPLE3.MAK to open the address data file:

```
    Open fileToOpen For Random As #1 Len = recordLen
```

The variable *fileToOpen* specifies the name of the file. This file name will be derived from the common Open dialog box. The *recordLen* variable specifies the length of each record in the file. You could simply specify 134 (the size of a record in the People array) instead of using a variable, but this method will help illustrate methods you can use to calculate the size of the file and the size of a record.

Here is a rundown of the steps you'll need to perform to open a file:

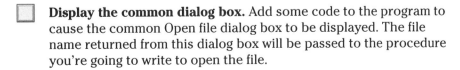   **Display the common dialog box.** Add some code to the program to cause the common Open file dialog box to be displayed. The file name returned from this dialog box will be passed to the procedure you're going to write to open the file.

☐ **Pass the file name to the FileOpen procedure.** You're going to create a new global procedure called FileOpen. The FileOpen procedure will open the file and input the data records into the array.

☐ **Close the file.** After you have input all of the records, you need to close the file.

The FileOpen procedure isn't very complex, but there are quite a few statements in it. Create the FileOpen procedure in the following exercise.

Creating the FileOpen Procedure

1. Continue working with the PEOPLE3.MAK project.

2. From the Project window, choose the PEOPLE3.BAS file, and choose the View Code button to display the Code window.

3. Choose **V**iew, **N**ew Procedure to display the New Procedure dialog box.

4. Choose the **S**ub option button, type **OpenFile** in the **N**ame edit box, and choose OK to create the FileOpen procedure.

5. Modify the OpenFile procedure to read as follows:

```
Sub OpenFile (fileToOpen As String)
     'Create a variable to store the length of a record
     Dim recordLen As Long
     'Redimension the array to 0 (one element)
     ReDim People(0)
     'Clear the variable that stores the name of the
     'currently opened file
     currentFile = ""
     'Set the error trap
     On Error GoTo noOpenFile
     'Clear the list box
     frmPeople!List1.Clear
     'Calculate the length of a record in the People array
     recordLen = Len(People(0))
     'Open the file
     Open fileToOpen For Random As #1 Len = recordLen
     'Calculate the number of records in the file
     numOfRecordsInFile = LOF(1) / recordLen
```

```
'Set the mouse pointer to an hourglass
Screen.MousePointer = 11
'Run through a loop that reads each record and adds each
'record to the array
For x = 1 To numOfRecordsInFile
        ReDim Preserve People(x - 1)
        'Resize the array to hold the new record
        Get #1, x, People(x - 1)
        'Retrieve record and store it in the array
        AddRecord (x - 1)
        'Add the item to the list box
Next x
'Close the file
Close #1
'Set the pointer back to its default
Screen.MousePointer = 0
'Store the name of the file for future reference
currentFile = fileToOpen
Exit Sub

noOpenFile:
    Close #1
    Screen.MousePointer = 0
    MsgBox "An error occurred opening the file.", 0, Str$(Err)
    ➥& ": " & Error$
    Exit Sub
End Sub
```

6. Choose the frmPeople form from the Project window, and choose the View Code button to display its Code window.

7. From the Object drop-down list, choose mnuFileOpen. Search through the mnuFileOpen procedure to locate the following line, and remove the apostrophe to change it from a comment to a statement (two additional lines are shown here for reference):

```
On Error GoTo NotOpenFile
'OpenFile (fileToOpen)        'Remove the apostrophe from this line
If Err GoTo NotOpenFile
```

8. Save the project.

Whew! That was a long one, but now you can open a data file. Before you start learning how the FileOpen procedure actually works, try out the program and see if it will open the bogus address file included on your *Understanding Visual Basic Disk.*

Testing the FileOpen Procedure

1. Run the program.

2. Choose **F**ile, **O**pen, and locate the file BOGUS.BOK that was included on your *Understanding Visual Basic Disk.*

3. Select the file, and choose OK. Address should appear in the list box (see fig. 14.5). Select names from the list box to view the associated addresses.

4. End the program.

Figure 14.5

The BOGUS.BOK address book.

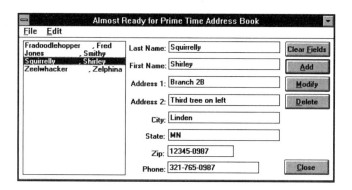

If you type all of the statements correctly in the FileOpen procedure, you should have just been treated to a look at a few strange addresses. Let's take a look at how the FileOpen procedure works.

Understanding the FileOpen Procedure

The first few statements in the FileOpen procedure set variables, dimension variables, redimension the array, set an error trap, and clear the list box:

```
Dim recordLen As Long
ReDim People(0)
currentFile = ""
On Error GoTo noOpenFile
frmPeople!List1.Clear
```

Why redimension the array and clear the list box? That's a good way of clearing out the array and reclaiming the memory it is using to store the current address book (assuming that one is open). The statements essentially prepare the program to accept a new data file.

The next statement calculates the length of a record in the array:

```
recordLen = Len(People(0))
```

The Len function in this example returns the length of a data record in the array. The array consists of only one record at this point because the procedure previously redimensioned it, so the statement uses People(0) as the "template" to calculate the record length. Even though the record is empty, the Len function still returns the total length of a record, which in this example is 134 bytes.

Why calculate the record length instead of specifying it explicitly? If you later change the data type, which will change the length of a record, you won't have to search through all of the code in your program to change all of the Open statements to use the new record size. Instead, the procedure will calculate the length of the record.

Next, the procedure opens the file using the following statement:

```
Open fileToOpen For Random As #1 Len = recordLen
```

You've already read about the Open statement. Notice that this statement includes the For Random keywords and specifies the record length using the *recordLen* variable that was calculated previously. The *fileToOpen* variable was passed to the procedure from the mnuFileOpen_Click procedure (which displayed the common Open file dialog box).

Next, the procedure calculates the numbers of records in the file by dividing the length of the file by the size of one record:

```
numOfRecordsInFile = LOF(1) / recordLen
```

Why do this? When the procedure reads the file, it needs some way to know how many records to read. You could instead use the EOF function in a Do...Loop structure to determine when the end of file is reached, but because we're using random access, we know that all of the records are the same length. By dividing the total number of bytes in the file by the number of bytes in one record, we get the total number of records in the file. The following For...Next structure uses the total number of records in the file to retrieve all of the records:

```
For x = 1 To numOfRecordsInFile
    ReDim Preserve People(x - 1)
    Get #1, x, People(x - 1)
    AddRecord (x - 1)
Next x
```

The first statement inside the loop redimensions the People array to contain the incoming record. The second statement uses Get # to read record x and store its contents in the People array. The third statement calls the AddRecord function to add the name to the list box. The important point to understand in these statements is the value of x as the loop is iterated. The array and list box both have a lower bound of 0. The first record in the file, however, is record 1. Record 1 must be stored in array element 0, record 2 stored in array element 1, and so on. By using the equation (x - 1), the procedure maintains the correct array and list box index number for each record.

Saving the Changes

Even though address book program can open a file, the program still is pretty useless because it can't save a new file or save changes you have made to an existing file. To save the file, you need to write a procedure that copies the contents of the array to a file. Here are the general steps the procedure should take:

Make a backup copy. To be safe, the program should make a backup copy of the original file (assuming the current address book was loaded from a file and not created as a new address book). A common practice is to create a new backup file name that uses the current file name and the BAK extension instead of the file's current extension (in this case, BOK). The procedure should then check if the backup file exists, and if the file does exist, the procedure should kill it. The procedure should then rename the existing file using this backup file name. Then the procedure can write the file to disk using the original file name. This maintains the same name for the file while ensuring that the original file is renamed as a backup file in case something goes wrong during the procedure.

☐ **Calculate record length and initialize variables.** As when opening a file, the procedure should calculate the length of one record so it can open the file properly. The procedure should also initialize any variables, such as the record counter, that will be used to store the records in the file.

☐ **Open the file and store only undeleted records in the file.** The procedure should step through the array one record at a time, checking to see if the record is deleted. If the record is not deleted, the procedure should write the record to the file. If the record is deleted, the procedure should simply skip it and read the next record. Because deleted records are not written to the file, they essentially are "thrown away."

That's it! Like the OpenFile procedure, the SaveFile procedure you are going to create for PEOPLE3.MAK isn't very complex, but there are quite a few statements in it.

Creating the SaveFile Procedure

1. Continue working with the PEOPLE3.MAK project.

2. From the Project window, choose the PEOPLE3.BAS file, and choose the View Code button to display the Code window.

3. Choose **V**iew, **N**ew Procedure to display the New Procedure dialog box.

4. Choose the **S**ub option button, type **SaveFile** in the **N**ame edit box, and choose OK to create the FileOpen procedure.

5. Modify the SaveFile procedure to read as follows:

```
Sub SaveFile (fileToSave As String)
    Dim recordLen As Long
    On Error Resume Next
    'Derive a backup name by stripping the .BOK extension from
    'the file name, then adding the extension .BAK to the file name.
    backupFile = Left$(fileToSave, (Len(fileToSave) - 4)) & ".BAK"
    If Dir(backupFile) Then    'If the backup file exists...
        Kill backupFile  '...kill (erase) it.
    End If
```

continues

```
        If Dir(fileToSave) Then   'If there is an original file...
            Name fileToSave As backupFile
            'Rename it using the backup name
        End If
        On Error GoTo noFileSave
        'Calculate the record length.
        recordLen = Len(People(0))
        'Set the record counter variable to 1 for the first record
        recordNum = 1
        Screen.MousePointer = 11
        'Open the file.
        'If the file doesn't exist, the Open statement creates it.
        Open fileToSave For Random As #1 Len = recordLen
        'Set the record counter variable to 1 for the first record
        recordNum = 1
        'Set up a loop to execute as many times as there are
        'records in the array.
        For x = LBound(People) To UBound(People)
            If People(x).Deleted <> 1 Then
            'If the record is not deleted...
                Put #1, recordNum, People(x)
                'Write the record to the file
                recordNum = recordNum + 1
                'Increment the record counter
            End If
        Next x
        'Close the file
        Close #1
        Screen.MousePointer = 0
        Exit Sub

noFileSave:
        Close #1
        Screen.MousePointer = 0
        MsgBox "An error occurred saving the file.", 0, Str$(Err)
        ➥& ": " & Error$
        Exit Sub
End Sub
```

6. Choose the frmPeople form from the Project window, and choose the View Code button to display its Code window.

7. From the Object drop-down list, choose mnuFileSaveAs. Search through the mnuFileSaveAs procedure to locate the following line, and remove the apostrophe to change it from a comment to a statement:

    ```
    SaveFile (fileToSave)
    ```

8. From the Object drop-down list, choose mnuFileSave and modify the mnuFileSave_Click event procedure to read as follows:

    ```
    Sub mnuFileSave_Click ()
          'Check to see if the file has been saved before
          If currentFile = "" Then
                'If the currentFile variable is blank, this file hasn't
                'been saved before, so "click" the Save As item in the
                'File menu. The user then can specify a file name in
                'the Save As dialog box.
                mnuFileSaveAs_Click
          Else 'Otherwise, currentFile is not empty, so this file
                'has been saved before. So, call the SaveFile procedure
                'and pass it the name of the current file
                SaveFile (currentFile)
          End If
    End Sub
    ```

9. Save the project.

Now you can save an address book to a file—your address book program is finally useful! Let's take a look at how the procedures work.

Understanding the SaveFile Procedure

First, consider the mnuFileSave_Click event procedure. If the *currentFile* variable is empty, the file has never been saved before, so the procedure "clicks" the Save As menu item, executing the mnuFileSaveAs_Click event procedure, which prompts the user to supply a file name. If the *currentFile* variable is not empty, the file has been saved before, and the procedure simply passes the file name stored in the *currentFile* to the SaveFile procedure.

How is *currentFile* set? I'm glad you asked! If the user opens an existing file, the OpenFile procedure sets *currentFile* to the name of the open file. If the user creates a new address book and then saves the file, the SaveFile procedure stores the file name in the *currentFile* variable.

Now consider the SaveFile procedure. The first part of the SaveFile procedure creates a backup file if the file being saved already exists:

```
backupFile = Left$(fileToSave, (Len(fileToSave) - 4)) & ".BAK"
If Dir(backupFile) Then  'If the backup file exists...
    Kill backupFile    '...kill (erase) it.
End If
If Dir(fileToSave) Then        'If there is an original file...
    Name fileToSave As backupFile
    'Rename it using the backup name
End If
```

The *backupFile* variable stores the name of the backup file. How can you be sure that stripping the right-most four characters from the existing file name will remove the file extension? The DefaultExt property of the CMDialog1 control is set to "BOK." When the user enters a file name in the Save As dialog box, the extension BOK is automatically appended to the file name. If the user has opened an existing file, the OpenFile procedure has stored the name of the file, including its BOK extension, in the *currentFile* variable. If the user selects the **S**ave item from the **F**ile menu, the mnuFileSave_Click event procedure passes the *currentFile* variable to the SaveFile procedure, and the procedure strips off its extension.

After the backup file name is created, the first If structure uses the Dir function to determine if a file with the backup file name already exists. If it does, the file is deleted with the Kill statement. The second If structure uses the Dir function to determine if the address file (with the BOK extension) already exists. If it does exist, the procedure uses the Name statement to rename the file using the backup file name.

The part of the procedure that actually places the records in the file is fairly simple. Here is the For...Next loop that accomplishes that task:

```
recordNum = 1
For x = LBound(People) To UBound(People)
    If People(x).Deleted <> 1 Then 'If the record is not deleted...
```

```
            Put #1, recordNum, People(x) 'Write the record to the file
            recordNum = recordNum + 1 'Increment the record counter
        End If
    Next x
```

The first statement in this code fragment sets the *recordNum* variable to 1. This variable will be used as a position locator to store records in successive locations in the file. The For...Next loop then iterates as many times as there are records in the array. The If structure within the loop tests the value of the *Deleted* element of the current record. If the record is not deleted, the Put # statement writes the record to the file at the position specified by the *recordNum* variable. The *recordNum* variable is then incremented by 1 for the next record.

The syntax of the Put statement is as follows:

```
    Put #recordNumber, record, variable
```

The *recordNumber* parameter specifies the file handle that you have specified earlier in an Open statement. The *record* parameter specifies the number of the record to be written in the file. The first record is record 1, the second is record 2, and so on. If you omit the *record* parameter, the record is written after the record is pointed to by the previous Put or Get statement. In other words, the next record is written right after the last record that was read or written. The *variable* parameter specifies the record data to be written in the record.

The If structure in the SaveFile procedure is what enables the procedure to "throw out" all of the deleted records. Only those records that are not deleted are written to the file. If you open an existing file that contains 100 records, then delete 50 of those records and save the file, only the 50 undeleted records are written to the file. The important point to understand is that you are not storing these records in the same file each time you save the file. The original file, which contains all 100 records (in this example), is renamed as the backup file. A new file containing the 50 good records is then created. This second file will require half as many bytes as the original, because it contains half as many records.

Some Final Tips about Random Access

Random access provides a good way to store records as long as the records are all the same length. You don't have to use a data type as I have in the PEOPLE3.MAK project, however. You can just as easily store single variables in a file, rather than data records that are defined by a data type.

When you are writing a procedure that uses random access to open or write to a file, keep these points in mind:

- [ ] If you omit the For Random keywords from the Open statement when you open the file, Visual Basic assumes you want to open the file for sequential access.

- [ ] You don't have to store your data in a data type to put it in a file. A record in a file can be a single variable or even a single character or number. Data types do, however, offer a great way to organize multiple related items; therefore, data types offer a great way to store records in a file.

- [ ] If you're using random access to read a file, always remember that each record in the file must have the same record length. This means that if you're storing a variable as a record in the file, you must define the variable at a fixed length or pad/truncate the record to the correct length. If you are writing a data type to a file, the data type must be declared using fixed-length variables.

- [ ] You can use the LOF function to determine the length of the file after you open it, then divide the length of the file by the size of one record to determine the number of records in the file. If you want to determine the length of a file *before* you open it, use the FileLen function. You can only use the LOF function if the file is already open.

- [ ] If you want to position the record pointer in the file without actually reading or writing a record, use the Seek function. The Seek function enables you to place the record pointer at the beginning of a specific record. A subsequent Get or Put statement can then begin reading or writing at that record.

For information on random access and the statements you can use to read and write files, search the Visual Basic Help file on the Open statement.

Using Binary Access

Now that you know all about random access and you're incredibly talented at reading and writing files, I have to tell you that random access is often wasteful. Depending on the type of data you're storing, you can waste a *lot* of disk space by storing your files using random access.

Why is this so? Consider the *Person* data type used in the random access example. Each last name is limited to 20 characters. What if you want to store the name of a close personal friend of mine, "Victoria Wojohovuna-kwizcianowski-Smith"? That last name is longer than twenty characters. The solution must be to increase the length of the LastName variable to a high enough number to store the longest possible name. We'll also increase the length of the FirstName variable to accommodate long first names. In other words, we'll change the *Person* data type as follows (I'll simplify the record to avoid boring you with details):

```
Type Person
     LastName As String * 30
     FirstName As String * 20
End Type
```

Now we can store a last name of 30 characters and a first name of 20 characters. Great! But what happens if you want to store the name "Abe Jones"? The names are padded with spaces to fill up the variable (see fig. 14.6) if the string is not as long as the declared length of the variable in the data type. With the current *Person* data type, this means you're wasting 17 bytes in the FirstName variable and 25 bytes in the LastName variable to store ol' Abe. Is that a big deal? Maybe yes; maybe no. If you assume an average of 20 characters for both the last and first names combined, you're wasting 30 characters to store each name. That's 1 KB of wasted disk space for about every 34 names. The actual amount will vary, but I'm sure you get the idea—you're still wasting disk space.

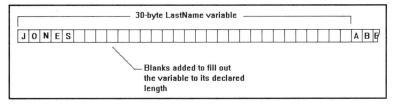

Figure 14.6

The last name is padded with spaces to fill its variable.

If the variables within the data structure were even longer, the amount of wasted disk space could easily increase. If you include a Comments field in a record, for example, and that Comments field can be as long as 512 characters, you should definitely use random access. If the user doesn't include any comments in any of the records, you'll be wasting 512 bytes for each record in the file. That equates to 1 MB of wasted space for every 2,048 records.

Your program's users aren't going to be very happy with you when their disk drives fill up and they find out that it is your program that's hogging all of their disk space. You might have to begin living under an assumed name, and those users will be calling you Left$("Assumed Name", 3). I won't spell it out for you; you know how the Left$ function works—you figure out what they're going to be calling you.

What's the solution? Use binary access instead of random access. If you use binary access, each record can be any size you like. Every record in a file could be a different length from every other file. Instead of using the same amount of space for each record whether you need it or not, you can use just the right amount of space to store the data, plus a small amount of space for some additional information to help you read each record.

Structuring the Data and the File

The structure of a file that uses binary access is different in structure from a file that uses random access. Every record in a file that is read using random access is the same length, but each record in a file that is read using binary access can be any length. Figure 14.7 shows a portion of an address book file that was written using binary access.

Figure 14.7

Part of a file created using binary access.

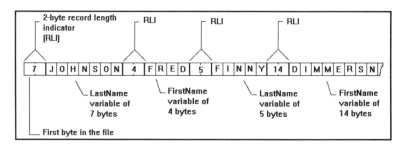

Using binary access keeps your file size to a minimum, but it requires a different method to write a record and read it back again. Assume you're using a data type like the one that follows:

```
Type Bonehead
     LastName As String
     FirstName As String
     Age As Integer
End Type
```

None of the variables in the type are of a fixed length, although the *Age* variable will always require two bytes of storage space because it is an integer. Assume that you create the following record:

```
Bonehead(0).LastName = "Jones"
Bonehead(0).Firstname = "Ferguson"
Bonehead(0).Age = 43
```

The total size of this record is 15 bytes; 13 bytes for the strings and 2 bytes for the integer. The next record will be different, and will likely have a different record length. If every record is a different length, how in the world are you going to be able to write or read a record? The trick is to store in the file the length (in bytes) of a record variable, then store the variable itself. Using this record example, you would write the integer 5 for the length of "Jones," then write the text "Jones." Next, write the integer 8 for the length of "Ferguson," then write the text "Ferguson." Finally, write the integer 43 for Ferguson's age.

Therefore, the trick is to first store the length of an element, and then store the element itself. What does that do for you? It enables you to retrieve the record from the file. When you need to read a record from the file, open the file and read the first two bytes, which tells you how many bytes long the first element is in the record. Next, read that many bytes to retrieve the first element. Then, read the next two-byte integer to determine how many bytes to read for the next element. Read that many bytes to retrieve the next element, then repeat the process until you've read all of the record.

Your *Understanding Visual Basic Disk* includes yet another address book project called PEOPLE4.MAK (I'm not very inventive with project names, am I?). The OpenFile and SaveFile procedures in PEOPLE4.MAK use binary access to read and write the data file. In addition, the PEOPLE4.MAK interface includes a Comments text box in which you can store a comment of any length about each entry (see fig. 14.8). The disk also includes a sample address book file called BINBOGUS.BOK that contains five sample addresses.

Figure 14.8
The interface
of the
PEOPLE4.MAK
project.

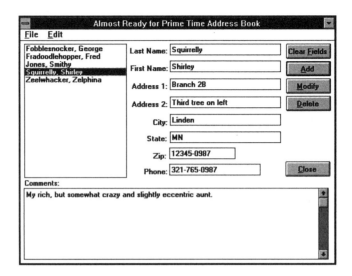

The OpenFile and SaveFile procedures are already completed in
PEOPLE4.MAK. In the next few exercises you'll examine these procedures.
First, however, read an overview of the project.

Overview of the PEOPLE4.MAK Project

The only major differences between PEOPLE3.MAK and PEOPLE4.MAK is
that PEOPLE4.MAK includes a few extra statements that copy the contents of
the Comments field into each record. Here's the data type used in
PEOPLE4.MAK:

```
Type Person
      LastName As String
      FirstName As String
      Address1 As String
      Address2 As String
      City As String
      State As String
      Zip As String
      Phone As String
      Comments As String
      Deleted As Integer
End Type
```

Notice that none of the fields is fixed-length, except for the *Deleted* variable which is two bytes (because it is an integer). Elsewhere in the cmdAdd_Click and cmdModify_Click event procedures, there are statements that copy the contents of txtComments into the Comments element of the current record. That's all pretty basic stuff (no pun intended).

The OpenFile and SaveFile procedures are simplified in some ways, but more complex in others. Neither procedure calculates the length of a record, because the record does not remain a constant length. The OpenFile procedure no longer calculates the number of records in the file, because there is no sure way to determine how many records are in the file. These differences simplify the main structure of the OpenFile and SaveFile procedures slightly, but the code required to read and write the file is more complex.

Opening and Reading a File

I know you're dying to get into the OpenFile procedure and check it out, so go for it.

Viewing the OpenFile Procedure

1. Open the project PEOPLE4.MAK that is included on the *Understanding Visual Basic Disk*.

2. Open the Project window, select the PEOPLE4.BAS file, and choose View Code to open the Code window.

3. From the Proc drop-down list, choose OpenFile to display the code for the OpenFile procedure. You should see the following code:

```
Sub OpenFile (fileToOpen As String)
    Dim bytesToRead As Integer
    ReDim People(0)
    currentFile = ""
    On Error GoTo noOpenFile
    frmPeople!List1.Clear
    Open fileToOpen For Binary As #1
    Screen.MousePointer = 11
    x = 0
```

continues

```
        Do
            Get #1, , bytesToRead
            If EOF(1) Then Exit Do
            ReDim Preserve People(x)
            People(x).LastName = Input$(bytesToRead, #1)
            Get #1, , bytesToRead
            People(x).FirstName = Input$(bytesToRead, #1)
            Get #1, , bytesToRead
            People(x).Address1 = Input$(bytesToRead, #1)
            Get #1, , bytesToRead
            People(x).Address2 = Input$(bytesToRead, #1)
            Get #1, , bytesToRead
            People(x).City = Input$(bytesToRead, #1)
            Get #1, , bytesToRead
            People(x).State = Input$(bytesToRead, #1)
            Get #1, , bytesToRead
            People(x).Zip = Input$(bytesToRead, #1)
            Get #1, , bytesToRead
            People(x).Phone = Input$(bytesToRead, #1)
            Get #1, , bytesToRead
            People(x).Comments = Input$(bytesToRead, #1)
            People(x).Deleted = 0
            AddRecord (x)
            x = x + 1
        Loop
        Close #1
        Screen.MousePointer = 0
        currentFile = fileToOpen
        Exit Sub
    noOpenFile:
        Close #1
        Screen.MousePointer = 0
        MsgBox "An error occurred opening the file.", 0, Str$(Err)
    ➥& ": " & Error$
        Exit Sub
    End Sub
```

4. Examine the code in the OpenFile procedure until your head starts to hurt and your eyebrows get red hot, then run the program.

5. Choose File, Open, and search for the file BINBOGUS.BOK that is included on the *Understanding Visual Basic Disk*. Choose the file, and choose OK to open it.

6. Examine the addresses in the file, and end the program.

A lot of the OpenFile code is the same as in PEOPLE3.MAK. The first major difference is the following line:

```
Dim bytesToRead As Integer
```

This statement declares an integer variable named *bytesToRead*. This variable will be used to read the record length integers from the file. Because the variable is declared as an integer, Visual Basic "knows" that the variable is two bytes in length.

The next difference between this OpenFile procedure and the one in PEOPLE3.MAK is the way the file is opened. Here is the statement that opens the file:

```
Open fileToOpen For Binary As #1
```

The `For Binary` keywords are used to open the file for binary access rather than for random access.

The Do...Loop structure is where the file is read. The statements in the Do...Loop structure continue to execute until the EOF (End Of File) marker is reached. Notice that the `Do` statement doesn't include any conditional code. Instead, the second statement inside the Do...Loop structure, which is an `If` statement, uses the `EOF` function to determine if the end of file has been reached. If it has, the Do...Loop structure is exited.

The most important concept to understand about the statements inside the Do...Loop structure that read the contents of the file is this: you control the number of bytes that the `Get` statement reads by specifying the length as a parameter of the `Input$` function. The `Input$` function uses the following syntax:

```
Input$(bytes, fileNumber)
```

The *bytes* parameter specifies the number of bytes (or characters) that will be read from the file. The *fileNumber* variable specifies the file handle defined in the `Open` statement.

The first `Get` statement inside the Do...Loop structure reads the first two bytes of the record. The first time through the loop, this statement reads the first two bytes in the file:

```
Get #1, , bytesToRead
```

How can we be sure it's reading the first two bytes? The *bytesToRead* variable is an integer variable. Because we've specified the name of an integer variable in the Get statement, the Get statement automatically reads two bytes.

Now, the *bytesToRead* variable contains the value of the number of bytes in the first record element. The next statement reads that many bytes from the file and stores the data it reads in the People(x).Lastname element:

```
People(x).LastName = Input$(bytesToRead, #1)
```

Next, the Get statement reads another integer. This integer stores the number of bytes to be read in the next record element. The process repeats through the Do...Loop structure until all of the elements have been read for the record. Then, the Loop statement causes the whole mess to be repeated.

NOTE How is the file read from beginning to end? The Open statement causes the file pointer to be located at the first byte in the file. None of the Get statements specify a pointer parameter (the second parameter in each Get statement is blank). And, the Input$ statements do not reposition the pointer after reading their specified number of bytes. Therefore, the pointer starts at the beginning of the file and the Get and Input$ statements move it sequentially through the file until the EOF mark is reached.

Saving the File Using Binary Access

Now you have the file copied into the array. How do you copy the array back to the file? It's really pretty simple. For each record in the array, write an integer that specifies the number of bytes in the first record element, then write the record element itself. Repeat this two-step process until all of the elements in the record have been written, then repeat the process for all of the other records in the array.

The SaveFile procedure in the PEOPLE4.MAK project uses just this type of process to store all of the records in the file. Here is the SaveFile procedure (if you want to view it on-screen, the procedure is located in PEOPLE4.BAS):

```
Sub SaveFile (fileToSave As String)
    Dim bytesToWrite As Integer
    On Error Resume Next
    backupFile = Left$(fileToSave, (Len(fileToSave) - 4)) & ".BAK"
    If Dir(backupFile) Then
        Kill backupFile
    End If
    If Dir(fileToSave) Then
        Name fileToSave As backupFile
    End If
    On Error GoTo noFileSave
    Screen.MousePointer = 11
    Open fileToSave For Binary As #1
    For x = LBound(People) To UBound(People)
        If People(x).Deleted <> 1 Then
            bytesToWrite = Len(People(x).LastName)
            Put #1, , bytesToWrite
            Put #1, , People(x).LastName
            bytesToWrite = Len(People(x).FirstName)
            Put #1, , bytesToWrite
            Put #1, , People(x).FirstName
            bytesToWrite = Len(People(x).Address1)
            Put #1, , bytesToWrite
            Put #1, , People(x).Address1
            bytesToWrite = Len(People(x).Address2)
            Put #1, , bytesToWrite
            Put #1, , People(x).Address2
            bytesToWrite = Len(People(x).City)
            Put #1, , bytesToWrite
            Put #1, , People(x).City
            bytesToWrite = Len(People(x).State)
            Put #1, , bytesToWrite
            Put #1, , People(x).State
            bytesToWrite = Len(People(x).Zip)
            Put #1, , bytesToWrite
            Put #1, , People(x).Zip
            bytesToWrite = Len(People(x).Phone)
            Put #1, , bytesToWrite
```

```
                    Put #1, , People(x).Phone
                    bytesToWrite = Len(People(x).Comments)
                    Put #1, , bytesToWrite
                    Put #1, , People(x).Comments
                End If
            Next x
            Close #1
            Screen.MousePointer = 0
            Exit Sub

    noFileSave:
            Close #1
            Screen.MousePointer = 0
            MsgBox "An error occurred saving the file.", 0, Str$(Err)
            ➥& ":" & Error$
            Exit Sub
    End Sub
```

The If...Then structure contains a number of statements that set the value of
the variable *bytesToWrite*. This variable stores, as an integer, the number of
bytes in each record element. Each record element is written using two Put
statements. The first Put statement writes the element length record to the
file, and the second Put statement writes the record element itself to the file.
When you later need to read the file, you can read the element length integer
to determine how many bytes to read for each record element.

Okay, troops! You're almost to the top of the ridge. You only have one more
chapter to go. You've learned about nearly all of the stuff you need to know
to write some pretty decent programs. Unfortunately, Murphy's Law is
bound to strike sooner or later, so you need to make your programs as
bullet-proof as possible. Don't wimp out now; read the last chapter. In it you
learn how to fix all of the "undocumented features" that will no doubt creep
into your programs.

15
CHAPTER

Da Bugs!

This chapter is not about Elmer Fudd's arch-enemy, Bugs Bunny. It's not about the creepy, crawly creatures that live under your refrigerator. This chapter is about program bugs, which programmers like to refer to as *undocumented features*. In addition to covering debugging (getting rid of bugs), this chapter also covers other types of program errors. Errors can happen for many different reasons in the programs you write. This chapter will help you avoid some of those errors, and also will help you detect and correct the ones you don't or can't avoid. The chapter covers the following topics:

- Types of errors and how they occur
- Testing and eliminating errors and bugs
- Other debugging and testing tips and procedures

This chapter doesn't cover every possible aspect of testing and debugging, but it should give you enough of an overview to make you familiar with the key issues involved in debugging a program.

Types of Errors

"You Can't Be Perfect." Naturally I don't say that about myself, but not everyone is as humble or modest as I am. When it comes to programming, however, errors seem to sometimes pop up from nowhere. Some happen as you are writing code, others happen when you attempt to compile the program, and still others happen when you run the program. Understanding how to get rid of errors and bugs requires that you first understand the types of errors you can experience when you're writing a program.

Syntax Errors

Visual Basic has the capability to check the syntax of the statements you write as you are writing them. By default, syntax checking is turned on. To turn syntax checking on or off, choose **O**ptions, **E**nvironment, and double-click on the Syntax Checking item in the Environment Options list.

If syntax checking is on and you make a typographical mistake, leave out a required keyword or punctuation mark, or make some other syntactical mistake, Visual Basic displays an error message. VB does this as soon as you exit from the line by pressing Enter or by moving the cursor off of the line using the arrow keys or mouse. Figure 15.1 shows an example of a typical error message generated by Visual Basic due to a syntax error.

Figure 15.1

An error message
generated by a
syntax error.

In most cases, the error message will give you enough information to fix the syntax. If you don't have enough information to fix the error, press the F1 key while an error message is displayed and Visual Basic will open the Help file and display a topic page about the error. This Help topic page should give you a clue about what's wrong with the syntax of the statement. If you still can't determine the error, switch back to the Code window and highlight the method, function, or keyword in the statement, then press F1 again. This will display a Help topic page with the correct syntax for the statement.

Why turn off syntax checking at all? In some situations you might want to create code that is incomplete. This often happens when you are cutting and pasting code between forms or procedures. If you don't turn off syntax checking, VB will generate an error message each time you enter an incomplete statement. I recommend that you turn off syntax checking only temporarily when you know you will be entering incomplete code, then turn it back on when you are beginning regular coding again. By checking the syntax as you go, you can eliminate errors that will crop up later.

Compile Errors

Compile errors are errors that occur when you attempt to compile the program into an EXE file. Compile errors are the result of incorrect code, which includes incorrect keywords, missing punctuation, or improperly constructed loops. Here's an example of a statement that won't generate a syntax error when you type it, but will generate a compile error:

```
Framistat
```

Framistat could be the name of a procedure or function. When you type the line, Visual Basic doesn't check to make sure the procedure or function exists, because you might not have written it yet. So, the only time Visual Basic can determine that there is an error is when you attempt to run the program or compile it. Figure 15.2 shows the error message that appears in this example because the Framistat procedure doesn't exist.

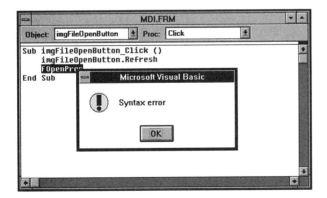

Figure 15.2

An error caused by a missing procedure.

Other compile errors can occur if you turn off syntax checking. Visual Basic tests the syntax of your program statements when you compile the program, displaying the same error message you would have received if you had left syntax checking turned on.

Run-Time Errors

Run-time errors occur when a statement attempts to perform an operation that isn't possible. Run-time errors can be caused by statements that are syntactically correct, but which can be impossible to execute. An example is division by zero:

```
tooBad = income / IRS
```

These statements work properly if the value of *IRS* is not equal to zero. What if the program for one reason or another has set a value for *income* but hasn't yet set the value of the *IRS* variable? You end up with a division by zero and a run-time error is triggered.

Avoiding run-time errors requires a two-step approach. No, that doesn't mean you have to learn country western dancing. It means that you need to do the following two things:

☐ **Avoid code that can generate a run-time error.** Think about the logic of your program as you're writing it. When you write a statement, think about all of the possible values for the variables in it. Is it possible that a variable might not be set when the statement executes? If so, try to rewrite the statement or change the logic of the program to avoid that possibility.

☐ **Add error-checking to your code.** If you need to leave the statement or logic the way it is, add some error checking to your code that can prevent the error before it occurs. In the previous IRS example, you could test the value of the IRS variable before executing the calculation. If IRS was equal to zero, you could construct the procedure to either set IRS to a valid number before executing the statement or skip the calculation.

Logic Errors

Logic errors are solely your fault. Sorry, but you can't blame them on Visual Basic, the phase of the moon, militant extremists, or nuclear proliferation. Logic errors occur because the logic of your program is flawed. A program can contain syntactically correct code and run without generating errors, but that doesn't guarantee that the program will generate the desired or anticipated results. If you write a program that is supposed to calculate interest on a mortgage but you use the wrong formula, for example, the results will be incorrect.

I ran across a logic error when I wrote the sample project PEOPLE3.MAK (okay, I'm not perfect after all). Here is the code I originally wrote to store undeleted records in the address file:

```
For x = LBound(People) To UBound(People)
    If People(x).Deleted <> 1 Then
    'If the record is not deleted...
        Put #1, x + 1, People(x) 'Write the record to the file
    End If
Next x
```

There is nothing syntactically wrong with these statements. Logically, however, they are completely screwy. Why? There is no relationship between the value of x (the loop counter) and the correct record number. This code resulted in record numbers being skipped in the file, which caused garbage records to appear in the file; VB had to fill in the skipped records, and it did so by filling them with junk. This was a stupid mistake, but I spent an hour trying to figure out why it didn't work. I finally resorted to showing the code to someone else, who spotted the problem almost immediately. The correct logic is to use a completely different variable to *sequentially* add records:

```
recordNum = 1
For x = LBound(People) To UBound(People)
    If People(x).Deleted <> 1 Then
    'If the record is not deleted...
        Put #1, recordNum, People(x)
    'Write the record to the file
        recordNum = recordNum + 1
    'Increment the record counter
    End If
Next x
```

The only way to detect logic errors is to run the program and test it extensively. If you are putting data into the program that you know is good but you're getting garbage or incorrect results, you have a logic error. If that's the case, it's time to review your program's logic and code to determine what is wrong. Don't assume that because your code makes sense and doesn't cause syntax errors that it is logically correct.

TIP When you're experiencing a logic error and can't seem to track it down, walk away from the program for a while. You can read the same flawed code many times without seeing the flaw. Take a nap, take a walk, or take a hike and forget everything you know about the program. When you come back, take a fresh look at the logic. You'll probably spot the error because you've thrown out any preconceptions about the code.

The Debugging Process

There is no set process for detecting and fixing bugs in your program, but there are some general guidelines that you can follow. Visual Basic also provides a selection of tools you can use to debug your programs. The first step in debugging your programs is understanding the three modes in which Visual Basic can operate.

About VB's Modes

Visual Basic provides three modes for writing, testing, and debugging your programs:

- [ ] **Design mode.** This mode enables you to create forms, draw controls, and write code. This is the mode in which you've spent the majority of your time in previous chapters.

- [ ] **Run mode.** This mode enables you to run your program to test it. You can view code as the program is running, but you can't change the code without first ending the program.

- [ ] **Break mode.** After entering run mode, you can enter break mode. Entering break mode suspends the program. After entering break mode you can view and modify code, restart the program, resume execution at the same point, or end execution.

You've worked almost exclusively in design mode in previous chapters. When you are drawing forms and controls and writing code, you're working in design mode. When you run a program (without first compiling it), you're working in run mode. Run mode enables you to test the program, but doesn't enable you to modify any of its code.

Break mode is useful for debugging. After you enter run mode, you can enter break mode. Entering break mode suspends execution of the program and saves the current state of the program, including its appearance and the value of properties and variables. Here is a list of things you can do when you're working in break mode:

☐ Examine the program's interface and determine which procedures have been called

☐ Control the statement that will be executed next

☐ Examine the value of properties, variables, and statements

☐ Change the value of properties and variables

☐ Modify code and run statements

You'll learn about these topics shortly. First, you need to know how to enter break mode. Getting into break mode is easy. After you start the program, you can press Ctrl+Break, choose Brea**k** from the **R**un menu, or choose the Break button on the toolbar. Figure 15.3 shows the buttons on the toolbar that apply to running and debugging the program.

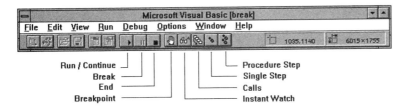

Figure 15.3

Toolbar buttons for running and debugging the program.

In addition to entering break mode manually using one of the three methods described previously, you can cause the program to enter break mode automatically if one of the following occurs:

☐ A statement generates an untrapped run-time error

☐ A breakpoint in the code (which you have set) is reached

☐ A Stop statement is executed

☐ A break expression that you have defined changes or becomes true

You'll learn about each of these four topics in the following sections. First, you need an explanation of what you'll see when the VB enters break mode.

What You See in Break Mode

When VB enters break mode, your Code window appears. The Code window's title bar displays the currently active form or module. The currently executing procedure appears in the Code window. The next statement to be executed is outlined in the code by a rectangle. Figure 15.4 points out these features in the Code window.

Figure 15.4

The Code window at break time.

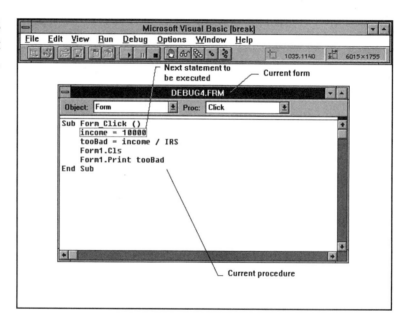

If you enter break mode manually, the Debug window appears. You'll learn about the Debug window later in this chapter.

Fixing Run-Time Errors

When a run time error occurs, it's often caused by incorrect variable or property values and, in some cases, by logic errors. Because the program is in break mode, you can modify the offending statement and continue execution to determine if the modification fixed the problem. Depending on the logic of the procedure, you can either resume execution with the statement that triggered the error, or start execution with a different statement. In the following exercise, you'll correct an error and resume execution with the same statement that triggered the error.

Fixing a Run-Time Error

1. Open the project DEBUG1.MAK that is included on your *Understanding Visual Basic Disk*.

2. Run the program and click on Form1. A run-time error will be triggered, and you'll receive an error message indicating a division by zero (see fig. 15.5).

Figure 15.5

A division by zero error.

3. Choose OK to close the error message dialog box. The Code window will appear with the statement highlighted that triggered the error (see fig. 15.6).

Figure 15.6

The Code window showing the statement that triggered the error.

4. Highlight the 0 in the statement `tooBad = income / IRS`, and type the number 2 to change the statement to `tooBad = income / 2`.

5. Choose **R**un, **C**ontinue (or press F5) to continue execution with the statement that triggered the error. The program continues execution correctly and displays the value 5000 in the form.

6. End the program.

This isn't a very practical example, because you wouldn't write the statement to divide by zero in the first place. It does illustrate, however, how you can change a statement and resume execution with that same statement.

In the next exercise, correct an error and resume execution with a different statement (one in which the error lies, but not the one that triggers the error).

Resuming Execution with a Different Statement

1. Open the project DEBUG2.MAK.

2. Run the program and click on Form1. This will trigger a division-by-zero error and display an error message.

3. Choose OK in the error message dialog box to close the error message.

4. In the Code window, change the statement `IRS = 0` to read `IRS = 2`.

5. If the cursor is not still located on the statement you just changed, click on it to select it.

6. Choose **D**ebug, and Set **N**ext Statement. This sets the current statement, which is `IRS = 2`, as the next statement to execute.

7. Choose **R**un, **C**ontinue, or press F5 to continue execution at the selected statement. The program will print a value on the form.

8. End the program.

You can make certain types of changes to a program and continue execution. Other changes, such as adding variables or changing variable declarations (changing an integer variable to a long, for example), require that you restart the program. If you make a change that requires restarting the program, Visual Basic displays a message informing you that the change will require restarting the program.

If you suspect that a certain statement might be causing a problem or you simply want to examine the state of the program at a specific point, add a Stop statement right after the statement you want to test, or right after the statement that places the program in the condition which you want to examine.

Tracing Procedure Calls

If your program contains calls to many different procedures or contains nested procedures, you might want to keep track of which procedures have been called but not completed. Nested procedures in particular can be difficult to follow when you are debugging, and being able to monitor which procedure calls have been completed makes it easier to track the execution of the program.

When Visual Basic is in break mode, you can open the Calls dialog box to display a list of the procedure calls that have been made but not completed (the called procedure has not finished executing). Figure 15.7 shows the Calls dialog box.

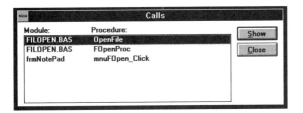

Figure 15.7

The Calls dialog box.

To display the Calls dialog box, first enter break mode either manually or automatically using one of the methods described previously. Next, choose **D**ebug, and **C**alls to display the Calls dialog box. If you prefer, you can press Ctrl+L or click on the Calls button in the toolbar to display the Calls dialog box.

When the Calls dialog box is displayed, it provides a list of all of the procedures that have been called but not yet completed. If you want to view the statement that called a specific procedure, choose the procedure in the Calls dialog box, and choose the **S**how button. Doing so causes the Code window to appear and display the statement that called the selected procedure. This ability is particularly helpful when you're trying to debug nested procedures.

When you want to close the Calls dialog box, choose the **C**lose button.

Stepping Through the Program

Another testing and debugging technique is to *step through* the program, not to be confused with stepping through a pasture. You don't have to be as careful stepping through a program. Stepping through the program enables you to execute statements one at a time, examining the results of each statement. This is particularly useful in helping you to identify logic errors.

There are two methods for stepping through a program. The first is the single step method.

Single Step

Single stepping through a program executes the statements in the program one at a time. Before each statement is executed, it is framed in the Code window by a rectangle to let you know which statement will be executed next. By single stepping through a program in this way, you can closely examine the logic and results of your program as it runs.

To single step through a program, choose the Single Step button in the toolbar or press F8. Visual Basic steps through the program one statement at a time. If a procedure makes a call to another procedure or function, execution jumps to the procedure or function and continues one step at a time. When all of the statements in the called procedure or function have been executed (according to the program's logic), execution returns to the original calling procedure and continues one step at a time.

Try out the single step method in the next exercise.

Using Single Step

1. Open the project DEBUG3.MAK that is included on your *Understanding Visual Basic Disk*.

2. Choose the Single Step button in the toolbar or press F8. The program starts and Form1 appears, but because there is no code in the Form1_Load event procedure, no statements are executed.

3. Choose the **Hello!** menu item. The Code window appears, displaying the mnuHello_Click event procedure. The statement msg = "Hello" is highlighted with a rectangular box.

4. Press F8 again. This executes the highlighted statement and highlights the next statement.

5. Press F8 again. Execution switches to the printStuff procedure and the printStuff procedure appears in the Code window.

6. Continue to press F8 or click the Single Step button until the Print statement in the printStuff procedure executes, placing some text in the center of the form.

7. Press F8 again and notice that execution returns to the mnuHello_Click event procedure.

8. Press F8 again to execute the Print statement in the mnuHello_Click event procedure.

9. End the program.

You can see that execution occurs one statement at a time. When no procedures are pending (such as when the program first starts), the program waits for you to take an action. When you take an action for which there is an associated event procedure, that execution jumps to that procedure.

Procedure Step

In the previous example, execution continues one step at a time through the printStuff procedure. That's fine if you want to debug the printStuff statement along with the rest of the program, but what if you already know that the printStuff procedure works properly? If it was a long procedure, or was one that was called often by the other procedures in the program, you'd probably get tired of stepping through it.

Instead of using single step in this situation, you can use *procedure step*. A procedure step executes statements one at a time until it reaches a call to another procedure or function. This called procedure or function then executes in its entirety rather than one step at a time.

To procedure step, press Shift+F8 or click on the Procedure Step button in the toolbar. You can switch between single step and procedure step as often as you like when debugging a program.

Try out procedure step in the next exercise.

Using Procedure Step

1. Continue working with DEBUG3.MAK.

2. Press F8 to start the program in single step mode. Form1 appears on the display.

3. Choose the **G**oodbye! menu item. The Code window appears with the first statement in the mnuGoodbye_Click event procedure highlighted.

4. Press F8 to step through the first statement in the procedure.

5. With the statement `printStuff(msg)` now highlighted (see fig. 15.8), press Shift+F8 or click on the Procedure Step button in the toolbar. The entire `printStuff` procedure executes and execution returns to the statement following the call to the printStuff procedure.

6. Press F8 to execute the last statement in the mnuGoodbye_Click event procedure.

7. End the program.

Figure 15.8

The printStuff statement ready to be executed using procedure step.

In a simple project such as DEBUG3.MAK, using procedure step doesn't save a lot of time, because the only called procedure, `printStuff`, is very short. If the program calls one or more long procedures, or calls many procedures that you do not need to debug, procedure step can save a lot of time.

Using the Debug Window

When you run a program in Visual Basic, the Debug window appears on the display automatically. Up to this point, we've been completely ignoring the Debug window. Now it's time to check it out.

You can use the Debug window to keep an eye on the value of expressions and variables. If you suspect that a variable is being set improperly and causing a problem or logic error, you can examine it in the Debug window.

The Debug window is available only in break mode, and consists of two panes: the Watch pane and the Immediate pane (see fig. 15.9). If you have not set any watch expressions, you will see only the Immediate pane.

Figure 15.9

The panes in the Debug window.

You can use the Immediate pane to enter statements to help test the program. If you suspect that a variable is not set properly, you can use the Print statement in the Debug window to print it. You also can set the value of the variable by issuing a statement in the Debug window. Try this out in the next exercise.

Using the Immediate Pane in the Debug Window

1. Open the project DEBUG4.MAK that is included on the *Understanding Visual Basic Disk*.

2. Run the program, and click on Form1. An error message will be generated.

3. Choose OK to close the error message dialog box.

4. Press Ctrl+B or choose **W**indow, and **D**ebug to display the Debug window.

5. In the Debug window, type **IRS = 2**, and press Enter. This sets the value of the variable IRS.

6. Press F5 to continue execution of the program. The program prints a correct result on Form1.

7. End the program.

You can see from this exercise that the Debug window can be a useful tool for helping you track down logic errors and run-time errors. In addition to letting you set values immediately as you did in the previous exercise, you also can use the Debug window to monitor *watch expressions*. A watch expression is an expression you define, and can be a variable, property, or any other valid expression. Watch expressions help you track the value of these types of items as the program is running.

Because this is just a primer on debugging, this chapter doesn't cover watch expressions in detail. While you are just starting to learn to use Visual Basic, the debugging techniques that are explained in this chapter should be sufficient to help you debug the majority of the programs you write. As you begin to write complex programs with higher numbers of procedures, watch expressions will become more important to you as a debugging tool. To learn more about adding and using watch expressions, check out the Debugging chapter in your Visual Basic *Programmer's Guide*.

If you've actually worked through this book from start to finish, congratulations. You've made the first *big* step toward learning how to program with Visual Basic. And no matter how you've used this book, I hope it has made the mystery of programming for Windows a lot easier. Let the people at New Riders Publishing know what you think. We want to help you *keep* learning the pleasures of programming in Visual Basic. Stay in touch.

INDEX

Symbols

! (exclamation point) single data type, 105
(pound sign) double data type, 105
$ (dollar sign)
   string data type, 105
   type-declaration character, 110
% (percent sign) integer data type, 105
& (ampersand) long data type, 105
^ (caret) exponent math operator, 122
* (asterisk) multiplication math
  operator, 121
+ (plus sign) addition math operator, 121
- (minus sign) subtraction math
  operator, 121
/ (backslash) division math operator, 122
@ (at sign) currency data type, 105
\ (slash) division math operator, 122
68 error, 311
71 error, 317
76 error, 311

A

Abort button (message boxes), 235
access keys, 179
  assigning to frames, 213
  assigning to menus, 179
accessing
  arrays, 321-322
  combo boxes, 227-228
  controls in dialog boxes, 204
  files, 348-350
    binary access, 348-349, 375-384
    random access, 348, 358-375
    sequential access, 348-358
  list boxes, 227
Action property (common dialog box), 243
activating
  menu items in menus, 183-184
  program window at program
    startup, 173
  toolbar buttons, 276
Add File command (File menu), 90, 174
Add File dialog box, 174

C

F

G

M

Understanding Visual Basic 3 for Windows
REGISTRATION CARD

Fill out this card to receive information about future New Riders titles!

Name _____ Title _____

Company _____

Address _____

City/State/ZIP _____

I bought this book because: _____

_____

I purchased this book from:

☐ A bookstore (Name _____)

☐ A software or electronics store (Name _____)

☐ A mail order (Name of catalog _____)

I purchase this many computer books each year:

☐ 1–5   ☐ 6 or more

I currently use these applications: _____

_____

_____

_____

I found these chapters to be the most informative: _____

_____

I found these chapters to be the least informative: _____

_____

Additional comments: _____

_____

☐ I would like to see my name in print! You may use my name and quote me in future New Riders products and promotions. My daytime phone number is: _____

New Riders Publishing 201 West 103rd Street • Indianapolis, Indiana 46290 USA

Fold Here

PLACE
STAMP
HERE

New Riders Publishing
201 West 103rd Street
Indianapolis, Indiana 46290
USA

WANT MORE INFORMATION?

CHECK OUT THESE RELATED TITLES:

	QTY	PRICE	TOTAL

PCs for Non-Nerds. This lighthearted reference presents information in an easy-to-read, entertaining manner. Provides quick, easy-to-find, no-nonsense answers to questions everyone asks. A great book for the "non-nerd" who wants to learn about personal computers.
ISBN: 1-56205-150-4.　　　　　　　　　　　　____　$18.95　_____

OS/2 for Non-Nerds. Even non-technical people can learn how to use OS/2 like a professional with this book. Clear and concise explanations are provided without long-winded, technical discussions. Information is easy to find with the convenient bulleted lists and tables.
ISBN: 1-56205-153-9.　　　　　　　　　　　　____　$18.95　_____

Windows for Non-Nerds. *Windows for Non-Nerds* is written with busy people in mind. With this book, it is extremely easy to find solutions to common Windows problems. Contains only useful information that is of interest to readers and is free of techno-babble and lengthy, technical discussions. Important information is listed in tables or bulleted lists that make it easy to find what you are looking for.
ISBN: 1-56205-152-0.　　　　　　　　　　　　____　$18.95　_____

Name _____

Company _____

Address _____

City _____ State ____ ZIP _____

Phone _____ Fax _____

☐ Check Enclosed　☐ VISA　☐ MasterCard

Card #_____Exp. Date _____

Signature _____

Prices are subject to change. Call for availability and pricing information on latest editions.

Subtotal　　_____

Shipping　　_____

$4.00 for the first book and $1.75 for each additional book.

Total　　_____
Indiana residents add 5% sales tax.

New Riders Publishing 201 West 103rd Street • Indianapolis, Indiana 46290 USA

Orders/Customer Service: 1-800-428-5331
Fax: 1-800-448-3804

- Fold Here -

PLACE
STAMP
HERE

New Riders Publishing
201 West 103rd Street
Indianapolis, Indiana 46290
USA

GO AHEAD. PLUG YOURSELF INTO
PRENTICE HALL COMPUTER PUBLISHING.
Introducing the PHCP Forum on CompuServe®

Yes, it's true. Now, you can have CompuServe access to the same professional, friendly folks who have made computers easier for years. On the PHCP Forum, you'll find additional information on the topics covered by every PHCP imprint—including Que, Sams Publishing, New Riders Publishing, Alpha Books, Brady Books, Hayden Books, and Adobe Press. In addition, you'll be able to receive technical support and disk updates for the software produced by Que Software and Paramount Interactive, a division of the Paramount Technology Group. It's a great way to supplement the best information in the business.

WHAT CAN YOU DO ON THE PHCP FORUM?

Play an important role in the publishing process—and make our books better while you make your work easier:

- Leave messages and ask questions about PHCP books and software—you're guaranteed a response within 24 hours
- Download helpful tips and software to help you get the most out of your computer
- Contact authors of your favorite PHCP books through electronic mail
- Present your own book ideas
- Keep up to date on all the latest books available from each of PHCP's exciting imprints

JOIN NOW AND GET A FREE COMPUSERVE STARTER KIT!

To receive your free CompuServe Introductory Membership, call toll-free, **1-800-848-8199** and ask for representative **#597**. The Starter Kit Includes:

- Personal ID number and password
- $15 credit on the system
- Subscription to CompuServe Magazine

HERE'S HOW TO PLUG INTO PHCP:

Once on the CompuServe System, type any of these phrases to access the PHCP Forum:

GO PHCP   **GO BRADY**
GO QUEBOOKS   **GO HAYDEN**
GO SAMS   **GO QUESOFT**
GO NEWRIDERS   **GO PARAMOUNTINTER**
GO ALPHA

Once you're on the CompuServe Information Service, be sure to take advantage of all of CompuServe's resources. CompuServe is home to more than 1,700 products and services—plus it has over 1.5 million members worldwide. You'll find valuable online reference materials, travel and investor services, electronic mail, weather updates, leisure-time games and hassle-free shopping (no jam-packed parking lots or crowded stores).

Seek out the hundreds of other forums that populate CompuServe. Covering diverse topics such as pet care, rock music, cooking, and political issues, you're sure to find others with the sames concerns as you—and expand your knowledge at the same time.

GRAPHICS TITLES

INSIDE CORELDRAW! 4.0, SPECIAL EDITION

DANIEL GRAY

An updated version of the #1 best-selling tutorial on CorelDRAW!

CorelDRAW! 4.0

ISBN: 1-56205-164-4

$34.95 USA

CORELDRAW! SPECIAL EFFECTS

NEW RIDERS PUBLISHING

An inside look at award-winning techniques from professional CorelDRAW! designers!

CorelDRAW! 4.0

ISBN: 1-56205-123-7

$39.95 USA

CORELDRAW! NOW!

RICHARD FELDMAN

The hands-on tutorial for users who want practical information now!

CorelDRAW! 4.0

ISBN: 1-56205-131-8

$21.95 USA

INSIDE CORELDRAW! FOURTH EDITION

DANIEL GRAY

The popular tutorial approach to learning CorelDRAW!...with complete coverage of version 3.0!

CorelDRAW! 3.0

ISBN: 1-56205-106-7

$24.95 USA

OPERATING SYSTEMS

INSIDE MS-DOS 6.2, 2E

NEW RIDERS PUBLISHING

A complete tutorial and reference!

MS-DOS 6.2
ISBN: 1-56205-289-6
$34.95 USA

DOS FOR NON-NERDS

MICHAEL GROH

Understanding this popular operating system is easy with this humorous, step-by-step tutorial.

Through DOS 6.0
ISBN: 1-56205-151-2
$18.95 USA

INSIDE SCO UNIX

STEVE GLINES, PETER SPICER, BEN HUNSBERGER, & KAREN WHITE

Everything users need to know to use the UNIX operating system for everyday tasks.

SCO Xenix 286, SCO Xenix 386, SCO UNIX/System V 386
ISBN: 1-56205-028-1
$29.95 USA

INSIDE SOLARIS SunOS

KARLA SAARI KITALONG, STEVEN R. LEE, & PAUL MARZIN

Comprehensive tutorial and reference to SunOS!

SunOS, Sun's version of UNIX for the SPARC workstation, version 2.0
ISBN: 1-56205-032-X
$29.95 USA

The *Understanding Visual Basic Disk*

Understanding Visual Basic comes with a cool disk that includes all the programs mentioned in the exercises. If you play along and work through the exercises as you go, you'll learn Visual Basic in the quickest way possible.

Avoiding the Big Mistake

You can make one mistake in installing this disk, so listen up: Install Visual Basic first (before installing this disk). If you don't, you'll have all the exercise programs sitting on your hard disk and no way of getting access to them. The setup program also needs some of the system files Visual Basic provides to run properly. So get the order right. *First* VB, *then* the cool disk.

Installing the Disk

1. Put the disk in your floppy drive.

2. Open the Program Manager's **F**ile menu and choose **R**un.

3. Type a:\setup in the Run dialog box. (Type b:\setup if you're installing from your b: drive.)

4. After the setup program starts, enter the source drive and the installation directory in the dialog boxes that ask for them.

5. When the installation program stops, click on the OK button.

Opening the Programs

To open one of the programs, follow the directions in Chapter 0. Basically, start Visual Basic. Click on the **F**ile menu and select the **O**pen option. Select the program you want using the Open dialog box and click on OK.

Have an Older Copy of VB?

The newest, most bug-free version of VBRUN300.DLL is on your disk in compressed form. If you purchased your copy of Visual Basic several months ago, expand this file and copy it to your \WINDOWS\SYSTEM directory. The procedure is:

1. Open a DOS window.

2. Execute this DOS command: cd \VB\SETUP.KIT\KITFILES.

3. Execute this DOS command: expand a:VBRUN300.DL_ a: VBRUN300.DLL (It's b: if the disk is in drive b:.)

4. Exit your DOS window.

5. Use File Manager to copy VBRUN300.DLL from your floppy drive to the \WINDOWS\SYSTEM directory on your hard drive.